True Coming of Age

*A Dynamic Process That Leads to
Emotional Well-Being, Spiritual Growth, and
Meaningful Relationships*

John T. Chirban

McGraw-Hill

New York / Chicago / San Francisco / Lisbon / London
Madrid / Mexico City / Milan / New Delhi / San Juan
Seoul / Singapore / Sydney / Toronto

*The **McGraw·Hill** Companies*

1 2 3 4 5 6 7 8 9 0   DOC/DOC   0 9 8 7 6 5 4

ISBN 0-07-142681-7

"Please Hear What I'm Not Saying" is reprinted by permission of the author. © Copyright Charles C. Finn, from *For the Mystically Inclined*, 1st Books Library, Bloomington, IN. April 2002.

"The Paradoxical Commandments" are reprinted by permission of the author. © Copyright Kent M. Keith 1968, renewed 2001, www.paradoxicalcommandments.com.

McGraw-Hill books are available at special quantity discounts to use as premiums and sales promotions, or for use in corporate training programs. For more information, please write to the Director of Special Sales, Professional Publishing, McGraw-Hill, Two Penn Plaza, New York, NY 10121-2298. Or contact your local bookstore.

 This book is printed on recycled, acid-free paper containing a minimum of 50% recycled, de-inked fiber.

Library of Congress Cataloging-in-Publication Data
Chirban, John T.
   True coming of age: a dynamic process that leads to emotional well-being, spiritual growth, and meaningful relationships/John Chirban.
     p. cm.
Includes bibliographical references.
   ISBN 0-07-142681-7 (hardcover: alk. paper)
   1. Self-realization. 2. Self-realization—Religious aspects. I. Title.
   BF637.S4C4975 2004
   155.2'5—dc22
                                             2004001872

For My Beautiful Wife
Sharon
And My Wonderful Children
Alexis Georgia
Anthony Thomas
&
Ariana Maria
My Greatest Blessings

CONTENTS

PART IV: INTEGRATING YOUR LIFE   207

FOREWORD

WE ARE A CULTURE IN SEARCH OF THE SELF. This is not a new quest. All cultures through the ages have had their philosophers, theologians, sages, and geniuses who brought forth new wisdom and spiritual scholarship. But at this time, in this era, the quest for the True Self, as John Chirban names it, has become one and the same with our contemporary spiritual society. Perhaps people have always been and will always be spiritually yearning for a more fulfilled life. But my sense is that we are living in an exquisitely rare moment in human evolution, perhaps among the rarest life has ever known. We are living in an era when the power and presence of the human spirit has come into its own.

My enthusiasm for *True Coming of Age* grew in quantum leaps as I progressed through each chapter, and I realized that John Chirban had succeeded in writing the essential guidebook for entering into a dialogue with one's deeper or True Self. In my own work as a teacher and a medical intuitive, I have encountered thousands of people seeking to find a way, a means, a system of thought that could help them organize their interior life. Many, if not most, of these individuals find themselves spiraling into places dark and lonely because they asked themselves the most authentic question of life, "For what reason have I been born?" I consider that question to be more of a spiritual invocation than a question, more of an invitation to the heavens to send in the winds of change and redirect one's life into a journey of substance and spirit. That is a mystical question and from such a prayer comes change in every form. There was a time when, in order to pursue the depth and nature of the human spirit, a person would have to retreat from society and seek shelter in a monastery, for heaven can be a demanding companion. Today—and this is one of the extraordinary characteristics of our contemporary spiritual culture—people pursue matters of the spirit while remaining in ordinary life. Yet, nothing remains ordinary when the spirit takes the lead in your life choices.

There is nothing simple about the quest for the True Self. This is an arduous journey that requires—no, demands—maturity of attention to the details of the Self. It is impossible to discover who you are, what you are, your hidden potential, and your untapped spiritual resources in a casual manner. One of the most difficult concepts for me to communicate to audiences is that the very nature of human consciousness is to be conscious of your own humanness. That is, to learn to enter into an observation mode through which you become aware of the subtle thoughts, feelings, emotions, and interior forces that form the whole of your being. You cannot accomplish this task without a guide, which is exactly what I consider this book to be. I remember years ago listening to a lecture in which the presenter commented that to truly know oneself was a lifetime's journey, and, even then, one would die having discovered just the beginning. I dismissed that comment, thinking, "How could any one not know who they are much less what they wanted out of their life?" I have since quoted that remarkable man's wisdom more often than I can count, having discovered how true it is.

For my part, I consider the pursuit of the spirit to be the most exquisite of all callings. I made the mistake of considering myself quite educated on matters of the spirit once I completed a graduate degree in theology. Five years after graduate school, I began my work as a medical intuitive and encountered for the first time people struggling with illness, depression, trauma, and often an impending death. Having planned a career as a journalist, I was hardly prepared for people asking me what they should do in order to survive cancer. Somehow fate had placed me in a position of needing to learn everything I would hold sacred bit by bit from all the wonderful people who came to me for help. Among the many jewels of wisdom I learned during those years was that there is an inherent yearning in each of us to become a whole person. Each of us longs to become animated with that sense of liberation that comes from achieving self-awareness, self-knowledge, selfhood. While there is no such thing—at least not yet—as an official diagnosis of "depression due to a lack of self," I am convinced that one day such a condition will be recognized as a legitimate spiritual crisis, because it is.

Through the years, I have seen the search for the self penetrate into every corner of society. The health movement and the model of mind/body/spirit as the goal of the balanced life is certainly an expression of this. But beneath the health craze and the popularity of therapy and all the other changes that have come to characterize the human consciousness movement is a much deeper and more profound shift occurring in the very fabric of human evolution. Simply put, the time has come for human beings to move their center of consciousness from "in front of their eyes" to "behind their eyes." We have entered into the era of the psyche and spirit, in which our fundamental paradigm of power is undergoing a transformation from dominantly external to primarily internal. We are living in such a heightened age of discovery, but the frontier is all internal. Our greatest challenge now is to pursue our True Self, and it is a challenge because, as I discovered in my own work, people fear their own empowerment as much as they are drawn to discover it. We are complex creatures, filled with contradictions and paradoxes, not the least of which is that we know that our interior being is our greatest resource, and yet we fear encountering our True Self because we know our lives cannot be the same once we have made the commitment to become whole.

Having directed as many people as I have through the years on their own paths, I know what questions to expect and I know where the pause in the journey is going to occur. One of the many reasons I am so enthusiastic about *True Coming of Age* is that it is written exactly the way a person experiences the path to the self and by an author who combines the warmth and pain of his own personal life experiences with the brilliance of his scholarship. In writing *True Coming of Age*, John Chirban has created a book that will become an archetypal guide for people who are serious about their own spiritual awakening.

CAROLINE M. MYSS
Author of *Sacred Contracts* and *Anatomy of the Spirit*

ACKNOWLEDGMENTS

EARLY IN THE PROCESS OF WRITING *True Coming of Age*, I realized that I would never finish this book without the support and encouragement of my family, friends, and colleagues. Indeed, *True Coming of Age* is a product of several important relationships. And it is now that I take great pleasure and enthusiasm in thanking those who I love most dearly and who have made this possible.

Most significantly, I am indebted to my amazing wife, Sharon, who balances, understands, and loves me. Her sensitivity, judgment, and empathy make her a blessing to all the lives she touches. Likewise I am continuously inspired and strengthened by the goodness and joy of my children—Alexis Georgia, Anthony Thomas, and Ariana Maria—who have released me from regular "Daddy duties" and encouraged me throughout the writing process. Their zest for life and their high spirits renew my heart and soul every day and make my purpose clear.

Most particular acknowledgment goes to my close friend, Ed Keane, whose title as "manager" insufficiently refers to his critical position as the sounding board for many of the ideas in this book. He is a true friend, the consummate critic, and an invested supporter behind the scenes.

I am most thankful to Jan Miller, the highly acclaimed and intuitive agent, who understood the idea of this book and committed to bringing its message to print before I even met her. Jan not only guided this project but also initiated this first-time writer into the world of trade publishing. And one editor stood out from among the rest: Nancy Hancock. Nancy guided me through the process of writing a trade publication and supported *True Coming of Age* even though it does not conform to time-tested formulae.

The list of researchers and staff who assisted in shaping this book is long. Among the talented individuals who helped me complete this project are Jeff Severs, whose excellent writing skills and objectivity helped me to refine my thoughts and express my ideas with clarity; and Tia Gubler, Gavriella Kroo, Lainie Schultz, and Gavin Stephens, whose competent suggestions far surpass their official standing as students: they have been superb critical readers who are kindred spirits with the ideas that I share.

Special gratitude goes to my family and friends who have supported and encouraged me all along the way. In particular, I want to thank Dr. Maria Pantelia, my unofficial Greek consultant, who knows the habits, customs, and traditions of the ancients and moderns equally well and has given me wise counsel.

Finally, I want to thank those who contributed their story to this book: Maya Angelou, Desi Arnaz, Jr., Lucille Ball, Billy Bean, Tom Brokaw, Shirley Chisholm, Eileen Collins, Bette Davis, Tom Hanks, Ron Howard, Jeane Kirkpatrick, C. Everett Koop, Jay Leno, Keith Lockhart, Sandra Day O'Connor, Mary Lou Retton, Jessica Savitch, Diane Sawyer, B. F. Skinner, Desmond Tutu, Rosalyn Yalow, and Anastasios Yannoulatos, in addition to numerous patients, students, acquaintances, and family members. The few pages that refer to their stories in this book cannot capture the time, commitment, and wealth of material they each offered to this project. I am greatly honored by their involvement and their trust; their lives embody and validate the ideas that this book addresses.

INTRODUCTION

WHEN I BECAME A PSYCHOLOGIST twenty-five years ago, the delicate balance between personal and professional life was a hot topic. This topic gained urgency as women pursued career goals previously attainable only by men. Concerns regarding the changing roles of women in society worked their way into my patients' sessions, into my students' papers, and into discussions that I had with both colleagues and friends. To understand some of these issues I organized a seminar to explore problems that confronted women in the workplace. Entitled "Women, Motivation, and Success," the seminar focused on stories of highly accomplished contemporary women and how they managed their professional and personal relationships. From their experience, I hoped that my students and I would clarify the costs and benefits that accompany our personal and professional choices.

As I searched for firsthand reports on this topic, I found few accounts about the impact work choices have on personal relationships. So I set out to interview notable women in athletics, business, entertainment, government, and journalism with the hope that we might learn from those who had opened doors and directly confronted these issues.

Yet while I was conducting these interviews, my personal life was suddenly ravaged: my mother was diagnosed with terminal cancer. She was given three years to live. My family was thrown into a state of emotional shock. My mother was the family's emotional and spiritual center—and the thought of her loss shook our foundation.

As we began to rearrange our individual roles and relationships, the dynamics of our family quickly changed, and old relationships took on a new depth. The children whom my mother once cared for were now her caretakers. And while my sister and I had previously been distant, we now began to develop a close relationship. My relationship with my father also changed. At one point, he flew from Chicago to visit me in Boston. During his trip he suggested that he might come live with me. I was taken aback as I watched him begin to plan a life without my mother. The commanding marine of my childhood was now dissolving before me; he was becoming a dependent figure.

Tragically, it was not long before our family was shaken once again: my father too was diagnosed with terminal cancer. Although his prognosis was more optimistic than my mother's, his illness advanced aggressively and took his life within a few years.

During my parents' illnesses, I became painfully aware of the limitations of time. Feeling the need to celebrate their every remaining moment, I tried to help them realize some of their dreams. I took my father on a safari in Kenya and joined him in living out his youthful fantasy of taking an adventure in the wild. I also traveled with my mother to Greece, the ancestral homeland she had always longed to see. The time I shared with my parents on these trips allowed me to express my love for them. I cherished the opportunity to be a part of these joyful moments that were scattered in the desert of their physical challenges.

Through these voyages, my perception of my parents changed. I began to see past the unassailable images of "Mom" and "Dad" and to know them differently outside their parental roles. Now we related as adult friends. With a fresh perspective, we found ourselves in a new place—one characterized by intimacy and understanding. These new connections were direct and powerful: the most powerful, in fact, that I had ever felt. It was more than the crises we faced together; it was the depth of the connections we now shared and the genuineness of those bonds. Reflecting on these times, I realize that while I was saying goodbye to them, I was also sharing a deeper experience of life with them.

Authentic Moments

What I had experienced were authentic moments: opportunities that provide the groundwork for direct connections—connections that give us access to ourselves and to others, and to assess what is of true value. In authentic moments we let down our defenses; these are the moments that create trust and allow us to feel open, to take risks, and to be vulnerable and honest. Authentic moments provide clarity and reveal the genuine qualities we hold within.

Authentic moments often result from crises that focus us toward what is most important and valuable in our lives, namely our most direct, clear, and honest relationships. For example, I witnessed my parents gain greater awareness of one another when their lives seemed to be ending. Their needs, desires, fears, and regrets led them to reach out and find one another.

My parents' suffering provided the impetus they needed to break through their ingrained habits and inhibitions and to bring more honesty and spontaneity to their relationships. Their newfound openness was a revelation to me as they discovered meaning in all they had endured and shared. They moved outside of their established routines—he joined her in grocery shopping and engaged in the neighborhood gossip, and she sat with him and cheered on the Chicago Bears, commenting on the plays with him as if they were lifelong buddies. The vulnerability brought on by their physical struggle led them to become much closer and to participate in each other's world as they never had before.

Authenticity Engaged

Authenticity is truth and genuineness; it means remaining faithful to your personality, spirit, and character and not letting your original self become corrupted with falsehood. You sense when you are being authentic. You know when you are doing something that feels honest and sincere, just as you know when you are playing a role or putting on a "game face." You also know when someone is "being real" with you. Authenticity is therefore something we all can recognize and something we all have experienced. In its simplest form, it is much like the heartfelt, honest enthusiasm of children who are eager to be with you when you show interest in them.

Following my father's death, my mother seemed determined to maximize each moment. Her three-year prognosis stretched into ten precious and vital years. During this time, and through several tumors and hospitalizations, she never once complained or expressed her fear to me. Her perseverance and strength moved me. For example, when we were in Greece, her determination led her on an arduous religious pilgrimage and a barefoot climb through the mountain cliffs of the Meteora monasteries to participate in Holy Week services. Physical limitations would not stop her desire to make contact with God. My mother was gaining a deeper understanding of who she was and what mattered to her, and was seeking genuine fulfillment in her life.

During the difficult period of my parents' illnesses, I experienced a deep sense of authenticity in both their deepening relationship and their openness to themselves, others, and God. Their honesty toward each other strengthened their relationship, and they could support one another even when things were at their worst. They were also honest with themselves. In particular, my mother's realistic appraisal of her situation gave her a genuine sense of peace. At one point, as the end drew near, I asked her about dying, and she confessed, "I don't want to die. I want to be with you and the family. But I know that we all will die. I know this life is just a visit, and I have to get ready for what's next. But for now I want to make the most of every day that I have."

Recognizing my parents' deeper awareness of themselves and of one another directly affected my own personal and professional relationships. It also influenced my research. By now it was apparent that this struggle for self-awareness and balance was not a theme for women alone. As I explored how people find fulfillment in their jobs and in their homes, I began to pursue the deeper, more personal themes I found in my interviews with both high-profile men and successful women. To my surprise, many of these celebrities welcomed the opportunity to consider how their more private (and sometimes painful) experiences awakened a need for authenticity in their lives. Tom Hanks, for example, willingly described the extreme loneliness in his early life in contrast to the vibrant relationships that he has developed throughout his career. Lucille Ball, moreover, discussed how she established a committed relationship through remarriage long after confronting the emotional devastation caused by her former husband's infidelity. Jay Leno connected his interest in entertainment to his childhood efforts to gain the recognition of his parents. And Sandra Day O'Connor credited her life on the farm for fostering the responsibility and values that guided her.

The search for authentic connections and meaning seemed to strike a nerve in each person that I spoke to. What intrigued them were not questions concerning the practical measures by which we succeed or meet society's expectations. I later realized that they were concerned with our ultimate challenge in life: maintaining integrity through our authentic nature and the depth of our relationships. By these means we retain authenticity in our search for fulfillment. For man or woman, famous or not, these are the struggles we all must equally face if we are to find peace in our life and with each other.

The profiles included in this book represent far more than individual stories of struggle, achievement, and success. They tap personal concerns that we all share in our quest for both authenticity and meaningful connections. The questions I asked in my interviews are the same ones that we should also ask ourselves: How do we know what to pursue in life and that we are following our true path? What can give our life purpose? Do we have meaningful relationships? Do we guide our life in accordance with our beliefs? How do we know that our beliefs are true?

Each person may have a different answer to the people and the choices that will bring them lasting fulfillment. Nonetheless, the quest for connection and fulfillment resonates equally for all of us, and we can learn from one another. Indeed, the challenge for each of us, regardless of gender, age, and our notion of "success" is to find our own understanding of meaningful relationships and to develop them. Our efforts to do so ultimately affect how, with whom, and to what extent we reach fulfillment.

Through the painful but transformative period of my parents' illness, I began to reassess my own principles of living. My own quest for fulfillment has led me to a lifelong study of medicine, psychology, and religion through research and teaching; clinical work with patients; encounters with the foremost leaders of our time; and improvement of the personal relationships in my own life. Yet while this has been my own odyssey, I have found that for all of us what is important in life—what is genuinely fulfilling—comes from understanding and taking ownership of our natural gifts and making authentic connections with our self, others, and God—our critical connections.

The journey toward fulfillment, as mapped out in this book, offers us an opportunity to grow by encouraging us to move beyond our ingrained habits and to discover the source of our True Self. And it challenges us to take charge of the way we define our actions. Our efforts in joining this quest give us a chance to understand our authentic nature and to engage our innate gifts. By initiating this process and following it through, we can all experience the depth of living authentically, or what I call True Coming of Age.

How to Use This Book

Antoine de Saint-Exupery wrote, "If you want to build a ship, don't drum up the men to go to the forest and gather wood, saw it, and nail the planks together. Instead, teach them the desire for the sea." This book intends to give you that "desire for the sea"—the passion and hope for a fulfilling life. *True Coming of Age* does so by helping you understand how you prevent yourself from fulfillment and recognize and embrace the power within you to create a fulfilling life. To accomplish these goals, *True Coming of Age* asks you to do three things:

First, look within these pages at people who recount their struggles to discover their direction, or their "desire for the sea." Look at them not in one-dimensional terms, such as a celebrity, a mother, a sister, or as a prisoner. Look at them instead with a view of their relationships and connections, that is, a sister who is also a mother, a film director who is also a father—people within the complex networks of life. As you read through each story you will undoubtedly recognize problems that directly and intimately concern you. From everyday men and women to notable Americans,[1] the stories featured here present people undergoing universal struggles. These people, as you will see, are looking back on their critical moments of growth and development. Some show strength when they try to connect to the True Self; others exhibit the disillusionment that persists when they do not. Discover with them the importance of reestablishing connections, opening your heart to your self and to others, embracing the Spirit, and integrating these accomplishments into your daily life.

Second, create the paradigm for fulfillment with which to chart your own authentic path. The book will explain to you what a paradigm is and how it determines your direction, either for good or for ill. The paradigm that you adopt will help you connect more effectively with yourself, others, and God. And through this book's various exercises you will evaluate the quality of the relationships through which your paradigm gets expressed.

Third, recognize that you already possess all the tools you need to lead a fulfilling life through your intrinsic gifts. This book will help you use these tools and deepen the opportunities that life has to offer. *True Coming of Age* will ultimately help you understand the fundamental questions of authentic existence. Yet while this book can guide you to these questions, you must do the asking and answering yourself and make the necessary changes for your life—for your voyage.

Each section of this book helps you maximize your critical connections. The voyage laid out in this book is a daring adventure on the ocean of life, a trip for which we need a worthy vessel. *True Coming of Age* helps us to build our ship to travel life's ocean and find our course on the sea. It teaches us how to navigate both life's storms and life's gentle breezes, how to sail through fear and uncertainty. Let me now tell you how that ship gets built.

Part I, "Knowing Your True Self," is like the rudder of your ship, for self-knowledge gives you direction in life. As you look honestly at yourself, you will rediscover your innate gifts —spontaneity, reasoning, creativity, free will, spirituality, discernment, and love. Knowing how we use these gifts reveals to us how we can chart our own course.

"Knowing Your True Self" proves that in order to reach a fulfilling destination we must use the innate gifts of our True Self to form genuine relationships. This section shows how we lose, confront, bury, or sell out our True Self. By examining the qualities of our successes and failures, we see how disconnection from our True Self affects our direction. Fulfilling others' goals, satisfying others' ideals, or pursuing our own misguided notions of success all tear us away from the True Self. Part I will help us assess the degree to which we are, or are not, connected to the True Self—and how we can reconnect to it.

Part II, "Opening Your Heart," is the hull of our ship. Because your heart holds the fullness of your emotions, the hull is the foundation of our ship that allows us to feel, to express ourselves, and to connect with others. Our heart is the part of the ship that holds everything together. More specifically, "Opening Your Heart" explores how our connection to the True Self affects the emotional quality of our two primary relationships—with self and another. "Opening Your Heart" shows that we build fulfilling connections when we allow our True Self to express who we are to others. In doing this, we chart a course rooted in clear and ready access to the full range of our feelings.

Here we will see how differently we progress when our relationships have an emotional connection to our True Self than when they do not. Living without an open heart disables our connections to self, others, and God. The stories in "Opening Your Heart" emphasize the costs of misunderstood communication, lost passion, and unrequited love, as well as the power of genuine intimacy, self-knowledge, and true acceptance. Through these stories we will explore how we create intimate connections and how others influence our emotional growth.

Part III, "Embracing Your Soul," is the mast. Like the mast of a ship, this part of the book will help support our sails so that they may be unfurled and filled with the breath, or the Spirit of God. Here we will find how our openness to spirituality forms our values and commitments. The Spirit is the force that will carry us forward in our voyage toward fulfillment and purpose.

Spiritual commitments often direct our course through life. If, for example, I believe that God determines my fate, then it would not make sense for me to try to change my destiny. On the other hand, if I believe that God helps those who help themselves, then I am likely to take responsibility for myself and for people and things that are affected by me. Connection to our soul results in clear commitments that bring a concrete realization of our values. Through this process, we allow the Spirit, or God, to be our compass. God navigates our voyage. We need commitment, focus, and discipline most in those moments when we feel abandoned, confused, or isolated because our relationship with God infuses our connections with grace and endurance.

True Coming of Age works from experiences common to many of the world's faiths but does not direct us to a particular religion. At the same time, this book does not espouse freewheeling religious eclecticism. In an atmosphere that pays lip service and courtesy to others without genuinely engaging with them, we risk losing the primary objectives of religion and spirituality that seek to help us connect with God. Also, because spirituality is in vogue, in many places we find openness to the importance of values, religion, and spiritualities; however, spirituality and religious systems may also be mired in political correctness or extremism and may not necessarily seek out the true nature of the Spirit. While an attitude of openness and tolerance is essential for engagement with others, we should not confuse it with our personal spirituality, for this can leave us estranged from the Spirit and disconnected from our True Self.

As many of us are born into different religious traditions, it is fair to ask if our inherited religion actually holds "the truth"[2] and whether it deserves our full commitment. If we were not born into our tradition, would we still stand in it? What distinguishes the quality of life in our tradition from that in others? How do we know the true path? The truth of our spiritual source is a mystery, the fountain of truth, the experience of wonder and awe for which we seek. The further we move away from the source of this experience, the less we are able to find fulfillment and purpose. We must learn to open our sails to experience the powerful breath of the Spirit.

Part IV, "Integrating Your Life," forms the bow and the stern. This section shows us how to connect all of our intrinsic gifts to our heart and soul and how to direct our actions. Our effectiveness in authentic living and our arrival at a safe harbor depend not on our potential but on our ability to apply what we know. Our level of fulfillment depends on how we put together all that we have learned on our voyage—how we organize ourselves and choose our priorities. "Integrating Your Life" helps us know and understand the basic connections among the pieces of our vessel. With a well-built ship, we know how to begin and are ready to make healthy and fulfilling connections, to explore and move through life with access to all of our potential, and to employ our talents and seize opportunities with direction and awareness. Guided from our True Self and critical connections we will arrive at where we want to be. "Integrating Your Life" brings our True Self, our open heart, and our fully embraced soul dynamically together so that we may make healthy, intimate connections. The culminating part of the book shows how to immerse our self in truth through practical applications in daily life.

Such integration helps us experience the amazing power of the Spirit, our compass, so that we arrive at a fulfilling destination characterized by truth in our purpose. Here we discover the unity of our True Self and access our intrinsic gifts more readily than we could when we began. We discover greater depth in our intrinsic gifts and express those gifts in our relationship to self, others, and God. It is here, in this moment, that the process of true coming of age becomes self-renewing. We find our fulfillment and understand our purpose.

True Coming of Age

True coming of age is a gift that only we can give ourselves. The voyage is personal. There comes a day for each of us when we must face one of life's challenges—we must choose a path. No matter how many people have had an impact on us, no matter what our station in life, no matter what else comes, this challenge will not go away.

We can hide from our true coming of age, avoid it, suppress it, and even fight it, but we cannot ignore the consequences of doing so: we will always know within ourselves that something is not right, not fulfilling. We cannot look to someone else for our answers—our answers must be found within. It is up to each of us to reconnect to our True Self and to let our True Self guide our motivations, our needs and desires, our story—to take charge, to remain open, and to embrace what life holds for us.

This book compels in us honest self-evaluation, understanding, and acceptance of how we are living, as well as of the actions we take. It awakens the desire to accept and embrace who we are, the insight to find our direction, and the perseverance to get where we need to go. It equips us to engage with heart, mind, and soul a dynamic process of finding meaning and value. Only through true coming of age can we live in truth, freedom, integrity, and clarity. And only then can we find both our purpose and our fulfillment. By entering within and discovering, accepting, and taking responsibility for our True Self in connection with others and God, we ignite the process of our emotional and spiritual evolution and experience our own true coming of age.

PART I

KNOWING YOUR TRUE SELF

Know thyself.
—THE ORACLE OF DELPHI

WHO AM I? Since the beginning of our history, we have struggled to answer this question of identity. Identity clarifies our purpose, our meaning, and our very reason for being. That is why this quest for self-knowledge is the most significant challenge in each of our lives. How do we find the answer to this urgent and elusive question? Education? Work? Therapy? Religion?

Many of us have embarked on at least one of these paths, hoping that by improving our self-understanding, we will be able to lead more meaningful and fulfilling lives. But some of us have begun these introspective journeys without having clarified our intentions or committed to a strategy. My work in counseling and in interviewing professionals from diverse perspectives and occupations has shown me that such clarification and commitment are crucial and that the first step toward personal fulfillment is to understand and affirm the means by which we get there.

The process of learning about ourselves begins early in life, as we negotiate our place within our home and our society: Am I who I think I am? Do "they" really understand me? To what extent should I reveal what I think and feel? Even though certain aspects of our personalities arise from genetic disposition and the families and cultures into which we are born, and while much of this early questioning occurs at an unconscious level, I truly believe that we shape much of who we are and who we become by the way we approach these questions throughout our lives. We therefore need to be systematic whenever we explore the self; we need to identify the innate qualities of the self and assess the extent to which these innate qualities find expression in our lives.

Part I breaks this self-examination down into three distinct parts: Chapter 1, "Finding Your True Self"; Chapter 2, "Owning Your Story"; and Chapter 3, "Connecting to Your True Self." In these chapters, we will also take the responsibility for recognizing and changing our behaviors, attitudes, and beliefs. We will understand how to identify our intrinsic gifts and how to overcome obstacles that emerge when we are not connected to these gifts. And we will discover what it means to be "true to oneself"—what we accomplish when we are "true" and what difficulties arise when we are not.

To fully understand who we are and why we make the choices we make, we must learn to identify (and sustain connection with) our genuine self—that part of us that I call the *True Self*. When we work on reclaiming and integrating our True Self, we learn to ignore or override impulses and influences that distract us from our authentic talents. When we allow ourselves to be centered and guided by our True Self, we begin to live in alignment with our goals, and we become more willing to assume responsibility for our actions.

What follows in Part I are stories of exemplary and courageous individuals who shared with me the challenges of securing their identities in their efforts to live authentically. Their stories give us insight into the process of knowing our True Self; and their examples show how we can confront and overcome even the greatest of life's obstacles.

The journey toward self-knowledge and fulfillment begins within you. If you are to understand your progress, you must ask yourself some basic questions:

- To what extent do others determine who I am?
- To what extent do I perceive my destiny to be decided by my past, my parents, or the actions of others?
- Can I make the choices and changes that will align me with my True Self and help me uncover my identity?

Confronting these questions may initially feel uncomfortable; change often requires sacrifice and risk because we need to let go of our familiar thoughts and behaviors if we are to take a new course. But asking these questions also allows us to take charge of our search for identity. By making this first step toward finding fulfillment, we come to discover the self we have hidden or lost, to know the self we seek, and to realize the self we want. With a secure rudder built on the solid material of the True Self, we will construct the ship on which we will sail toward our True Coming of Age.

1

⚜

FINDING YOUR TRUE SELF

Dig deep; the water—goodness—is down there.
And as long as you keep digging it will keep bubbling up.
—MARCUS AURELIUS ANTONINUS

OUR AMAZING CAPACITY TO understand and grow is greatly influenced by our environment. In fact, we are incredible receptors; we assimilate and adapt to our surroundings and make the ideas of others our own. The Greeks have a saying, *"Pes mou ton philo sou, na sou po pios eisai"* ("Tell me who your friend is, and I will tell you who you are"); also, from Plato's *Symposium*, *"homoion homoioi aei pelazei"* ("Like draws to like"). Because of this impact of our setting and our malleability, it is reasonable for parents to be concerned about the friends their children choose, the television shows they watch, and the teachers who give them guidance. Such interactions have critical effects on children's perception of themselves and the world.

Likewise, depending on our influences, we either consciously learn or unconsciously adapt to the particular perspectives that will guide us. Thus, some people come to believe that their lives promise only simple or limited choices—or maybe even none at all. Others will be convinced that there are limitless options from which they can choose their own course. These realizations and perspectives form the map—or paradigms—which we knowingly or unknowingly set for our life's course.

Models, Maps, and Paradigms

Our paradigm is the map that guides us through life. One simple paradigm might be, "I am on this earth to serve others"; another might be, "Others are basically out for themselves, and I have to be too." Do you see how each paradigm would either expand or limit its holder's options in life? We may not always be aware of the models, maps, and paradigms that are directing our lives, but they are present nonetheless. Each of us must ask: What is the paradigm for my life? How do I envision my voyage? Who has determined the paradigm that establishes my possibilities?

A paradigm for living consists of a mental picture or metaphor for envisioning what's going on. It influences our outlook on life. Our paradigm may be such that we imagine life as a great sea, a vast expanse of opportunities for exploration. Others, operating under different paradigms, may not see any water at all, much less envision a sea; they may perceive life as a desert. Those who do not share our vision will ask, "What sea? What voyage?" We may think of them as living on a dry dock, disengaged and unaware that there are extraordinary opportunities toward which they may chart their vessel. Still others, who partially share our paradigm, may conjure for themselves the image of a small pond on which they would lead their lives simply and safely. They seek only to paddle a canoe, without pursuing range or depth. Those of us who can see the ocean will need to prepare ourselves by building a vessel worthy of our voyage. We must identify our coordinates and secure a plan.

What, then is your worldview? Do you see the sea? Have you constructed a vessel? Do you envision a voyage? Do you have a particular paradigm?

We learn from our experience what opportunities are possible. Our view and approach to life form our paradigm; the framework in which we place ourselves determines our boundaries. As we take stock of our paradigm, we need to determine if adjustments to it are necessary. Our paradigm establishes our purpose. It gives us identity. Our paradigm is our religion in the deepest sense of the term—the system and cause of our commitments, attitudes, beliefs, and practices. Therefore, it is incumbent on us to take ownership of our paradigm and

- to realize what paradigm we have embraced
- to assess whether or not our paradigm meets our needs
- to know that our paradigm leads us to fulfillment

Many have been indoctrinated into a particular paradigm, neither feeling any vitality in their course nor recognizing the existence of more meaningful options. While the canned answers to life's riddles may leave us dissatisfied, most of us will continue to pursue the path that offer the least resistance. Therefore, once we have been socialized into a paradigm, we are rewarded for playing out our given roles, regardless of how authentically we actually live. For example, a parent may groom a child to manage the family business. But this may not take account of that child's own intrinsic motivation or calling. The demand to please the family and follow the family tradition may cost the individual the invaluable pursuit of figuring out his or her own purpose and destiny. Constructed or solidified in crucial moments of decision like this, our paradigm can become much larger and more influential, affecting our family life, our work, and our values.

Our paradigm of the sea—or whatever image represents our personal philosophy—has real-world implications.

The Paradigm of Self, Others, and God: Our Critical Connections

The fundamental paradigm for fulfillment put forth in this book is the connection between self, others, and God—what I call our critical connections. These areas are our most important relationships for personal development. This paradigm is broad and universal, embracing insights common to us all from the great religions of the world.

The paradigm of self, others, and God is not meant to replace your belief system; it does not supplant or collapse the rich unique elements of particular traditions or orientations. Rather, this paradigm identifies and draws together core aspects of our nature. Accepting this paradigm means recognizing that:

1. We are a unity of physical, emotional, and spiritual dimensions. Our well-being requires that we awaken these aspects of our self and integrate their interdependent dynamics.
2. We are authentically independent as individuals, yet parts of our lives are truly interdependent; therefore, our well-being requires attunement to our connections with our self, others, and God.

The paradigm of self, others, and God invites us to examine the depth of both our independence and our relationships. Being connected can be a difficult task in practice but one that may help us understand our identity.

Let me illustrate how the paradigm works. The figure below shows concentric circles around each of three relationships—to self, others, and God. Our ability to know our self in these relationships is tied to

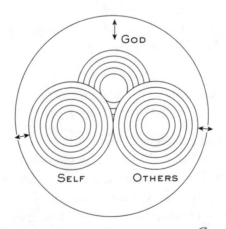

CONNECTING TO SELF, OTHERS, AND GOD

the depth of our understanding of each of these connections. The more we develop our relationship in one of these spheres, the larger the concentric circle. Therefore, we ask: What is the quality of my relationship to myself? To others? To God? While we may feel that we know ourselves, that we have friends, and that we know God, the fact is that such knowledge is an ongoing process. We are never finished becoming our authentic selves. We must ask: To what extent am I engaged? How directly do I know others? How deeply do I feel connected? As we grow in understanding of each sphere and its connections, we experience increased self-awareness, helping us to understand others and increasingly to live out our beliefs and values. In other words, connection in one sphere enhances the potential to connect to the others.* Fulfillment comes from bringing together these critical connections.

Because our engagement with self, others, and God is dynamic— that is, changing and evolving; increasing in one area, decreasing in another; deepening at one time, static or disengaging at other times— we need to monitor these engagements and learn how to develop them.

To visualize our critical connections to self, others, and God and to understand how they lead to fulfillment, let's think of our life as a large

---

*We may know our self, others, and God in varying degrees (as reflected in the layers of concentric circles). Fulfillment increases from depth and directness of the interaction of these connections. Psychologists and scholars have helped us to understand change of growth in our relationships along a spectrum of variables (areas): psycho-sexual development (Sigmund Freud), psychosocial development (Erik Erikson), intellectual growth (Jean Piaget), relational development (Robert Selman), moral development (Lawrence Kohlberg), faith development (James Fowler), and integral development (Ken Wilber), among others. Some of these models reflect changes in stages of growth that are discrete (with clear definitions), whole (descriptive of definable periods in life), and hierarchical (progressing in sequential order toward different variables). Spiritual growth may not correlate with intellectual growth, moral development may not correlate with relational development, and so on.

sphere containing the three spheres of our critical connections. The previous figure illustrates both different levels of engagement in our connection to self, others, and God as well as the dimensional and organismic interaction of our critical connection. The more synchrony created among these concentric circles, the greater our critical connections integrate, the more wholeness and peace we find. The more unity of the circles with one another, the more we experience self, others, and God.

The Self Sphere   Our self sphere contains all that we possess inside us: our thoughts, our emotions, all that we are and all that we have become. It also includes the seven intrinsic qualities (spontaneity, reasoning, creativity, free will, spirituality, discernment, and love). Our growth and development of these qualities form the basis of direct communication with our self. In this way, the True Self plays a critical role in all of our connections. Until you possess the ability to connect to your True Self, you cannot begin to understand who you are and why you make the choices you make—or how to engage others or God in a real and meaningful way.

The Others Sphere   Our others sphere contains all the relationships in our life, past and present: parents, friends, coworkers, spouse, partners, children. These are both people whom we have known and with whom we have relationships today. The degree to which we are able to make emotional engagements with others depends on how much influence our True Self exerts on our self.

The God Sphere   Our God sphere contains all that makes up our experience of spirit: religion, belief systems, existential ideas, pursuits, and our relationship to the higher power. More importantly, this sphere concerns how we bring faith, spirit, and spirituality, as gained through our relationship with God, into all our relationships.

Fulfillment depends upon our rootedness in all three areas, which expands our awareness of self, others, and God—and makes us whole. This does not mean that our understanding of each sphere needs to be all-encompassing and complete. We do not need to have all our questions answered about one sphere before we can address the others. Often, growth in one sphere leads to growth in another. The spheres will not have the same influence (size) at all times. However, it is the extent of our development of each sphere and the strength of the bonds between them that determine the health of our relationships and the fulfillment we achieve. In the chapters that follow, you will understand how our fulfillment grows as we draw these spheres together. The starting point to ignite this whole process is to establish a more direct connection with our self—with our True Self.

What Is the True Self?

The qualities that define us stem from the realization and actualization of our True Self. This authentic solution is available to each of us—it is inside us. By understanding and responding to our True Self, we

- attune to our talents and develop our character
- align our self with our objective—make direct connections to self, others, and God
- live authentically—thrive and experience fulfillment

We discover our own voice through our True Self. It is our voice that leads to authentic actions. At times it may lead to decisions that set us apart from the group, as the author of the Paradoxical Commandments discovered.

THE PARADOXICAL COMMANDMENTS
Kent Keith

1. People are illogical, unreasonable, and self-centered. Love them anyway.
2. If you do good, people will accuse you of selfish ulterior motives. Do good anyway.
3. If you are successful, you will win false friends and true enemies. Succeed anyway.
4. The good you do today will be forgotten tomorrow. Do good anyway.
5. Honesty and frankness make you vulnerable. Be honest and frank anyway.
6. The biggest men and women with the biggest ideas can be shot down by the smallest men and women with the smallest minds. Think big anyway.
7. People favor underdogs but follow only top dogs. Fight for a few underdogs anyway.
8. What you spend years building may be destroyed overnight. Build anyway.
9. People really need help but may attack you if you do help them. Help people anyway.
10. Give the world the best you have and you'll get kicked in the teeth. Give the world the best you have anyway.

Finding and staying connected to the True Self involves, most fundamentally, going within and generating such principles. While it is good to listen to and consider the opinions of others, those others may not understand our goals or facilitate our growth. We must look inside ourselves to ask who we are and whether we are living a life that is consistent with the qualities of our True Self. We cannot afford to mistakenly or impulsively arrive at an answer, for far too much is at stake.

Because we naturally yearn for fulfillment, we will feel a sense of rightness as we begin to take ownership of our True Self. By doing so we will feel a new sense of integrity in our actions. We will feel confident, for we will know that we are living our life in truth.

The True Self is innate in each of us. To engage it, we must first experience the qualities of our nature that define the True Self. It is the source of two basic truths: first, the intrinsic gifts that make us unique and distinguish humanity from the rest of creation; and second, the interdependent relationships among self, others, and God—our critical connections.

Qualities of the True Self

Our True Self is defined by seven intrinsic qualities. I initially identified these qualities during my own study of Christian anthropology while in seminary. As I went on to study psychology and religion at Harvard, I found these qualities confirmed in the great religions of the world and in the modern study of psychology. These qualities are:

- spontaneity
- creativity
- discernment
- reasoning
- spirituality
- love
- free will

Human beings possess these qualities, and they are given to each of us equally. The True Self is not reserved for those who have devoted their lives to becoming mystics. We are born with these resources, and they are available to all of us at any time. By developing them, we engage the critical connections with self, others, and God.

These seven intrinsic gifts form the rudder on the ship of self for our journey to our true coming of age. We may recognize, treasure, nurture, and implement these gifts, or we may ignore them, dismiss them, and take them for granted. If we choose the former course, our lives will be filled with meaningful opportunities. If we choose the latter, we will remain wanting, functioning at a level far lower than our potential. Nevertheless, even if we fail to use them, these qualities lie dormant, for we never lose them. They merely wait for us to awaken them.

Spontaneity

> Children are born true scientists. They spontaneously
> experiment and experience and re-experience again.
> — R. BUCKMINSTER FULLER

Spontaneity is our ability to express ourselves without hindrance. We preserve and develop spontaneity when we feel safe, cherished, and free from distress. Spontaneity captures the innocence, readiness, and freshness of a child. The spontaneous person embraces humor and joy just as children, who are less inhibited and socially constrained and naturally express their authentic and visceral feelings. Those who are spontaneous beyond their childhood years retain honest access to the full range of their emotions. People may attribute spontaneity to those with a youthful character; but while spontaneity involves innocence, childlikeness, and having fun, it also entails resilience and the ability to heal, mature, and expand our competence. Our spontaneity spurs us to growth because we are destined to express our aliveness.

Psychologists have identified six universal emotions that are expressed cross-culturally: happiness, joy, surprise, anger, sadness, and fear. While we often associate access to the positive emotions as a sign of maturity, awareness of and access to the full range of one's feelings more accurately characterize one who is spontaneous. To assess our spontaneity, we must ask: Do I feel openness and readiness in my activities? Do I possess a freshness and enthusiasm in life? Do I have access to only certain emotions? Do I feel greater restraint or greater ease with certain emotions?

Reasoning

The first reason for man's inner slavery is his ignorance, and above all, his ignorance of himself. Without self-knowledge . . . man cannot be free, he cannot govern himself and he will always remain a slave, and the plaything of forces acting upon him. This is why in all ancient teaching the first demand at the beginning of the way to liberation was: Know Thyself.
—George Gurdjieff

Reasoning is sound thinking; it accounts for our understanding of the world and our place in it. Through reasoning, we can discover endless ways to explore and engage the world with vitality and creativity and find solutions to a multitude of problems.

Our ability to reason includes the capacity to reflect, understand, and take action, which leads to knowledge. Reasoning, therefore, involves wider considerations than our intellect alone. Reasoning requires contemplation, prudence, and judgment. For example, we all know that we can rationalize immoral behavior or justify contradictory actions. But reasoning, as derived from the True Self, is attuned to our needs as well as those of others, and to God, providing us with perspective. In the guise of reasoning, some may argue that their logic (which they say is based on what they say is true and good) leads them to drastic actions that harm others. However, this is not reason but a rationalization, because reasoning does not lead us to destroy others. Reasoning thus enables us to gauge our concerns, thoughts, and actions in view of their ultimate implications.

Creativity

> *Creativity is . . . seeing something that doesn't exist already.*
> *You need to find out how you can bring it into being and that*
> *way be a playmate with God.*
> — MICHELLE SHEA

Creativity is our unique ability to express something original. Although we cannot, like God, create *ex nihilo* ("out of nothing"), we have the power to generate and transform things: to convert our ideas into new forms, to make our dreams realities, to shape our self and our world—to inspire, excite, incite, calm, and originate. When we create in connection with God, we feel inspired and empowered. Through creativity, we can develop skills that we often do not fully understand or engage. By applying our abilities to new possibilities, we build self-awareness and strengthen our identity.

When we create, we take risks and embrace new possibilities. The creative process taps the source of both our intrinsic nature and our individuality. This permits us to discover and express more of the other intrinsic gifts and more of our self. Creativity helps us to recognize those qualities and to harness their power.

We often feel that what we create is who we are—it is a part of us. We often call our creation art and equate the product with our self-worth. One of the miracles of each of our lives is the possibility of leaving our distinct mark through our creative expressions. In sum, creativity is a unique expression of our own experience and achievements.

Free Will

> *The most tremendous thing granted to humanity is:*
> *the choice, freedom.*
> — SØREN KIERKEGAARD

Free will is our ability to choose. Moreover, it entails thinking outside ourselves—gaining an observational sense of our situation. Exercising free will, we recognize that we can draw on our own voice rather than just echoing what we have been told. By examining the choices we have, we can establish our voice in relation to others and feel integrity in our position.

To not make choices is to give up a part of who we are. Those who feel as if they have lost their will often feel trapped. If we feel that we have no choice or are locked in, we need to examine what constrains us. By drawing on our spontaneity, reasoning, and creativity, we can release ourselves from these shackles.

Spirituality

> *A return to reverence is the first prerequisite for a revival of wisdom. . . . Wisdom comes from awe rather than shrewdness. It is evoked not in moments of calculation but in moments of being in rapport with the mystery of reality.*
> —ABRAHAM HESCHEL

Spirituality is our response to God's call—our communication with the spirit of life's mystery. Spirituality is a mystery not only because it involves something beyond our mind and our knowledge, but also because it comes from our experience of God. The power of that relationship to spirit is unique for each of us; each of us must fashion our own spirituality from encounters with God that give us a clear vision and an understanding of life. This is why there are so many different paths to spirituality.

Our ability to grow spiritually is made possible through a recognition of and commitment to developing our relationship with God. To engage our spirituality, we must engage our personal relationship with God and make this relationship central in our lives. By penetrating beyond the temporal and engaging the mystery, we can be guided in our journey toward fulfillment.

Your relationship to Spirit may be a personal commitment to an organized religion or simply your own way of giving meaning to your life. I call the Spirit God. Let me be clear: I do not say that one religion's God stands over another's. In fact, religion may not even be the best or most direct means through which you can experience God. But whether you subscribe to a particular religion, develop a personal understanding of Spirit, deny all divinities, or are an atheist, there exists one certainty: Things occur in life over which you have no control. You can attribute these things to fate, randomness, nature, or God. I personally believe, however, that it is the Spirit that provides the answers for us in all things.

We find the Spirit when we discover and actively engage our True Self: When we connect to our self, others, and God and hear the voices of our thoughts (our mind), our feelings (our heart), and our spirit (our soul), we both explain and understand our nature and how these connections bring us fulfillment.

Discernment

The supreme end of education, we are told, is expert discernment in all things—the power to tell the good from the bad, the genuine from the counterfeit, and to prefer the good and the genuine to the bad and counterfeit.
—CHARLES GROSVENOR OSGOOD

Discernment is our ability to distinguish good from bad—and to choose the good. When we choose between good and bad, we demonstrate the principles that guide us. Discernment is thus the ability to take moral positions and act according to them. It is not judgmental or disdainful moralizing; it is judgment driven by truth. Discernment emerges from knowing, choosing, and acting on the good.

According to psychologists who study moral development, the simple ability to distinguish right from wrong begins at age three. Even from our earliest experiences, we learn how to discern by developing virtues; and the extent to which we develop virtues (such as kindness, justice, caring, truthfulness, and courage) also determines our ability to discern. Discernment and virtue are mutually reinforcing. While our individual temperament may be drawn to one virtue rather than another, refining our personality through the discipline of enacting virtue shapes both our character and our ability to discern.

The intrinsic relationship between virtue and discernment helps us become more aware of those around us and of the power of God in our life. As we develop the capacity to make moral judgments and to live moral lives, we experience our connection with others and God. Through our discernment, we express our connection to others and define our character.

Love

> One word, though, makes every burden lighter to bear,
> and that word is love.
> — SOPHOCLES

Love is the culminating point of living—the place where we put the True Self to its greatest use. Love is a profoundly caring, intensely passionate, and personal connection that generates respect, honesty, and reciprocity. Love also involves physical, emotional, and spiritual attraction to an other. We are driven by the powerful urge to love and to be loved, for love is intrinsic to our social nature. By trusting another to know our own self through their eyes, we free our self to union—to love and be loved. Loving connections convey the ultimate expression of our authentic existence through an active engagement of self, others, and God. But while love is frequently identified as life's most fulfilling experience, it can also be our most difficult pursuit—because it often gets confined to only one of the three crucial relationships to self, others, or God. Authentic love may begin by engaging only self, only others, or only God. But authentic love always leads to the other two.

Loving is a sacred connection—the highest human function, entrusted to us by God. When that sacred trust is broken, by us or by another, we feel it. When a lover does not act with the kindness and respect that we expect in sacred love, we feel that opening up to that person was a mistake. Although loving may include sex, a relationship based only on sex is not love. Love is a connection that opens the inner floodgates of one's being to another. Because of the inherent vulnerability of exposing the self in a relationship, you feel love when you feel safe and are comfortable enough to "let go" of your defenses. In this healthy expression of love, both people are accessing their True Self.

Finding the True Self

Many sacred traditions and great thinkers have identified inner knowing—the engagement of self with others and God—as the means by which we find purpose. The True Self reinforces the authentic connections we share with others and God as expressed in the seven innate qualities, which have stood the tests of time as the key elements of authentic living. Our ability to express the seven innate qualities of the True Self depends largely, though not exclusively, on how they are nurtured in our early development. Most of us are affected by the kind of nurturing that we receive from others—by their opinions and criticisms as well as by their guidance and support. Our connection to our True Self continues from childhood on and manifests in how we perceive ourselves. This perception encourages us either to access the character-building elements of the True Self or drives us to lose contact with them.

Charting Your Course

He who knows not, and knows not that he knows not, is a fool;
   Shun him.
He who knows not, and knows that he knows not, is simple;
   Teach him.

He who knows and knows not that he knows, is asleep;
   Wake him.
He who knows and knows that he knows, is wise;
   Follow him.

—PERSIAN PROVERB

To help you evaluate your starting point in your true coming of age, take a few moments to reflect on where you are in your life's journey: What relation do you have to the paradigm of critical connections? How would you plot your course in conjunction with the coordinates of self, others, and God?

Perhaps you are a person for whom the self sphere seems overdeveloped. You always put yourself first, have no discernable relationship to God or spirit, and feel lonely. On the other hand, some of us may have an overdeveloped God sphere. Such people pursue their faith so wholeheartedly that they can barely talk to people outside their faith without condemning or confusing them.

Let me give an example of the seven intrinsic gifts at work in interpersonal dynamics. Often in the face of a crisis, because we are at risk, we feel vulnerable. We may fear sharing ourselves and avoid trust and exchange. When I think about how my sister and I became closer to our parents during their battle with cancer, I realize that our perceptions of our parents changed as our self-perceptions changed as well.

Most significant was how we experienced one another. My parents' increased connections to their True Self affected the quality of their daily lives; they felt close to each other, understood each other, and shared more of life together. I believe that this connection greatly affected my mother's long-term health—her three-year prognosis was extended to ten. My parent's growth in spontaneity, creativity, spirituality, and love changed the quality of their lives and the fulfillment they found. They seemed less self-focused and more available to each other. They were more interested in doing things and strengthening their connections with family and friends.

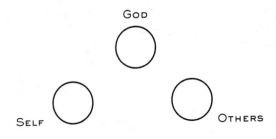

IDENTIFYING
YOUR COORDINATES

Spiritual life deeply strengthened my parents' new openness. While all my life I had observed my father's respectful but reserved stance on faith, I was struck by his pursuit for connection with God. On one occasion, there was a news report of a miraculous icon of the Virgin Mary weeping in a Chicago church. In the past, he would have reacted skeptically toward this kind of news. But now he not only waited patiently in a long line to see the icon but also was conspicuously moved by the encounter. He was willing to change his bent and seek a spiritual connection—and in so doing bring transforming experiences to his life. He revealed new hope and openness to new encounters in life.

Consider the coordinates above. Do all three coordinates appear on your map? Some people may find only the self; their lives are fully consumed by their daily agonies and triumphs. Little besides themselves seems to exist. Some will image only others. Absorbed by the continual demands that others place on their lives, these individuals are totally enveloped by others—as if nothing else exists, not even themselves. Still other people may be absorbed in their focus on God or some idealized truth. Yearning to do what is right, this group has inadvertently lost the basic point for which their Truth holds significance. Typically, the coordinates in our lives will be skewed, not balanced between self, others, and God. Do any of the following models illustrate the coordinates of your life's map?

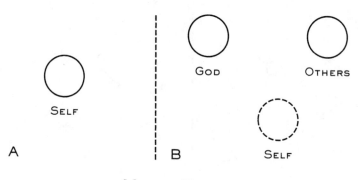

MAPPING YOUR
COORDINATES

Now take a look at the diagram above. If we map our course as in A, we see neither the journey, others, or God. There exists no genuine connection. We are preoccupied with our self and our burdens, and we are immobilized. Here we engage in life without recognizing it. We see our own needs, but are unable to recognize the needs of others. This is the perspective appropriate to a young child.

In B, our self is undefined and misunderstood. We relate to others indirectly. We are clear in principle about the significance of the others and God, but self, others, and God are not understood personally. We can think about them, but we cannot experience them. We have not made the connections.

In C, on the next page, our awareness relates both to our needs and those of others. But there is nothing else. Life is about attending and engaging our self and others as we agree with the other.

In D, on the next page, while self, others, and God are charted, we define God in the service of our own image and likeness. Others exist, but they are of little significance to us. In this model, we have a one-way relationship to God; we feel assured of how we interpret our actions. Yet there is no relational development between self, others, and God.

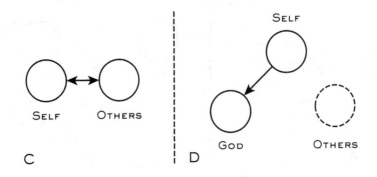

DRAWING YOUR COORDINATES OF YOUR CRITICAL CONNECTIONS

How would you identify the coordinates in your life? Make a drawing of how you see your self, others, and God spheres connecting. Is one bigger than the others? Or does one sphere not even exist? What life choices have led to the distortion of your coordinates—or the problems in your paradigm? In the course of this book, you will see how to redirect your coordinates and to create a meaningful paradigm.

As we have seen, the seven intrinsic qualities of the True Self are the means by which we acquire our authenticity. But as we have also noted and will see later, these intrinsic qualities may lie dormant or become disfigured and unrecognizable. As we will see, permutations or distortions to these qualities occur as a product of life experience. Sometimes, as noted in the Persian proverb on knowing, we may be unaware of our lack of knowledge, or unaware of our dormant gifts, or, in fact, may have a solid hold on our True Self. What about you?

Assessing the Intrinsic Qualities of the True Self

To what extent do you express:

	Yes	No
1. Spontaneity		
• Do you take charge of your life rather than respond in reaction to circumstances?	☐	☐
• Do you engage freely and naturally?	☐	☐
• Are you open to new ideas and activities?	☐	☐
2. Reasoning		
• Do you think through your options before acting?	☐	☐
• Do you take steps to increase your ability to reason?	☐	☐
• Do you learn from your experiences and assimilate what is new?	☐	☐
3. Creativity		
• Do you generate ideas, projects, and plans?	☐	☐
• Does your work tap into your ideas?	☐	☐
• Do you have ways to express your creativity?	☐	☐
4. Free Will		
• Do you think you have choices?	☐	☐
• Do you take opportunities to express your freedom?	☐	☐
• Do you take advantage of your opportunity to choose?	☐	☐
5. Spirituality		
• Do you believe in something greater than yourself?	☐	☐
• Do you bring your spiritual or religious beliefs to your action?	☐	☐
• Does spirituality affect your relationships?	☐	☐

ASSESSING THE INTRINSIC QUALITIES OF THE TRUE SELF, CONTINUED

	Yes	No
6. Discernment		
• Can you judge good from evil?	☐	☐
• Do concerns of right and wrong guide you?	☐	☐
• Do you see more than one side to problems or opportunities?	☐	☐
7. Love		
• Do you have someone with whom you love and share?	☐	☐
• Does loving enhance your life?	☐	☐
• Does your love reflect a connection with self, others, and God?	☐	☐

How did you do? Do you have these personal qualities in the self sphere? Do you have deep connections to your social engagement (others sphere) and in spiritual matters (the God sphere)? Do you realize that the relationship between these innate qualities is within your grasp? Many of us recognize the significance of the individual qualities of the True Self but neglect to make the connection between how the qualities that we possess can bring us increased fulfillment.

2

❧

OWNING YOUR STORY

First tell yourself what sort of man you want to be;
then act accordingly in all you do.
— EPICTICUS

WE DO NOT ALL START FROM the same point in life. Possessing different abilities, educational backgrounds, and support systems, we embark either well-equipped or ill-equipped for our voyage. Yet however we are launched, we need to take stock of ourselves and determine how we will proceed in our journey. We need to gain self-awareness. To do this, we must answer some basic questions and attend to our innermost thoughts and feelings: How does my childhood affect my life? Am I interacting with others now as if I am still responding to those from my earliest relationships? Do I understand myself? Do I have access to my True Self? Do I know and feel comfortable with who I am?

While our parents and caregivers usually intend to equip us with what we will need for our voyage, they too are limited in what they have been taught, in what they know, and in what they are able to do. If we follow only their dreams for us or repeat their mistakes, how can we pursue our own journey? If those who nurtured us did not know their True Selves, how will we? We must each answer, "How did I get here?" and perhaps more importantly, "How can I go from here to where I need to go?" This is the process of owning your story.

Our past relationships shape our current self-awareness. As experiences have formed our self-esteem and character, our earliest moments may have suppressed or awakened our True Self. In this chapter, we will consider how realizing our True Self today, regardless of our history, enables us to actualize our potential. By studying our past, we can gain a current hold on our self-awareness.

Let me begin by telling the stories of two children who, though deprived of parental love, both found professional success—but with very different levels of fulfillment and very different attempts by each to reclaim their True Self.

A Child of Divorce

Only five when his parents divorced, this forty-two-year-old man downplayed the separation's consequences for his life. Rather, he began our interview by enthusiastically sharing his first powerful childhood memory, an event that took place in an auditorium:

> I think I was in fourth grade. All I did was read about Sir Francis Scott Key, who wrote the Star Spangled Banner. But to get up and just read four paragraphs in a microphone and have everybody standing there and looking at me made my little head come off. I immediately warmed to the task that was there. Everybody stopped what they were doing, everybody looked in one place, and they looked at me. It was wondrous, exciting, thrilling; and it was just extraordinarily special—unlike anything else in my youth.

His father, whose time was heavily invested in the restaurant business, was frequently missing in his life. Moreover, his parents fought and divorced, his father married five times, and the family moved frequently. He described his pursuit of theater during adolescence in terms of communal, creative efforts. In high school, the chance at a group identity drew him in, to an "eclectic and romantic clique who knew how to do this. It looked," he said, "like the most fun you could possibly have, and certainly a lot more fun than being on the track team."

But the attention he craved and gained on stage seemed to me to have its roots in a deeper lack. He reported nonchalantly that he grew up living almost exclusively with his father since he was four years old and characterized his mother's absence as inconsequential. It struck me as odd that he made no connection between his lack of parental attention and his enjoyment of the spotlight:

> I don't really know what growing up without my mom around was like; it was normal. We visited her four times a year. In some ways I remember having the mistaken impression that I had an advantage over a lot of my friends because I got to go somewhere. I actually liked it. I'm sure I missed a lot by not having an everyday close relationship with my mom until much later. But I honestly had nothing to compare it to.

It was apparent to me how sensitive this man was to what other people thought and felt about him. So his neutral reaction in response to what sounded like his mother's rejection made little sense. I asked him whether he thought his attraction to performing filled a need for attention left unfilled by his parents. He confided: "Well, I thought so when I was in my twenties and thirties. . . . I enjoyed that form of attention when I was reading Francis Scott Key because I wasn't getting any at home." Now he admitted that his parents' divorce had fostered in him a sense of loneliness, insecurity, self-reliance, and a search for emotional connections.

Where families often generate their own community, nurturing fellowship, establishing rituals and celebration, he had felt a vacuum. When I asked what it was like or what he did during the painful or lonely times of childhood, he reiterated that nobody was there for him. He did not know if it was right to have the feelings that he had or, more importantly, if his feelings even mattered to anyone. This made him uncertain about himself and awkward with others. While acting was easy, interacting was not. He was self-conscious and self-doubting.

Thus, he understood the origins of his skill to engage and disengage emotionally from others as an adaptation to the emotional demands of his early life. These experiences in emotional detachment provided him with invaluable professional skills for acting. But he distinguished this training from his own yearnings to seek out genuine connections and personal fulfillment. He acknowledged that his extraordinary ability to pour himself into roles has been a double-edged sword. Professionally, it has been a strength, containing his own person (itself hidden in a cocoon) from getting in the way of his characters. Personally, however, this mechanism has hindered his discovery of his own identity and genuine connections: "While I usually told myself that my search for authentic portrayal was about acting, I'm only now wondering if this search exposed something I missed from my past."

This man was able to make a turn in his life, though. He got a second and even a third chance:

Every example of my family, as I was growing up, [taught] that something could happen that would make you get kicked away from the table. The marriage would explode, the father would stop loving the mother, or would move away; maybe take you with him, or maybe not take you with him. That is not a brand of unconditional love. That's the way it was when I was five years old, when I was ten, when I was fifteen years old. My parents divorced quite a bit, and I even had a failed marriage of my own.

My daughter, from my first marriage, who lived with me for a while as an adult, said, "I was really worried there, I thought that something was going to happen. I thought that someone was going to get kicked out. I thought that someone was going to have to move." And I said, "You know what, babe, I know exactly why you think that but that doesn't happen anymore."

This is the power of the union, the friend that I made in my second wife, and the background that she comes from. There is a way of thinking with her that sometimes can be confounding to me but at the same time is unshakable. There is this, "You belong to this family. At this table you can say anything you want. You can be angry over any reasons that you want to be angry.

You can verbalize those things, you can act them out, you can say what you have to say, but you are always going to be welcome in this house and at this table and you will always be loved."

That's a powerful thing. But it's only powerful if it is practiced as long as you live. And I came to that late, I must say. Even when I was married— we'll have been married for fourteen years in April—even in the earlier years of my marriage, I felt I had too many decades of living in the other type of operation, always an inkling of fear that something is going to happen and that someone is going to leave.

This is how Tom Hanks described navigating the challenges of his childhood, establishing himself as an actor, and pursuing his personal goals as they have become clearer to him. His awakening of self-awareness helped the qualities of the True Self to take hold on his identity and led him to an honest confrontation with reality.

Tom is a deeply thoughtful person known by those in his industry for approaching others with great sensitivity and individual attention. While his own needs for emotional nurturance were not met in his early development, he manages to attune himself to the complex needs of others. This attention has enabled him to address his own emotional deficits: "I fret over everything. I go to bed at the end of the day thinking, 'Have I done the right thing? Did I make things better?'"

The watershed in Hanks's transformation came in his second marriage. In this relationship he has felt showered with love and experienced the goodness he had heard about in church. He found the safety and support he needed to delve into his pains and to find genuine connection with another—someone who shared in his search for honest engagement for most, if not all, of the intrinsic qualities that constitute the True Self.

In his life story we see the repeated theme of professional success overlapping and impelling personal success. A short-changed personal life can often build transformative professional skills. How we use those transformative skills to tap our personal qualities and generate new personal growth demands self-awareness.

Hanks has awakened and changed. Now, in response to his daughter's apprehensions about home life, he knows and can tell her, "That does not happen anymore." When he became more confident, he could begin to examine his earlier relationships and how they had impacted his identity. As he deepened his understanding of his own motives and captured his True Self, the connection between his parents' divorce and his longing to know himself became clearer to him. He now "owns his story" and is able to take hold of his feelings from his early home life, to recognize the achievements made possible by knowledge of his True Self, to distinguish between unfulfilling and fulfilling relationships, and to know what is important in his life.

Not every attempt to own your story, however, finds such a peaceful path.

Being Seen but Not Heard

This woman spoke with me when she was well into her seventies. Like Tom Hanks, she was a child of divorce. Eventually she experienced four divorces of her own. With arm and hand outstretched, she looked directly into my eyes and greeted me with vigor and cadence that compelled attention. Her life was a study in contrast: the highs of professional success and the lows of minimal personal fulfillment. She discussed her loneliness in the third person, reserving her "I" sentences for stories of her strengths. Possibly to protect herself from difficult memories, she characterized people and situations with exaggeration:

> My father was totally brilliant, just brilliant. He was one of the most well known patent lawyers in this country. But he was not a real father. Humanly, he lacked warmth, no question. What kind of a father comes home at night

and doesn't go to see his children? He was a monster of a father. He felt children should be seen and not heard. He didn't want to hear them, see them, or have any contact with them. Not a real father. He walked out on us. My parents divorced when I was six years old. Probably the greatest gift given to me by my father was the day he said to me "You can never become an actress! It is ridiculous!" He told me to go to secretarial school. I never forgot it.

Deeply affected by a lack of emotional contact with her father, she painted a picture of herself as a little girl longing for a loving embrace—an embrace that never came. Her story, however, was not that of a sad person but rather of one who fought fiercely with everyone and always with the same energy that she had used to get her father's attention.

As a child, she tried to get his attention by proving his callous predictions for her wrong. With vivid clarity she related a time when he saw her perform on Broadway. Afterward he came backstage and "expressed admiration for everyone in the cast except me." Then she recalled, "I asked for his words of praise." Very animated, she explained, "I wanted to shake him, to say, 'I was good, too!'" Withholding the love and acceptance that she most desired, this woman's father was laying the foundation for her drive and her fight for success, as well as her apprehension of finding true intimacy. I could see and feel her deep hurt.

Even more starkly, her father never gave her much-needed recognition. Attention instead came from outside the family. Her appetite for approval and for honest recognition was ferocious, and her labors to find it knew no bounds; in fact, she had won every possible accolade in her field. So I was surprised when she characterized herself as "empty and boring." When I asked her to elaborate, she cleared her throat. Pausing, as if waiting for help with an answer, she considered:

I don't really like myself very much. I'm a totally split person in that I am one person personally and one person in my work: totally split. In my work I have utter security, utter belief—not true of me personally at all.

After she began a fluid discussion about her professional confidence, I asked her if she could say a little bit more about her personal insecurities. She replied, "Well, I am very grateful for the adoration of the people, and certainly, I have it"—as if to reassure herself before biting this bullet—"but I don't like myself. No, I don't like myself. I don't really know why. I'm a coward. I mean, for me to fire a servant, I cannot tell you what that is like."

Not associating the pain of her father's rejection with her own self-rejection, she confided, "I loathe the way I look—I just loathe the way I look. To get me to look at a show I have done, well, it's just murder . . . never could stand my face. Never. Terrible." I could not help but ask her if she believed there was a relationship between her feelings of physical and emotional inadequacy and her father's rejection.

Haunted throughout her life by her father's abandonment, her despair and anxiety over unrequited affection caused conflicts in her personality and behavior, and she ended up repelling what she sought most—intimacy. This was Bette Davis, acclaimed film star, owner of the world-famous eyes. Davis had a profound awareness of what drove her—the heartbrokenness from which she came—but no ability to support or overcome its effects. As we spoke, we both were gripped and saddened by the extent to which she had relived for seventy-five years the rejection from her father. Whenever genuine affection was within reach, from her suitors or even from her own children, she recoiled to a safer, inner sanctum, lest she revisit the vulnerability of her childhood.

In these brief glimpses, we see the incredible obstacles in Hanks's and Davis's encounters. By identifying certain similarities and differences in their separate journeys, perhaps we can find how similar situations in our own lives can affect self-awareness, form our identity, and develop our True Selves.

Both Hanks and Davis came from humble backgrounds and challenging childhoods. Both channeled their natural talent toward their own emotional defense. Both have been drawn to the portrayal of complex characters. Both struggled in their earliest personal relationships and fought to achieve intimacy. Both wrestled with loneliness, depression, and self-loathing while exhibiting powerful charisma.

As their stories amply illustrate, turbulence in the home often pushes us to extremes. Tom continued always to strive for connection in his personal and professional life, while Bette concluded that "you can't have it both ways." Both, however, were very sensitive emotionally. And while gaining access to their inner worlds was complex, their sensitivity honed their acting skills, which found a safe and enthusiastic reception on stage.

Rousing the True Self

Both our families and our environments deeply affect how we know our True Self. If our parents or society ignore rather than celebrate the qualities of the True Self within us, it becomes difficult to reclaim our True Self.

We all seek affirmation and recognition. If we understand this and are generous in our distribution of it, we will usually find the experience returned. Many people are motivated by power or things that ultimately give them a false sense of self. By engaging our True Self, we are in touch with our authentic nature. Psychologist William James said that we are only half awake, using a very small portion of our brain to direct ourselves, and that we fail to use much of our ability and potential. So how do we pursue our potential and direct ourselves toward fulfillment? To what extent do we know and incorporate our True Self?

I used to work with a college quarterback who came to me with complaints of his obsession with checking the weight of footballs. Later I learned that when he had been five, his father had watched him struggle to pick up a grocery bag, telling him with disdain, "You'll never be able to lift two pounds!" Now in his twenties, this bright and talented young man was seized with doubts every time he made a pass in a game. In fact, his father's insult had dug into his psyche so deeply that when he lifted a book or a bag, he would obsessively ask himself, "Does this weigh two pounds?" His father's comment had instilled in the young man a feeling of inadequacy and incompetence. When he finally confronted his father in therapy, he could not believe that his father had no recollection of the comment. For years the son had been tormented by the compulsive ritual the comment had created and by what he believed his father's words truly expressed—that he was weak and unworthy.

Off-hand comments rarely remain significant outside their context after solid relationships have been established; nor do they become powerful metaphors unless they symbolize the dynamics of a relationship more generally. With Bette Davis and the quarterback, we see extreme manifestations of how seemingly inconsequential comments have lasting effects. Hurtful experiences can take on monumental significance and directly undermine the emergence of the True Self.

Parents should remember that there is plenty margin for error in child rearing as long as the child knows how much he or she is valued. While we will undoubtedly make errors, we can correct them. Positive messages, effectively communicated, will establish self-awareness, as well as a child's access to the qualities of his or her True Self. Here are some important messages to convey:

- I love you, and I act in ways that show it.
- I see you. You are important, invaluable, and you know it.
- I recognize you, and I take the time to give you the attention you deserve.
- I see in you, and in all others, the True Self that gives you dignity, identity, and direction.

Through active involvement with their children and with each other, parents can convey these messages to a child while modeling, reinforcing, and sharing the living truth of these messages.

Engaging the Critical Connection

We all need to be recognized and appreciated. We often grow closest to those who give us a warm reception, affirmation, and support. We get the message that we are good when we are supported and nurtured. In kind, we can support and nurture others. We have all heard that you cannot give what you do not have.

To not give the messages of support and affirmation puts a child into a state of perpetual limbo, as Bette Davis's story illustrates. Adults who have not received such messages continue to feel rejection and develop the unconscious repetition of those negative patterns experienced in youth. When caught in such a trap, we re-create the situations that are most familiar to us, thereby sabotaging our efforts to connect with our True Self and with others. This negative dynamic may be a way of re-creating the distorted intimacy that had been experienced. We set ourselves up for maintaining the status quo: lack of self-awareness, diffusion of identity, and an inability to recognize the qualities that give us access to our True Self. Many patients in therapy will often accuse their unsuspecting (and often innocent) spouses of exhibiting the same hurtful behavior they had experienced as children. Therapy is often about understanding the nature of such cycles, reexperiencing the feelings that first set them in motion, mourning the loss of missed opportunities, and building the structures with which to proceed in life.

Davis illustrates this process. She in essence "raised" her own mother and was in turn "raised" by her own daughter. Even though she described her mother in very caring terms, she at times felt like her mother's keeper—a phrase that, to Bette's shock, was hauntingly echoed by her own daughter's book. In B. D. Hyman's *My Mother's Keeper*, we observe the assumption of caretaking duties by the next generation and Davis's difficulty in creating bonds of genuine intimacy in her mother-daughter relationships.

A warm embrace helps to produce the safe environment that we may have missed in our youth and creates a place where we can grow and connect with others. Bette Davis never had such a source of care and understanding; and as a result proceeded through life alone. Bright and competent in many ways, she recognized the unhealthy nature of her marital relationships but remained helpless to change them.

Another way that we cope with our pain from early relationships is to unconsciously hold onto them and incorporate our negative self-image into future relationships. In this way, we also hold onto our parents, our roots, and our history, even when it is damaging. We incorporate the negativity we feel with ourselves into our new relationships.

I recall a patient who I once treated for anxiety. On one occasion, the woman shared with me that she had once taken a knife to her son's neck when he was seven and felt vague about her motives. While years had passed and no similar incidents had occurred, she felt guilt and concern for what damage she might have caused her son. At this point he was thirteen years old. While meeting with him for a few sessions alone in the course of offering a consultation to the family, he never commented on the incident that his mother had shared in a family meeting. At one point, I asked him directly if he could recall the time when his mother had taken a knife to his neck. He said that he did, but he had thought that his mother "was only playing around because I was acting up." It was too difficult for him to imagine that she had a serious problem or that she had violated him in any way. To confront such thoughts, at age seven, he would have felt deserted. In such ways, we often—as children and as adults—assume responsibility for negative experiences rather than risk being alone or dramatically change our view of someone we hold dear.

Dramatic changes, such as divorce, invariably affect us despite our attempts to resist or minimize our feelings. Frequently, when I review with patients the impact of an impending divorce, they want to diminish its significance in the lives of their children, comforting themselves with the common refrains, "Most families experience divorce," "All of my kids' friends are children of divorce," and "At least my kids will only go through one divorce—hopefully." Buried under an avalanche of their own feelings of despair, parents often cannot bear to face the turmoil they have brought upon their own children as well. Speaking to the children, I often learn of their worry over finding their structure of support divided. Even if a child's quality of life is improved by divorce, and the separation is preferable to an environment of marital agony, the chasm produced nevertheless has many consequences.

Despite their professional success, Hanks and Davis continued struggling with intimacy and meaningful relationships as adults. Their own words belied their more confident facades as they spoke of "utter loneliness," "depression," "self-loathing," "sadness," and "emptiness."

Abandonment or violation of this sort can deeply scar any of us, regardless of the success we find in other areas of our life. Each of us must recognize our own response to feeling alone. Each of us must manage the depression and anxiety of our loneliness and understand the impact of others' actions on us—and our responses to them. Hanks quoted director Vincent Dawling as saying, "All the great stories are about loneliness." It may be in part because Hanks and Davis identified with the depths of such pain that they became great actors and artists.

Fear of loneliness teaches many of us to fill our lives with things and activities, lest we confront the loneliness head on. In assessing our situation, we need to distinguish depression and loneliness that arise from severe rejection, trauma, and loss from the aloneness that everyone— however healthy—will face in a life of union, separations, and ultimately death. To do this, we need to be self-aware.

Self-Awareness: Connecting the Dots

The discovery of one's True Self is a process. Although you may not have actively explored your intrinsic qualities, you may bump into them, even without guidance. These inherent abilities, such as reasoning and creativity, are often the means for our success and the tools with which to solve our problems and form healthy intimacy. So we must connect the dots—connect the qualities of our True Self with actions.

All of us have both positive and negative qualities. Self-awareness brings us to a realistic place from which to start. Just remember:

+ Do not idealize yourself.
+ Do not judge yourself.
+ Be honest with yourelf.
+ Direct yourself to the good.

Tom Hanks and Bette Davis used their creativity to move from their stagnant worlds to new opportunities. Their craft so powerfully propelled them that they were totally absorbed in their careers. And their reward for their singular focus was a profound sense of accomplishment and a distance from a difficult past. And the more they achieved, the greater potential each had for growth in the True Self.

Most lives have many facets. While we often feel the need to burrow into one area (consciously or unconsciously) because of the rewards we find, self-awareness makes us cognizant of our individual qualities and the full range of our self in all our relationships: with others at work, at home, and with God. Self-awareness rouses us to take an inventory of the extent to which we have connected the dots and found consistency in our feelings, character, beliefs, actions, traits, and demeanor. It entails distinguishing between attributes and roles we have "tried on for size" from those qualities that we possess and own. Our self-awareness is an ongoing process of discovery, and it is especially available to us when we act in ways to truly understand who we are.

Some people start toward fulfillment by developing, perhaps overdeveloping, one quality of the True Self. For Hanks and Davis, creativity became their lifeline, the vehicle for their outer lives and the tunnel to the inner self. As Bette Davis put it, "It's not the most talented people who make it to the top; the ones who make it are those with drive: I had a deep desire to make it." Engaging the experiences of any of the qualities of the True Self may provide the springboard out of this malaise in which we find ourselves and introduce us to the deepening of other parts of the True Self we did not know existed.

Tom Hanks put it this way—essentially commenting on our True Self and our critical connections:

> We have to inch closer to brotherhood.... or else we are missing out on a great opportunity in the only place in which we get to change our lives and the world. The only secret of happiness is honesty, you know. Be honest all the time [and] you might have actually found the secret of happiness. And that is hard to do, hard to do all the time. Also, there is the power of unconditional love. And that is not a magic thing. That is literally saying, no matter what you do, or what you say, I am still going to love you. But I was an old—older man before I truly felt as though I was sitting at a table at which unconditional love was practiced. Before this there were an awful lot of feelings of loneliness that I had.
>
> I believe in the Great Mystery that's going on. There's going to be a time when it's going to be explained to us in ways that we can understand it, but right now, I [have] just got to believe that there's a reason for everything we're going through. There's a line in the song "Amazing Grace": "Through all life's dangers, toils, and snares, we have already come. 'Twas grace that brought me safe thus far and grace shall lead me home." Grace is something that you can accept from a great piece of art; it's a healing acceptance that says, "You're going to be okay."

Hanks feels this; he knows this; he lives this. Its power cannot be contained by the influence of religion. It's a spirit, the grace available to us in life once we connect to it. The power of Hanks's spiritual perception comes not from the story's end, with the emotionally imperiled poor boy making it big, but his recognition of its progression. Or, in his own words, it is a knowledge you gain from "feeling responsible for all the things that have gone incredibly well and for all those things that have gone badly: the struggles, the difficulty . . . always accepting yourself no matter where you go . . . and [creating] as best you can, when you can." In truth, many directions can serve you in your search for the True Self.

Sinners, Stars, Saints, and Spectators:
Getting Real, Being True, and Having Self-Awareness

The power of the True Self lies in its availability to all. Every physician, counselor, and confessor knows from all of those who come to see him or her that each of us is flawed. We all face challenges from which we can grow. The goal is not to become an idealized star or perfect saint, because these are illusions (fantasies rather than realities) or destructive delusions (unrealistic ideals that we pursue).

Awareness of the True Self keeps us from idealizing good and evil. It is certainly appropriate to be skeptical at times. Sometimes religions have idealized their heroes—either out of respect or in an effort to provide glowing examples of good deeds. But perhaps our skepticism inadvertently takes us off the hook: "Since I am not, nor can ever be, that holy or good, I will stay on the sidelines and watch." We thus become spectators.

There is a story in the literature of the Desert Fathers about a man who went out to meet Saint Anthony, the renowned monastic who had overcome the temptations of the devil and to whom many miracles had been ascribed. As he searched the barren desert, the man came across an elderly wanderer and sought his advice as to where he might find the revered saint. The old man said that he didn't know of such a person, nor had he heard of any saint. In despair, the pilgrim continued his search. After time passed, he returned to his village and shared his lack of success with the religious elders. To his surprise, the elders replied: "You met him. Saint Anthony was the old man with whom you spoke." Do we see the opportunities within our reach? The potential before us? The potential within us?

We often seek truth outside of ourselves and pass it by when it's right in front of us. When we have access to our True Self, we immediately recognize truth because it resonates with our own intrinsic qualities. The True Self cannot be confused with a glorified ego because the True Self is grounded in our connections with others and God. As we found with Hanks and Davis, fulfillment is not equated with accolades and attention. Fulfillment is instead rooted in the combination of self-awareness and expression of the True Self. The True Self leads us to recognize the only dependency and connection that we can count on—God. We cannot ultimately depend on the connection with others or even with our own self. How many times have others disappointed us? And how many times have we taken a position that we said we would stick to only to change that position soon after? In this chapter, we have seen that the engagement of our self-awareness may take a highly circuitous route. Yet we have seen the significance of the True Self in this process: how we may develop great skills and achievements but not necessarily develop the perspective to connect the dots and how in even the most complicated and devastating situations the qualities of our True Self provide the means for achieving our potential.

In the lives that we have begun to consider, we have seen the importance of recognizing and developing awareness through the True Self. If the True Self goes unrecognized, we must seek to bring its qualities forward, but in a manner that permits us to actively participate in life. Seeing within our self the sinner, the star, and the saint, we are not "spectatoring," but living.

The following exercises will help you to reflect on your early development and to consider how your experiences have affected your voyage.

The Self-Awareness Exercise

This exercise helps us recognize and understand the source of our concerns, fears, and desires, identifying where we began and how we got where we are. Reconnecting to childhood can be a profound experience. It can resurrect forgotten hopes, remind us of lost innocence, and help us understand our story so that we can better understand where we need to go. Recall your memories and dreams and the way you viewed the world as a child: Anything was possible, hopefulness was second nature, and fulfillment seemed just a day away. Let's reconnect to those dreams.

Think back:

- What did you want to be? How did that make you feel?
- Have you become what you wanted to be?
- Have you become whom you wanted to be?
- Were you introduced to an ocean of possibilities by your parents or by other influential people in your life?
- Who helped prepare you for life's journey, and what was the impact of those lessons on your journey?

Now ask yourself these questions: As you think about your path and the turning points you confronted, do you think you were adequately introduced to the qualities of your True Self? Have qualities of the True Self appeared to you in others? Do you wish to further develop your True Self? Do you take the opportunities available to you?

The Quiet Storm Exercise

This exercise helps us to see and resolve lingering problems that create undercurrents—internal problems of identity related to our connection with the True Self that we must identify, "the quiet storms" of life.

Consider these questions: To whom do you turn when you're in need? Why do you turn to that person? How do you overcome undercurrents, internal and external, that hold you back? Can you think of ways that engaging the qualities of your True Self can change your situation?

The "I Am" Test

Complete the following twenty sentences, describing yourself with the first associations that come to mind.

I am _____

I am _____

I am _____

I am _____

I am _____

I am _____

I am _____

I am _____

I am _____

I am _____

I am _____

I am _____

I am _____

I am _____

I am _____

I am _____

I am _____

I am _____

I am _____

I am _____

Was it difficult to come up with twenty responses? Pauses can signal a quandary, a change of focus, or a shift from feelings to thoughts, or vice versa. Did you pause between responses? If so, what were you thinking during your pauses?

Look at what you have written. Does it reflect the aspects of your physical, social, psychological, and spiritual self? Note descriptions such as "I am fat" (physical); "I am a dentist" (social-vocational); "I am cheerful" (psychological). Try to understand what you see, the particular areas that you identify, and the patterns that they reflect. How many responses are negative? How many are positive? How many focus on the physical? How many focus on the psychological? How many focus on the spiritual?

Frequently, when students and patients present their problems, I ask them to take this self-examination. For some, the statements are negative, ambiguously so at times: "I am lost," "I am ugly," "I am stupid," "I am unlovable." And yet others may write, "I am hopeful," "I am nice." This exercise gives us a snapshot of our self-awareness. Your responses indicate how you view yourself.

THE "I AM NOT" TEST

As in the "I Am" test, take a pencil in hand and complete the sentence beginning "I am not" twenty times.

I am not _____

I am not _____

I am not _____

I am not _____

I am not _____

I am not _____

I am not _____

I am not _____

I am not _____

I am not _____

I am not _____

I am not _____

I am not _____

I am not _____

I am not _____

I am not _____

I am not _____

I am not _____

I am not _____

I am not _____

The ways in which we perceive ourselves in the "I Am" and "I Am Not" tests may describe the ways in which we either idealize or limit ourselves. Often, because we lose connection with our innate spontaneity, we may not be able to see ourselves as changeable. The "I Am" and "I Am Not" tests also reflect our sense of being fluid and show us those areas in which we may be stuck. Engaging our True Self can change this picture.

3

❦

CONNECTING TO YOUR

TRUE SELF

The day we stop resisting our instincts,
we'll have learned how to live.
—FEDERICO GARCIA LORCA

WE HAVE SEEN WHAT HAPPENS when the True Self does not develop. But what does it mean to grow? Where should we place our efforts? To develop our minds? Our hearts? Our souls? And what if we were never given a chance to grow physically, intellectually, and spiritually? Are we thus condemned and disadvantaged?

As we learned in our discussion of paradigms, our perception of the world can determine where we look and what we see. Our experiences in childhood and as young adults can distort our vision and keep us from connecting to our True Self.

In this chapter, we will look at some of the reasons we pursue empty promises in our search for fulfillment. We learn, above all, that an abiding sense of realism in the face of pressures and expectations is key to our search. We will also distinguish between the qualities of the True Self and those of our individual talents. We will further learn how pursuit of "perfectionistic" goals can be superficial and lead us away from the True Self. Finally, we will also explore the significance of our physical body in our total development—especially the body's role in integrating the heart and soul.

Nurturance

Nurturance is affectionate care and attention that promotes our physical, emotional, and spiritual development. We are affected by our every experience, good and bad alike. Our senses, as our windows to the world, color and shape our inner life. Good nurturance, moreover, keeps us open to new experiences and able to adjust to life's vicissitudes. On the basis of troubling experiences, then, certain receptors of our soul can become blocked, resulting in the contamination of our inner being. What nurturing experiences supported your growth? What troubling experiences have closed you off or shut you down?

Before you begin answering these questions, think of human development through the metaphor of a seedling: thriving when given sun, water, and soil, but dying in the absence of any of these. To continue the metaphor, while we human seedlings are designed to seek out light (the spirit) and to reach out to achieve our potential, our leaves and branches cannot grow without the "water" (nurturance from our caretakers) and rich "soil" (a loving home) to support development of strong roots. Those who nurture us in our early years can either strengthen or impede our development. In the same way, our larger environment will either enhance or jeopardize our ability to thrive.

As we see in the figure on the next page, plants need light just to survive, let alone to flourish. Light is our spiritual resource, that extraordinary source of energy toward which we all naturally turn. Our ability to receive light, however, is limited by our ability to perceive it, and the circumstances of the past and present may hinder the functioning of this process. Such inhibitors to our light absorption may originate in our past, but they may also stem from more recent sources. Where

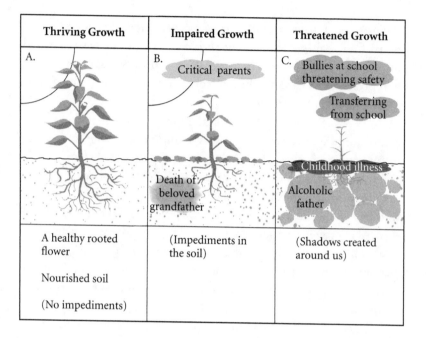

Thriving Growth	Impaired Growth	Threatened Growth
A. *A healthy rooted flower* / *Nourished soil* / *(No impediments)*	B. Critical parents / Death of beloved grandfather / *(Impediments in the soil)*	C. Bullies at school threatening safety / Transferring from school / Childhood illness / Alcoholic father / *(Shadows created around us)*

and how we are originally planted obviously matters a great deal, for damage from early relationships can make substantial flowering difficult; at the same time, to survive, each of us becomes, in our own way, adaptable and resilient. Changing ourselves, removing contaminants, or transplanting to new, well-fertilized soil—all of this can give us ground to flourish. As we saw in the stories in Chapter 2, even in the face of extreme challenges, people are able to persevere and overcome obstacles. Inherent within us are the yearning to survive and the strength to flourish.

Regardless of the individual challenges we meet—whether physical, emotional, or spiritual—we all share a common vitality, a source of opportunity, wonder, and excitement. No life is perfect; we all emerge from challenges, difficulties, and hardships that we have encountered. Life becomes tragic, however, only when we resist dealing with our imperfections or are overwhelmed by them. These are struggles against the process of growth, and their results are stagnation and spiritual death. Our challenge is to find our optimal source of nourishment and to rely on it when we face conflicts. We have already seen how one can find professional success while personal growth remains impeded by a lack of quality nurturance.

To take the analogy even further, we must remember that plants come in multiple varieties—growing in different seasons and in different conditions, their blossoms covering a spectrum of colors. Experienced gardeners know that they cannot care for their plants as though they were all the same. Because I succeeded at growing roses last year, watering and fertilizing them in a particular way, does not mean I will succeed in growing carnations this year following the same plan. Gardeners need to determine what the plant needs by monitoring its response to their care. In the same way, it is necessary to understand another's unique qualities and growth process and to nurture these at the same time as we recognize the qualities of the True Self we all share in common. By doing so, we attend to characteristics that vary from person to person and support the entire True Self by letting each individual's talent and authenticity thrive.

IMAGING NURTURANCE IN YOUR GROWTH

You are now ready to consider your own nurturance. Draw a plant that captures the conditions of your early childhood and imagine the flowers that emerged from this first period of life; let each petal represent a particular achievement or meaningful event. Identify the personal and environmental conditions that may have created obstacles to your development or produced disillusionment or stress. For example, you may represent an angry parent as a cloud or lightening bolt that hits or nearly misses you. Now draw the conditions of your current life. Compare these drawings.

In our childhood, we feel as though our parents are the sun and our homes the universe. Depending on our environment in our youth, we

	EARLY LIFE DRAWING	CURRENT LIFE DRAWING
ENVIRONMENTAL FACTORS (PLANT)		
INTERNAL FACTORS (ROOTS)		

may feel drawn to a mixture of both authentic and artificial lighting, such as decorative lights on a Christmas tree that may be attractive and superficially illuminating but would not support the plant's need for natural light. Of greater concern, however, is that we may be shaded from light entirely, acclimating ourselves as adults to the permanent, unnoticed dimness of our lives. This next story illustrates how nurturance requires more than a well-intentioned plan.

Creating a "Good Home"

Peter stood out among the teenagers I counseled who had been in trouble with the law. An energetic, lively nineteen-year-old, he was neat and poised, carrying himself with confidence and self-assurance. Underneath this controlled facade, however, lurked a youth who had been charged with assault and battery and possession of illegal drugs. His court record described him as "argumentative and aggressive." In therapy, we discovered that Peter's environment, his soil, had been contaminated in large part by his parents' demanding nature. Peter found himself stifled by the very environment that should have encouraged growth.

During our first sessions together, Peter was reserved and withdrawn. His responses were terse, and he appeared preoccupied. An only child, he said that his parents shared a good marriage, held "important jobs," and were "very religious." His own relationship with each of them, however, was much less benign. "They bought into all the rules," he told me. Rules were what it was all about. Since the age of twelve, he had been on a reinforcement schedule; his father literally engineered his life with a token economy, rewarding each accomplishment and doling out punishment "when things weren't done to his satisfaction." Although Peter was an A to B student, his grades were a disappointment to his father, who demanded he receive all A's if he was going to "amount to anything." When Peter reached high school, his father increased his burden of obligations, "making it impossible to see any reward." His father's word, it seemed, had become strict doctrine. Meanwhile Peter's mother remained passive and distant.

Peter said that his parents made him feel like a failure. Although immersed in what he described as a "religious home," Peter had had no positive spiritual experiences. In his mind, God and church were his parents' whip, the means by which they dictated their standards. In a plea for attention, he once told the nuns in his Roman Catholic high school that his parents practiced witchcraft. While his tricks initially garnered support and concern for him at school, Peter's behavior inspired the opposite reaction from his parents. On another occasion, Peter, along with his other unlicensed buddies, "borrowed" his father's car without permission. Outraged, his father pressed legal charges and had his son tried in juvenile court, where the judge reprimanded Peter and placed him on probation. Discontented with the decision, Peter's father convinced the judge to send him to a juvenile facility for delin-quents. From that time on, Peter's crimes escalated.

When I asked Peter what was most important in his life, he answered, "Happiness, honesty, and reaching for something meaningful." When I asked what was not important, he replied:"Religion, society, and family." The very institutions designed to guide us toward fulfillment—toward happiness, honesty, and reaching for meaning—had deserted Peter; he saw them as nothing but hollow and insincere. But without them I won-dered how Peter would gain what was most important to him."I'm still searching," he admitted. His quest had brought him to sex, drugs, and heavy metal, but Peter acknowledged that these provided no real answers.

The vacancies in Peter's family and religious experiences made it difficult—at times even impossible—for him to connect to the qual-ities of the True Self. Although his parents actively participated in their religious community and strove to provide for their son, Peter experi-enced these interactions as rigid and cold. He looked up and did not see any outside light toward which to grow. His soil was contaminated. He was not nurtured in the seven intrinsic gifts. Because he did not learn about his intrinsic gifts, Peter did not nurture them in himself.

People who are emotionally and spiritually fulfilled typically do not steal, because they have what they need; they do not assault, because they can relate well with others; they do not take illegal drugs, because they have access to naturally uplifting encounters. Peter's entire fam-ily shared the consequences of his emotional shortcomings: missing critical moments in his development, Peter failed to forge the con-nections that could have helped him in his search for meaning and purpose. His parents, meanwhile, suffered as their own efforts to aid in their son's struggle caused more harm than help.

And yet, despite the oppressive forces of his surroundings, Peter persisted in searching for his own voice and for genuine connections. While his story is painful, it illustrates the force of our innate drive to live authentically. The search for fulfillment is motivated by no less than a desire for truth, the light that attracts and sustains us.

Peter's story shows that everyone has access to more than one voice—some of which speak from our past, others from our present, and the one from within our True Self. When Peter mastered a streetwise attitude and made himself "cool" through this image, he was seeking genuine connection with his peers. Initially, these voices were louder than his own true voice within, which he associated with his difficult upbringing and so rejected it.

Peter came to distinguish these multiple voices as he confronted several paradoxes in therapy with me. First, though his parents felt that they had found a meaningful path, they could never convey to Peter its vitality. Second, his contrarian position nevertheless allowed him to access qualities of his True Self. He was forced to disentangle the baggage of home from those intrinsic qualities he desired and valued. He refused to participate in empty rituals and chose to follow the immediate feelings and experiences that gave him proof that he was alive: happiness, honesty, and reaching for meaning. While he projected an antisocial exterior to his community, internally he was struggling to achieve genuine relationships. At the crossroads now before him, Peter would have to make a choice: to denounce his inner awareness, submit to his parents, and continue to choose false promises while denying himself; or to transform his exterior disposition to be consistent with his internal objectives.

I have no doubt what path Peter decided to travel. During the several months I worked with him, he remained steadfast in his efforts to understand the directions in which his inner awareness led him. The remarkable progress he made was a testimony to his fight to survive and thrive. He systematically read about different religions and visited a variety of groups to find out whether he could fit in. The transformation included his growth in self-awareness and his exercise of free will and discernment to assess his real needs and to recapture the other qualities of the True Self: spontaneity, reasoning, creativity, spirituality, and love.

Like Peter's parents, we often fail to understand people who are close to us because we presume to already know them. Upon first sight, we interpret a person's appearance, assessing the individual and determining his or her identity based solely on our first impressions. Sometimes "the mask" that we observe has developed because (like Peter) the one we see has become an outcast from society and family and so we put on a mask—an outsider seeking connection. Our ability to know others—and to know our self better—is predicated on our ability to look beyond the masks, biases, and stereotypes and to make contact with the true person.

PLEASE HEAR WHAT I'M NOT SAYING

Don't be fooled by me.
Don't be fooled by the face I wear.
For I wear a mask, a thousand masks,
   masks that I'm not afraid to take off,
   and none of them is me. . . .

So I play my game, my desperate pretending game,
   with a façade of assurance without,
   and a trembling child within.
So begins the glittering but empty parade of masks,
   and my life becomes a front.
I tell you everything that's really nothing,
   and nothing of what's everything,
   of what's crying within me.
So when I'm going through my routine
   do not be fooled by what I'm saying.
Please listen carefully and try to hear what I'm not saying,
   what I'd like to be able to say,
   what for survival I need to say,
   but what I can't say. . . .

Who am I, you may wonder?
I am someone you know very well.

> For I am every man you meet
>   and I am every woman you meet.
> — CHARLES C. FINN

"Feeling Alive" Through the True Self

In the 1950s, psychoanalyst Donald Winnicott deepened our understanding of the struggle for authenticity by explaining how a child's bodily language can be an expression of the true self (which I am distinguishing from the True Self elsewhere in this book).[1] The British child psychoanalyst explained how the true self is suppressed from a very early age. Relating to the very functioning of the infant body, which represents the baby's natural inclinations, the psychoanalyst observed that a parent's response to the child's needs, expressed by the child's cries and body language, had a deep impact on the development of the child's true self. Winnicott emphasized that a child's behavior—crying, wiggling, testing out body parts—reveals his or her true self; the caretaker can either affirm and encourage this identity or destroy it by denigrating, ignoring, or outright rejecting it. According to Winnicott, the questions we must ask are: Do we recognize, engage, and support the actions of our children which support the true self, or do we oppose them and squash the true self? Do we acknowledge their personal efforts to express their needs, or do we respond to them only in some generic and socialized manner? Or do we reconstruct, redirect, or replace their voice and actions?

Some of the most memorable experiences I shared with my infant children occurred while we played our own version of "follow the leader." As we lay together on the floor or in bed, I would gently mimic their every gesture and coo. During these moments, they were the center of my universe, and their delighted responses assured me that they knew this. But this was not just recreation; for child's play is serious work. Our reactions to our children's attempts at self-expression are critical to the development of their sense of themselves in the world, and our attunement to our children helps them feel recognized and valued. Attunement is our primary attentiveness to another; it evokes awareness, harmony, and responsiveness. By communicating to my children my attentiveness and reaffirming their self-expression, we produced mutual feelings of connection, and I honestly could not say who enjoyed the interaction more. Contrast this, then, with the relationships established by parents who perceive their child as a responsibility rather than a person, as an object, plaything, or treasure they must isolate, protect, or control.

Let me use Winnicott's notion of the true self as a model for the kind of nurturing and development of the True Self I have been talking about, extending well past our days of merely being able to coo and scream. Indeed, the true self Winnicott describes is the underlying foundation for the True Self I describe. Although based more on biological considerations than on innate qualities, Winnicott's true self contains within it a fundamental axiom: that the whole person is an intricate combination of body, mind, and soul. Initially, before we have verbal language and other tools, we may express our self fundamentally through our body; these expressions have a lasting effect on our self and soul. Importantly, Winnicott explains that when the child's true self—or the expression of his or her bodily inclination—is disturbed or frustrated by the adult's will, the infant unconsciously puts his or her own needs below those of the adult. Winnicott argues convincingly that when children abandon their natural inclinations, they only nurture a false self.[2] In this way, the false self comes to dominate the true self in Winnicott's definition— and ultimately the True Self as we are addressing it in this book.

Both as an infant and further on in life, when a child cannot get what he or she genuinely needs, the child takes whatever he or she can get in its place. We observe such compromise, for example, in adolescents' compliance with social pressure regarding the word *love*, which they commonly use to refer to mere physical pleasure. Although an adolescent may desire deeper union, many are not prepared to express more than their basic physical, sexual needs in order to comply with a peer-supported notion of love. By contrast, with possession of Winnicott's true self, the child would develop greater self-assurance and probably make his or her own choice regarding love. To strengthen the child's True Self, the caretaker must respond in ways that acknowledge and affirm the child's bodily communication.

Often, we, like Peter, see ourself as dependent and possibly inadequate. If we listen and follow what others have to say, we may denounce ourselves; yet sometimes we are in need of advice and change. How do we know what is right? Unable or unwilling to accept who we actually are, we instead seek fulfillment outside of our self.

Winnicot suggests that we live in a world that rewards people for compliant behavior and that children begin to suppress emotion and rationalize wounds suffered by conforming to outside expectation. For example, if a child's formative experiences suggest that his behavior conflicts with the behavior of others, the child will deduce that something is "bad" or wrong with him. This rationalization ultimately seduces the psyche away from its relation to the body, creating a mind-body divide. Compliance with social forces that suppress emotional, physical, and sexual expression thus leads to the individual's alienation from his or her own inner qualities, emotions, and desires. People then become removed from the actions of life and instead engage in a world of ideas disconnected from experience. The effects of that initial split are ongoing and far-reaching. We *talk* about living rather than actually living; and while our religions teach goodness and life, this is not part of our genuine experience.

While only some of us are parents, all of us are former children who can reflect on how our parents' approach to these concerns affected us. The balance we seek cannot be found either in the extremes of conformity or rebellion. Too many people have warned my wife and me to enjoy our children while they are young, "because once they're teenagers it's all over." Putting aside the natural angst of adolescence, we must remember that every action creates an equal and opposite reaction: if children are controlled or squashed by their parents, whether consciously or not, it follows that as teenagers and adults, their character will form as a reaction to that suppression. Acceptance and support from playpen to adolescence will always produce better results than control and unilateral dictate.

While we must encourage childrens' awareness of and comfort with their body, as they begin to integrate it with their mind and soul, we must also be sensitive to the various ways in which each child experiences this process. I personally learned this lesson from my firstborn child. Throughout her infancy, I wanted to play with my daughter every day. From almost the moment she arrived home from the hospital, no day began or ended without stretching, tickling, or other such games. Our play gave me a solid sense of connection to her, which she returned with joy in her eyes and her smiles. This bond led us toward more adventure in our games. Before long, when she was not yet two, she would balance, standing on my hands, straight up in the air and over my head. Her trust seemed without limit. Looking back, it is clear that such physical and emotional interactions with my daughter enabled her to be trusting in physical and social settings later on. Winnicott's ideas only reaffirmed my understanding of my actions. There is no question that the body is central to our "aliveness." As we proceed, we will learn that connecting to our body and understanding its messages serve as the cornerstone for authentic connection to both our heart and soul. We will see how engagement of our physical self opens the door to the True Self and how reexamining this engagement is essential for our fulfillment.

In following the stories of athletes Mary Lou Retton and Billy Bean, we will see how their physical connection to their talents presented challenges to know themselves, to fit in, and ultimately to find their True Self.

A Real Life: Excellence over Perfectionism

For many of us, Mary Lou Retton is the woman who brought American gymnasts to the forefront of Olympic competition, the first American to win the gold medal in the women's all-around gymnastics competition, and the winner of the most medals in the '84 Los Angeles Olympics. In her own eyes, however, Retton is just an "ordinary young woman" from an "average family," a woman blessed with an athletic gift and a profound sense that hard work pays off.

Unlike some of the people we have considered, Mary Lou came from a close and happy family with what she describes as "the usual kidding and craziness of most homes." She comfortably owns her reputation as "happy," "motivated," "likable," and "someone who strives for perfection without being a perfectionist." What is this paradoxical state Retton describes of striving for perfection without being a perfectionist? How does it manifest itself in her life? What can we learn from it?

From childhood, Retton knew she wanted to be a gymnast and understood that her "God-given athletic ability required my decision to master my drive and develop a strong work ethic" if she was to achieve her goal. As her young daughters darted into the room for last-minute hugs and counsel before my first interview, I saw the down-to-earth and unpretentious warmth in Mary Lou that conveyed the heart of her message: total love and commitment and total focus on the task before you. For Mary Lou, at that moment, it would be the interview; for the girls, it would be playing with their nanny and practicing their own gymnastic exercises.

At the same time, however, I noticed Mary Lou was also reserved. While vivacious and fun, she also distinguished between emotional spontaneity and emotional vulnerability. Whenever anything that smacked of "self-pity" threatened to emerge, she repeated her mantra: "Suck it up" and "put the experience in its place." She did not deny the existence of adversity or failure in her life. She instead expressed a focused and constructive philosophy: that no event is truly negative. When things do not progress as you desire, learn from the experience and then transform it into something positive.

Mary Lou believes that consistency, discipline, and self-confidence make champions in any field. Although these were the elements in her experience that led Mary Lou to leave her hometown at age fourteen to train for the Olympics, the power of her access to her True Self spoke to a development that was more complex than simple hard labor.

The foundation that began in her early life permitted her to take risks and to step outside of her comfort zone. As she spoke, I realized that freedom, self-discovery, and true coming of age often come from moving beyond the place that you believe to be your goal. Thinking in this way, Mary Lou said:

> We spend most of our lives in a comfort zone, told to avoid the unknown, and actually learn to avoid risks. It's only when you get out of your comfort zone and perform that you become a real champion.

I wanted to amend that to "champion of your life," excellence not just in sports but in living. In fact, Mary Lou thinks the same way, now serving as a consultant and motivational speaker, helping people to make the connection between athletics and life.

Mary Lou's story is not simply that of an extraordinary athlete who did well. Her Olympic achievement occurred after being told that she probably could not compete because she required knee surgery six weeks before the games. Recovering swiftly and surpassing her medical prognosis, she trained with consistency, discipline, and confidence, completing three months of rehabilitation in three weeks. The pressure, however, only continued to mount as the carrot was held before her: already having come in first in every other gymnastic event, she was preparing to complete the vault and had to beat a 9.95 score if she was to win her gold medal. Her skills—and principles—led her to a perfect score and the win!

It seemed evident that Mary Lou neither internalized nor externalized difficulties. Internalizing occurs when your action is criticized and you take it personally, as if losing a game or performing poorly means that you are a bad person. Externalizing occurs when someone delivers a message to you that you don't want to hear and you project that the problem has nothing to do with you, feeling that they don't know what they're talking about, or that "they're out to get me."

Mary Lou's emotional life seemed rather clear: she had access to a fullness and richness of emotional experiences. However, when instances of negativity might create grounds for externalizing or internalizing, she did neither and simply went to work, saying to herself, "I'll prove them wrong." She possessed few false notions of who she was:

> I knew that I wasn't the sweet, slender, little princess ballerina who would float onto the floor; I was a strong, muscular, stout athlete that they really hadn't seen before and that didn't fit their image: But I was determined to show them.

This may seem simple, but Mary Lou's story is not one of "living happily ever after." Retton described in detail her pain and sense of personal failure when she left the world of athletic competition and began to pursue her college education. Studying at the University of Texas, Mary Lou anticipated having time to enjoy the normal social life and educational opportunities in college that she had missed in high school. But Mary Lou's first failure would soon unfold:

> My friends really didn't like the fact that I wouldn't join in the sorority life, and slowly I was becoming more and more ostracized. The jealousy and games became so unpleasant that one day I just up and left. I really could not stand to be at college anymore. It wasn't the academics; I was a good student. It was just the pettiness and lack of kindness. It wasn't at all what I had prepared myself for.

I couldn't help asking if she applied the principles that had guided her in athletic challenges to her social situation and how it played out. She replied, "You know, it's funny, but I never thought of it." Strangely, then, the champion of her own life had missed an opportunity.

Often, in the areas in which we feel most vulnerable or most emotionally dependent, it is difficult, if not impossible, to distance ourselves from challenges or threats and gain proper perspective of them. To live authentically, to survive, to overcome obstacles, to truly live, we must tap that innate drive.

Mary Lou developed an authentic emotional antidote: her relationships with God, her husband, and eventually her children. Mary Lou's husband, Shaun, was a University of Texas quarterback who she met at college. She described her relationship with him as "a connection with a soul mate that will continue for the rest of my life." With her children, she described "a Godly love that is unconditional."

While I knew that Mary Lou had participated in religion from youth because she described her mother as "a very devout Roman Catholic" with whom she "would go to Church regularly," I asked if she could compare her spiritual life at fifteen, twenty-five, and now in her mid-thirties:

Well at fifteen, I was focused on gymnastics and caught up in the Olympic win. My faith at this point was really formal religious practice and not very personal. While I had some feelings and thoughts about religion and politics, my handlers at the Olympics always emphasized that I should never reveal them: just keep smiling and play out the image of America's little sweetheart.

At twenty-five, all that I had described at college had passed. I had made my commitment to Shaun and now worked through a much more personal understanding of my faith in life. I established the priorities that I needed to feel good about myself and to have a clear direction and life. And that meant: my number one relationship is with God; my number two relationship is with my husband; and my number three relationship is with my children. And everything else comes after that.

Now, at thirty-five, I'm deepening all of these relationships. I'm not willing or able to be directed as I was at fifteen—to tell people what others tell me that they want to hear. I tell people what I know, who I am, what I believe. The priorities of my life lead me to the greatest fulfillment that I could have ever hoped for; and while success is different for everyone and cannot be defined, I cannot think of how it can be better than feeling the success that "I love you" is shared for me in all these levels of these relationships that I defined.

Play, the Body, and Discontinuity

Play is essential for expressing our self and developing self-awareness. In play we learn to converse with others and understand our self. Through play we feel physical, emotional, and social competence. Play opens the door for developing our creativity, discipline, and confidence in the True Self, as well as working off frustrations and tensions.

Access to play is a vehicle for awakening our True Self throughout life. Play takes on several forms, all of which are invaluable to the formation of our identity:

1. *Sensory motor play and practice play*—activities from which infants derive pleasure and activities where new skills are learned.
2. *Symbolic play*—transforms the environment into symbols and draws on our creativity, another quality of the True Self.
3. *Social play*—involves social intervention with peers.
4. *Constructive play*—combines other forms of play to construct a product or solve a problem.
5. *Games*—activities engaged for pleasure, involving rules and competition.

It is quite understandable that adolescents feel preoccupied with their body. Not only are they still building on their awareness of physical play from childhood, but during this period biological triggers stir an avalanche of change across several areas of development (physical, emotional, social, and spiritual). The physical—whether as their self-image or athletic competence—provides areas in which they often feel compelled to control. In fact, because we inevitably experience discontinuity in our bodies according to the different settings of family, peers, and intimacies, we may abandon our True Self for a safer image.

Possessing physical beauty and athletic prowess often supports a positive concept of one's self. But like anything else, we can overinvest or wrongly invest in beauty and prowess. Certainly, access to one's physicality strengthens identity. Although the attainment of significant physical accomplishment and maintaining beauty may be a dream come true for adolescents, the challenge of continuity with one's body remains critical. We have considered how our body may enhance our confidence and our awareness of our True Self; however, the complexity of life may generate discontinuity between our physical mastery and our effort for fulfillment. Let's look how one major league athlete confronted this challenge.

Hitting a Home Run

Billy Bean was an All-American boy: a great athlete, straight-A student, and high school valedictorian. His childhood dream was to play major league baseball. And by virtue of his relentless work ethic, he made his dream come true.

Pursuing studies at Loyola Marymount University, Bean was one of the very few athletes to make it in the major leagues. He played from 1987 to 1995 for the Detroit Tigers, Los Angeles Dodgers, and San Diego Padres. He also at that time married Anna, "the perfect girl from a well-to-do family." The handsome outfielder seemed to have it all. Three years ago, however, he publicly admitted his lifelong struggle: Billy Bean is gay.

Describing how he had avoided and suppressed sexual feelings in his youth, Billy told me that he always felt something was missing: "I felt a restlessness that I couldn't define or shake." Although he was happy with Anna, who "fit the image" he had created of "the proper woman for a baseball star," locker-room talk of sexual exploits made him uncomfortable. In spite of his concerns about his sexual identity, he said, "I hoped that by making my marriage a priority, I could get beyond the gay thing." Within a year, however, he divorced.

Billy managed to keep his secret from everyone, including friends and family. Oppressed over what would happen if his teammates and management found out—much less his fans—Billy spoke with me about how he carefully orchestrated his role as a jock inside the clubhouse—what he called his "tough exterior"—even as he maintained a relationship with his first companion, Sam. This split lifestyle pulled him into a perpetual conflict. His dilemma was most dramatic when Sam died from AIDS; Bean left Sam's bedside on the day he died because he felt that he could not miss a game. On top of that error in judgment, he chose to miss Sam's funeral rather than face potential exposure. This, however, was a turning point. He vowed that were he ever to establish another meaningful relationship, he would leave baseball and confront the duplicity in his life.

Billy had confronted duplicity before as a child. His biological father was not a part of his life. Raised by his mother and stepfather, Billy had to adjust to new family dynamics.

As a child and teenager, Billy had difficulty understanding himself because he lacked a visual image to relate to in his place in the family. He said, "I looked different than everyone else in my family" because he looked so much like his biological father. He frequently wondered, "Why wasn't I good enough for him to stay?"

Billy tried to compensate. He characterized himself as the type of child that was so organized "it looked almost funny . . . laying your clothes out the night before or showering before school at the age of seven or eight." His "manic behaviors" of always trying to improve in order to feel acceptance and to alleviate his perpetual self-doubt are the pivotal reasons he became such a successful athlete. His Little League coaches became men he admired and looked up to for acceptance. He told me that his drive toward becoming a great player started as a result of his need to find attention from a male role model as a child. In high school, Billy was "a very, very late bloomer" to the point of being "painfully late." Being smaller and weaker than most of his classmates, Billy worked even harder than they did to compensate by creating his goals and setting forth a regimen in order to accomplish them. He said:

> The reason I became such an exceptional athlete right at the end of my
> high school career . . . was because I was forced to keep up as a prepu-

bescent kid. I always identified myself as little Billy Bean. Even when I became 6 feet tall, 170 pounds, Billy Bean with a deep male voice and a mature male body. I always looked at myself as that little kid trying to keep [up] with my heroes who were my friends.

He explained his experience of trying out for the 1984 U.S. Olympic baseball team:

At nineteen, if you don't have some feelings of inadequacy, I don't think you're a human being. You're looking at Mark McGwire and Barry Bonds, and these guys who are guaranteed to make the team, and you're trying to take one of five spots. I think that's what pushes you to fight to the death ... to run a ten-mile run, or to go to the gym six days a week, or not eat when you want to eat something, because you're constantly feeling if I could be just as good as that guy. . . .

Billy only began to fully accept himself and the limits of his own athletic capabilities when he started playing for the Padres in 1997. Finally, he realized, "It doesn't matter how hard I try. It doesn't matter how hard I focus and concentrate. There are just guys who are better than others and it's easier for them." He was finally happy with the level of success he had achieved, and stopped comparing the small details of batting averages and outs. He explained:

I'm here and I've achieved a certain level of success. There's a lot of guys that ... end up beating themselves up because they think that there are adjustments to make. But some guys just have a better swing, and shorter stride, and they see the ball a little bit better. Those are the things you learn to accept.

For him, life's most simple, yet hardest lesson was to learn to be completely comfortable with who he was.

But how could he reconcile this life of success that forced him to deny his True Self? He was struggling to be genuine and real while fighting against the very authenticity he valued. Billy credits Sam and his passing for helping him admit his sexuality to his family. Billy then decided that if he became involved in another long-term relationship, he would retire from baseball because of the potential conflicts between the profession and his sexuality. Billy followed through with this promise that he made to himself. When he developed an honest, genuine relationship again, he knew that he now had to leave baseball to live an honest life. His honesty gave him inner peace.

Although Billy displays an easy-going charm, he still mutes the "voices" in his life from his own internal dialogue to find acceptance in our society and the media as a major league baseball player. Continuity may not be as easily achieved even after negotiating social demands of extraordinary physical achievement. The individual challenges that we face in the system in which we "play" may not always offer us compassion. Paradoxically, it was Billy's great achievements in the physical realm that led him to confront a deeper conflict within himself in relationship to his body and his sexuality.

Individuality, Personal Characteristics, Talents, and the Pressure to Fit In

We've seen how our soil can be well fertilized and how it can be depleted. Now let us look at the challenge we face as individuals who are also part of the whole. We know that we are unique, but early on we get the message that our specialness is limited and that we need to fit in. We have explained that our earliest efforts to claim our voice may be strengthened or weakened by our caretakers. Following that contest in early childhood, we face the world on our own two feet, distanced from our primary caretaker, to confront the forces of what Freud called "the group mind." Freud explained how every group establishes its identity and how, much like with individual identity, the group is pressure toward consistency. As Charles Finn's "Please Hear What I'm Not Saying" describes, we "wear a mask, a thousand masks" in our efforts to avoid the sting of not fitting into the group. To some extent, conformity provides order; but the pressure of the group mind can also prove both devastating and deadly to our individual identity.

GROUP PRESSURES AND THE NEED TO BE "ME"

Reflect for a few moments on five poignant moments from the past in which you deferred to the group mind. In the left column, note the situation; in the middle column, note your feelings and thoughts that directed your decision; and in the right column, explain how you would handle this situation today.

	INCIDENT	FEELINGS AND THOUGHTS AT THE TIME	RESPONSE PROJECTED TODAY
1.			
2.			
3.			
4.			
5.			

When we defer to the group mind, we usually feel disengaged from ourselves, because we have felt bullied by the group and consequently not recognized, valued, or understood. Sometimes the force of the group communicates (directly or indirectly) that we should conform rather than express ourselves; sometimes we fear retaliation of the group and try to become acceptable to it. Recognition of these dynamics are well understood by big business, which often anticipates and feeds on fears when it markets its products. Submitting to the group mind is not necessarily a function of shyness, weakness, or humility; it may also conceal the power of narcissism or manipulation. Such group force has little regard for the True Self: our authentic voice. Only by entering into the group and communicating our self can we properly experience genuine engagement. So whether we contrive our behavior toward a particular social end or join a group out of fear, our True Self may be compromised.

To be self-aware, we need to know our individual characteristics, including our temperament and personality, our virtues, habits, and hobbies, and all that we have acquired. By recognizing our personal characteristics (both positive and negative) that have developed from understanding our story, we increase our self-awareness and can evaluate how these qualities stand up before our True Self—and know what we may need to do to reclaim our True Self.

ASSESSING YOUR PERSONAL CHARACTERISTICS

Listed here are 100 characteristics that you may or may not feel you possess. Rate yourself on a scale of 1 to 5 for each quality. This list is not comprehensive; you can add more traits.

	Low		Average		High
1. ACCURATE	1	2	3	4	5
2. ADVENTURESOME	1	2	3	4	5
3. ALERT	1	2	3	4	5
4. AMBITIOUS	1	2	3	4	5
5. ANALYTICAL	1	2	3	4	5
6. AMIABLE	1	2	3	4	5
7. ARTICULATE	1	2	3	4	5
8. ARTISTIC	1	2	3	4	5

	Low		Average		High
9. ASSERTIVE	1	2	3	4	5
10. ATHLETIC	1	2	3	4	5
11. ATTENTIVE	1	2	3	4	5
12. ATTRACTIVE	1	2	3	4	5
13. BRAVE	1	2	3	4	5
14. BROAD-MINDED	1	2	3	4	5
15. CAPABLE	1	2	3	4	5
16. CHEERFUL	1	2	3	4	5
17. COMPETENT	1	2	3	4	5
18. COMPETITIVE	1	2	3	4	5
19. CONFIDENT	1	2	3	4	5
20. CONSCIENTIOUS	1	2	3	4	5
21. CONSISTENT	1	2	3	4	5
22. CONSTRUCTIVE	1	2	3	4	5
23. COOPERATIVE	1	2	3	4	5
24. COURTEOUS	1	2	3	4	5
25. CREATIVE	1	2	3	4	5
26. DECISIVE	1	2	3	4	5
27. DEPENDABLE	1	2	3	4	5
28. DETAILED	1	2	3	4	5
29. DETERMINED	1	2	3	4	5
30. DISCIPLINED	1	2	3	4	5
31. EFFICIENT	1	2	3	4	5
32. EMPATHIC	1	2	3	4	5

	Low		Average		High
33. EMOTIONAL	1	2	3	4	5
34. ENERGETIC	1	2	3	4	5
35. ENTHUSIASTIC	1	2	3	4	5
36. EXPRESSIVE	1	2	3	4	5
37. FAIR	1	2	3	4	5
38. FAITHFUL	1	2	3	4	5
39. FLEXIBLE	1	2	3	4	5
40. FORCEFUL	1	2	3	4	5
41. FREE-SPIRITED	1	2	3	4	5
42. FRIENDLY	1	2	3	4	5
43. GENEROUS	1	2	3	4	5
44. GRACIOUS	1	2	3	4	5
45. GREGARIOUS	1	2	3	4	5
46. HELPFUL	1	2	3	4	5
47. HONEST	1	2	3	4	5
48. HUMOROUS	1	2	3	4	5
49. INDEPENDENT	1	2	3	4	5
50. INFORMED	1	2	3	4	5
51. INNOVATIVE	1	2	3	4	5
52. INSIGHTFUL	1	2	3	4	5
53. INSPIRING	1	2	3	4	5
54. INTELLIGENT	1	2	3	4	5
55. JUST	1	2	3	4	5
56. KIND	1	2	3	4	5

	Low		Average		High
	1	2	3	4	5
57. LOGICAL	1	2	3	4	5
58. LOYAL	1	2	3	4	5
59. LUCID	1	2	3	4	5
60. MATURE	1	2	3	4	5
61. MECHANICAL	1	2	3	4	5
62. MORAL	1	2	3	4	5
63. MOTIVATED	1	2	3	4	5
64. MUSICAL	1	2	3	4	5
65. NURTURANT	1	2	3	4	5
66. OBJECTIVE	1	2	3	4	5
67. OPTIMISTIC	1	2	3	4	5
68. ORGANIZED	1	2	3	4	5
69. OUTGOING	1	2	3	4	5
70. PATIENT	1	2	3	4	5
71. PERCEPTIVE	1	2	3	4	5
72. PERSEVERING	1	2	3	4	5
73. PIONEERING	1	2	3	4	5
74. PLEASANT	1	2	3	4	5
75. POISED	1	2	3	4	5
76. POLISHED	1	2	3	4	5
77. PRACTICAL	1	2	3	4	5
78. PRINCIPLED	1	2	3	4	5
79. PROFESSIONAL	1	2	3	4	5
80. PUNCTUAL	1	2	3	4	5

	Low		AVERAGE		HIGH
81. REALISTIC	1	2	3	4	5
82. REFLECTIVE	1	2	3	4	5
83. RESPECTFUL	1	2	3	4	5
84. RESPONSIBLE	1	2	3	4	5
85. SENSITIVE	1	2	3	4	5
86. SERIOUS	1	2	3	4	5
87. SINCERE	1	2	3	4	5
88. SOCIAL	1	2	3	4	5
89. SPIRITUAL	1	2	3	4	5
90. SPONTANEOUS	1	2	3	4	5
91. STABLE	1	2	3	4	5
92. TACTFUL	1	2	3	4	5
93. THOROUGH	1	2	3	4	5
94. TOLERANT	1	2	3	4	5
95. TRUSTFUL	1	2	3	4	5
96. TRUSTING	1	2	3	4	5
97. TRUSTWORTHY	1	2	3	4	5
98. UNIQUE	1	2	3	4	5
99. VERSATILE	1	2	3	4	5
100. OTHER	1	2	3	4	5

Think about the characteristics you possess. Having completed this exercise, select your ten most prominent characteristics. Do you see how your physical, emotional, and spiritual qualities support your True Self? Are they apparent to others? Do you feel comfortable presenting these qualities to the various groups in your life?

PART II

OPENING
YOUR HEART

It is also good to love: because love is different. For one human being to love
another human being is perhaps the most difficult task that has been entrusted
to us, the ultimate task, the final task and proof
of this work for which all other work is merely preparation.
—RAINER MARIA RILKE

WE ARE READY TO BUILD the hull of the ship. The hull is the ship's very
body. Your hull should not only *appear* seaworthy, like the façade of a
ship on a Hollywood set, but also it has to *be* seaworthy. It has to provide the framework to connect you to all the other parts of your ship
that secure you on your voyage. Our hull is literally our heart, the source
of our love. It is so basic to our voyage that, much like a ship without
a hull, life without heart is not a viable life.

What is love? It is the powerful lifeline that permits us to connect
our inner being to others. But who among us has not heard someone
say "I love you" and wondered, "What does that mean exactly?" I need
you? I lust for you? I want to share my life with you? Do these words
express something eternal, or have they been blurted out in the heat of
the moment? And how can we ever know?

The ancient Greeks tried to solve the riddles of love by distinguishing between its physical, emotional, and spiritual manifestations with different terms. Indeed, no single Greek word embodies the many meanings of the English word *love*. Instead, the Greek vocabulary for love includes *eros*—love of a thing, material desire, passionate joy; *philia*—love of a friend, feelings of affection; *storge*—love of a family, the connection between parents and children; and *agape*—brotherly love, charity, unconditional love; and several other kinds of love as well.

These subtle differences in love point out the complexity an individual faces in expressing the meaning of love. The challenge is not limited to figuring out whether a person loves you as a friend, as an object, or as a partner for life. You also have to determine if your lover is capable of understanding what *you* mean by love and if your respective views of love agree. By honestly confronting our experiences of love, we will better understand the process of attaining real love in our True Self.

In Part I we reached within, looking to connect to the True Self. In Part II, we will explore how to reach out to another, using the True Self to build authentic relationships. Here we will explore the relationship between our feelings of love and our critical connections to self, others, and God. Relationships involve the interdependence of the body, mind, and soul, because we have the ability to express our love physically, emotionally, and spiritually. When we love in this way, we extinguish any false alliances between body and soul and between sexuality and spirituality. We see how our personal histories can disguise themselves in our efforts to express love and sexuality when our actions speak from our past selves. Finally, we will discover how opening our heart enables us to forge genuine connections that usher in fulfillment.

Because opening your heart requires the integration of your body, mind, and soul, it must begin from a deeper understanding of your connections to others and to God. To begin opening up your heart, you must ask these questions:

- How has my experience of receiving love affected the way that I offer love?

- What signals or resources guide me in assessing my love and the love of others?
- Do I really want intimacy? And do I pursue it effectively?
- How do my relationships with self, others, and God affect each other and my quest for fulfillment?

The stories in Part II compare the experiences of both those who have and those who have not explored these vital questions. The stories underscore the cost of failing to express the full range of love, and they reveal the importance of both understanding and accepting our sexuality. By strengthening our skills of communication and embracing our passions, we can forge bonds of intimacy and reconnect with our "aliveness."

While we each begin life with an open heart, keeping it open is one of our greatest challenges. Fashioning our sexual identity and learning how to give and receive love can put our heart at risk. But when we allow the heart to close, we cut ourselves off from the energy and vitality that inspire us in life. Opening the heart requires taking the risk to love as fully as we can physically, emotionally, and spiritually. Are you ready to look at yourself in these ways?

4

❧

FIRING UP YOUR PASSION

Give all to love; obey thy heart.
—Ralph Waldo Emerson

THE WORD "LOVE" conjures up a range of images associated with happiness, contentment, and joy. Love is something we feel, and the power of this feeling is limitless. Saying "I am in love" resonates with the force of Juliet's promise to Romeo, "My bounty is as boundless as the sea." But what defies borders also escapes definition. What unleashes this emotion potent enough to inspire Anthony to forfeit the Roman Empire for the love of Cleopatra? How is it that our lives can be turned upside down—one day flying high as our fantasy wedding becomes reality, while the next day crashing down in a gut-wrenching divorce? How can we know when our love is grounded in our True Self?

Love is a complex and sacred connection between human beings. It is both an instinctive, psychological expression of our sexuality and an emotional expression of the multiple aspects of our self. Intimacy requires personal investment, understanding, sensitivity, and, most importantly, trust. When that trust is broken, by ourself or by another, we feel it. This is because love is more than sex or sexuality; it is a connection that opens the inner floodgates of our being. Loving involves vulnerablility; thus, it is possible only when we feel safe enough to let down our defenses. Only when we can step out from behind these protective walls can we, and our lovers, see ourselves and embrace our True Self.

When we love, we take a risk. And though we may not succeed in protecting ourselves from heartbreak, we can nevertheless improve our chances of experiencing the wonders of love. By understanding what lies beneath our needs, desires, and behaviors that characterize our love, we will know our own heart. In this chapter, we explore how our love of self and relationships with others are expressed through our sexuality; the different forms of love and how connecting them to the True Self leads to warm, deep, and lasting relationships; and why we remain trapped in painful, inauthentic love and what we need to do to escape and establish fulfilling relationships.

The stories here are of people who have striven to open their hearts through their relationships. Together, these stories reveal our tendency to turn to others for the nurturance, recognition, and love we all need. From the lessons these stories provide, we will learn how to avoid repeating some of our most common mistakes and approach the joy of love with confidence.

The Different Sides of Love

Understanding, accepting, and integrating your sexuality into your loving is the only way to know yourself and to express genuine love. Let's take another look at the Greek categories of love to help us further understand their meanings and interconnections.

Eros Eros is a passionate love that evokes powerful physical attraction. Because of its association with the body, eros is often related to sexual attraction, and thus also to the word *erotic*. In Plato's writings, however, eros refers to a certain beauty, the true beauty that can be found only in the afterlife. The images we see in this life are only reflections of this ideal eros. And so Plato deemed physical love for a person, an idea, or an object a lesser emotion; erotic love pursued an imperfect representation of beauty.

Today, eros refers to our sexuality and sexual drive; it is not a lesser kind of love, but a different one. Frequently associated throughout history with something inherently evil, and misinterpreted and feared by those who believe they must suppress their physical impulses, physical love is a basic human experience that contributes to fulfillment in life; and it extends far beyond the erotic. Erotic love that is part of a larger whole does not have to be ego centered. We move beyond the ego when we do not merely obey our sexual impulses but unite them with our principles. In this way, sexuality can be transforming and uniting, giving greater meaning to our relationships.

With eros, we can direct our sex drive toward purposeful goals: finding friendships with our lovers, creating long-lasting relationships, or starting a family. And while the tangible pleasures of eros are enjoyable, alone they are not sustaining and they may misguide us. Inevitably, we all bring our own histories and our own struggles to our expression of love and sexuality. If we wish to open our hearts and access our love, and our sexuality, we must align them with the True Self, so that they might point us toward our authentic goals.

Philia   Philia encompasses our fondness of, appreciation for, and faithfulness to others. It is reciprocal relationship and loyalty. The Greeks saw philia as the inspiration to care for someone else, doing, as Aristotle said, "kindnesses, doing them unmasked, and not proclaiming the fact when they are done." Aristotle also perceived that for someone to have philia, he or she must first have love for him- or herself. This is not eros as hedonistic or self-serving but something rooted in an awareness and connection to the qualities of the True Self.

Storge   Storge is a nonsexual love, an attachment based on profound friendship and affection. It is instinctual, as in the love a parent feels for his or her child. It exists for its sake alone and is not conditional like eros, nor does it require the reciprocity of philia. Where philia demands, "I will love you if. . . ." storge says, "I will love you because. . . ." One who loves with storge is self-surrendered to other; the self is denied *because* I love you. This love still delivers whether it be self-love, appreciation, reciprocity, or philia.

Agape   Agape is a generous love that does not seek payment in return. Deeper than eros, philia, and storge, agape transcends them all. Agape is God's love for humanity and the potential of our love for others. Agape challenges us to "love your neighbor as yourself" and establishes the possibility that we can extend the love we desire for ourself toward another. Agape is morally centered, motivated by our own intent and our sense of a wider good and truth. It is a giving of the self that transforms ordinary experiences into something meaningful and fulfilling. Agape is not a single moment but a vision, belief, experience, and reality that permits us to know and feel the divine.

Love in the True Self is the culminating point of living. But love in the True Self develops over time; we do not manifest it from the outset of every relationship. Every relationship instead contains the potential to experience love in the True Self. Realizing this potential requires our engagement with self, others, and God.

As these next stories show, when we say, "I love you," we need to know what we mean. An erotic feeling? A warm, fuzzy encounter? A deep liking of another? A commitment to experiencing an ideal? While songwriters, poets, philosophers, and psychologists tell us that all we need in life is love, understanding and expressing love is not so simple. Most of us dabble in the multiple definitions of love, but when pressed to answer the question of what love is find ourselves confused. As you read the following stories, consider if they reflect your own experience and if your loves, past and present, have been in agreement with your True Self. You may also recognize people trying to understand and find love, allowing us to see how the True Self guides in this most important task.

"We Will Always Love One Another—
I Just Can't Live Life with Him"

He cheated on me from the first month we were married. But you begin to think it's your fault. And you're not sure. You think, "I'm jealous." [So] I worked on myself. [But] I couldn't find any answers. He did everything and nothing in moderation. I had to deal with it all—booze, broads, and gambling. It sounds vulgar . . . and I just couldn't tolerate it anymore. When the children got to an age where they were asking questions, I got fed up with saying, "Daddy isn't feeling well."

He just would not take care of himself, and he never honored our marriage. He still loves us, but he plays around. It took me a long time to realize it was a lost cause, because, to avoid confusion, we stayed married nineteen years. But the last six years, it was just sort of finishing our commitments, business-wise.

This is how Lucille Ball, icon of *I Love Lucy*, recounted her personal life with Desi Arnaz. Although decades had passed since their divorce, the intensity of Lucille's emotions revealed that her wounds were still raw and that Desi's memory had never faded. Few performers, past or present, have been loved so dearly as this woman, who humorously captured the experiences of friendships and marital relationships. As I prepared to interview her, I recalled that her TV character struck a chord with so many. We identified with her longing for attention and affection, her need to feel accomplished, her passion about her friends with childlike spontaneity, and most of all, her love for her husband, family, and friends. Lucy and Ricky's on-air affection appeared so natural. But here she was, in front of me, recounting her marital grief some twenty-five years after they split up. What went wrong for Lucille and Desi?

The famous marriage began like a fairy tale: two actors meeting on the set of a Broadway play, head over heels for one another. Lucille said, "The chemistry was irresistible," and "the sparks were flying." Six months later, the two were married.

But the title of the play that introduced Lucille and Desi in 1940, *Too Many Girls*, proved to be an eerie prophecy. Desi's infidelities, together with the strain of his absence while on tour, provoked "terrible fights" and prompted Lucille to file for divorce. Instead of separating, the couple managed to patch things up and eventually create the *I Love Lucy* show. Their renewed love had drawn them into a masterful creative collaboration. Together they hoped that their carefully planned filming schedule would provide the stability they needed to work on their relationship and begin a family. Yet despite their efforts to balance their professional lives and their family commitments, Desi and Lucille's love was unable to sustain the happiness that they sought.

Many of Lucille's relationships seemed to follow a pattern: while externally she engaged herself with others (working tirelessly in show business), internally she remained isolated and preferred to bear things alone. Facing her problems alone always inhibited her engagements with others. "The only way you can have principles is to not put yourself in a position where you have to borrow, beg, steal. . . . Learn to take care of yourself, physically, mentally, financially, emotionally."

Sitting down with Lucille, I wanted her to be the Lucy I had watched on TV as a little boy, giving to me the same warm and joyful feelings now as she did then. Listening to her, however, I felt the distance between the independence she spoke of so convincingly and the loneliness her independence had wrought. Lucille appeared to have never clearly connected her desires and emotions with the realities of her personal life: "I had a great childhood, although my father died when he was twenty-three and my mother was five months pregnant with my brother." Lucille was four at the time and her family was poor. Her mom, DeDe, went to work six days a week while Lucille lived with her strict, eccentric grandfather. Her Aunt Lola died in the house shortly after her father died. Lucille escaped into her imaginary world. Just like the woman who was capable of creating such believable characters on screen, Lucille had constructed a believable persona to engage the problems of her inner self. But she did not know how to create the good life for herself.

Reluctance to confront the disjunction between reality and expectation hurts our closest relationships. Desi's infidelity, along with her own isolating sense of independence, left Lucille feeling humiliated and betrayed. Worried about the effects of her marital problems on her children, she finally filed for a divorce in 1959, after eighteen years of marriage.

The televised life shared by Lucy and Ricky could not have contrasted more with the marriage between Lucille and Desi. Yet both Lucy and Lucille loved their husbands passionately. Even when Desi humiliated Lucille and caused her emotional agony, her romantic desire for him never lessened.

It would be several years, however, before Lucille would even begin to understand that Desi's conception of love, marriage, and family had differed dramatically from her own:

> Desi was a very generous man. He gave us the world. . . .[In] fact, gave us four or five homes—but they were houses to him, never homes. They were homes to us, but they were houses to him. He was never in them. He was always off someplace with someone else. He still has never settled.

Lucille's love for Desi blinded her from reality, and she suffered the consequences of it. The pain of her loss never quite left her.

Like Lucille, we have all persisted in relationships beyond the point of logic, hoping our expectations will someday be matched by reality. But why do we stay in relationships that bring so much pain? Why do we fail in finding constructive connections? And how are we to understand love when it seems to persist even in contradiction to the qualities of our True Self? To answer some of these questions, let us consider the process by which Lucille and Desi fell in and out of love.

Lucille's love for Desi began initially with physical attraction. While we are all capable of distinguishing between relationships based on physical desire and those founded on spirit, we sometimes let the potency of sexual attraction trick us into believing we have found a deeper connection. In our search to make genuine connections, physical cues are by far the most prominent signals that we have found someone of potential interest. Our blood pressure rises; our heartbeat increases. The measures of what physically attracts us are easily discerned: our body, our whole being tells us "yes." In general, our sexual response is an excellent indication that we feel attraction—an attraction that we may further associate with our emotional and spiritual wishes for love. But physical attraction does not provide information about the potential emotional and spiritual content of our love. It is all too easy to misinterpret our body's message. Lucille and Desi were physically attracted to each other, and they established their relationship because of it. But neither partner attended to the emotional or spiritual implications of their attraction. Instead, the two merely transferred their own emotional and spiritual expectations onto each other, binding each other up in the words "I love you."

Love at First Sight   This reminds me of a couple that met when they began their MBA program. Their romance, too, began as "love at first sight": they studied together; they lived together; they were inseparable and "totally in love." They were going to marry right after graduation. They came to see me, however, because of "one little thing": he was Jewish, she was Protestant, and both were practicing believers. For two years they danced around the difference, reassuring each other that they would participate in both traditions and even attend each other's religious services. As their graduation approached and wedding plans were established, however, they could no longer deny their families' discomfort with the mixed marriage and the avalanche of concerns it brought to their blissful relationship: Which faith would the children follow? Could they really celebrate both Christmas and Hanukkah? Were their cultural roots and traditions truly insignificant in the face of their romantic love? Reality, it seems, was bursting the romantic bubble in which they had been floating.

Their family members and I verbalized for them the concerns they felt but feared to confront. I saw their sexual and religious identities pulling at each other. They enjoyed the emotions of loving each other, but these feelings seemed irreconcilable with the separate love of their unique families and traditions. After they finally raised the questions they feared, they argued intensely, revealing critical parts of their values that the euphoria of their romantic love had veiled. Their plans for a future together unraveled.

The physical, emotional, social, and spiritual dimensions of our love are intertwined. But sometimes they get entangled and mismatched. Depending on how attuned we are to each of these areas, whether to physical, emotional, or other cues, they may enhance or detract from our love. It is therefore important that we understand these variables and recognize the role they play in our sexual behavior.

The Message of Passion

Like the word *love*, the word *passion* is enigmatic. The term *passion* stems from the Greek word *pathos*, literally "denoting suffering."

Passion is critical to love because it grounds our idea of idealized love in our emotions and body. Passion makes the unbearable possible: a parent gives his life for his child. Passion means committing to someone at a cost: doing something very special for someone you love may exact hard work—but it's worth it! The Greeks were right: passion is an integral component of love.

Love is inherently passionate and connected to our sexuality. To experience fulfilling love, we must acknowledge that sexuality contributes to love. Because sexual behavior and attraction defies any simple explanation, we must look at the many components of sexuality:

Biological: This is made up of the hormonal and organic factors that affect a person's bodily desires. For example, a high level of testosterone in a man often results in a sexual appetite greater than would occur if his body did not produce as much. A woman's sexual appetite can also be greatly affected by hormones.

Emotional: Our emotional needs often manifest themselves in our sexual expressions. We therefore may enter a physical relationship out of a desire to feel reassured, safe, and comforted. On the other hand, fears and anxiety can make us uncomfortable with others and sexually dysfunctional.

Relational: Strong feelings of trust, care, and understanding often promote and sustain sexual interest; conversely, mistrust and uncertainty can produce communication problems that often result in reactions, ranging from lack of interest to sexual disorders. Even simple miscommunications may prove detrimental. For example, a man may experience sensitivity and vulnerability as he touches his girlfriend affectionately, but his girlfriend may interpret the gesture as rude and offensive.

Social: Acceptable expressions of masculinity and femininity are often shaped by our culture and force us to sometimes assume roles that do not resonate with our personal desires or intentions. Subcultures within the larger society may confuse us further, and we may feel pressure somehow to negotiate their often conflicting demands. For example, a young girl may experience tension by trying to comply with the differing standards of dress dictated by her home, her church, her school, and her peers.

Spiritual: Religious experience can produce for some a constructive sexual expression; while for others it may be destructive or denying. For the former, the spiritual community assists them in understanding how to integrate their feelings of love and sexuality and how to form a meaningful relationship between their values and their behaviors. For the latter, religious codes create feelings of guilt and fear, causing people to disclaim their sexual being and to disconnect from their True Self in body, heart, and soul.

Our sexuality, then, is no mere appendage. Our comfort with our sexuality enhances our personality, communication, and love. Moreover, our sexual lives have spiritual and religious components. These often greatly influence intimacy, love, and our feelings of passion. In fact, the spiritual components of love and sexual identity often serve as blueprints for how we express our True Self. Although discussing sexuality can be difficult for all of us, understanding it is vital, as it also indicates our emotional and spiritual needs and longing.

Speaking one day with a seminarian, I heard him make the mistake of separating himself from his sexuality, as he told me in all seriousness, "You know, if I didn't have sexual urges, I really think I would be holy and probably a saint. I think that our sexual urges, which are simply biology, lead us to sin—to think or to act in ways that we shouldn't." This young man suspended his sexual feelings and dissociated from them, rather than trying to understand them.

In reality, the seminarian's sexual urges were not an obstacle to his sainthood. His sexual dilemma and the particulars of his fantasies revealed his emotional concerns by pointing out his struggles with impulses and his need for others. His sexuality was not in his way; it was his idealized notion of himself that was in his way. His challenge rested in recognizing the dissonance between his ideals and his reality and integrating them both into his True Self. Having a way to express sexual impulses and wanting to engage in fantasy are common, so I suggested that he approach his fantasies as expressions of yearning or struggle within. Without attending honestly to his feelings and thoughts, and clinging instead to an idealized vision of himself, he would doubtless end up in trouble when his suppressed needs returned in another form.

Sexuality is not something we merely acquire at puberty; it is the product of our total history, the relationship between our physical expressions of love and our innermost motivations—and so much more. With that deeper understanding, we can appreciate why our love lives get so complex and why simple rules of "should" and "should not" can neither fully motivate our emotions nor be the final standard for evaluating our actions. Instead, we must commit ourselves to understanding the many messages our sexuality conveys.

Why Am I Fighting Myself? The passionate struggles in the story about the intimate life of Lucille Ball and Desi Arnaz revealed the many ranges of loves we have all felt—eros, philia, storge, and agape. This marriage could not bring together each partner's True Self in a harmonious whole. Such problems with intimacy are often found in relationships that we are born into. The next story is a clear of example of this.

Lou, a handsome and polite young man in his early twenties, came to therapy to address his sexual dysfunction. Lou overcompensated for feelings of inadequacy in many areas of his life. In school and at work, he was a perfectionist. He was bright and athletic. Not only was he a kickboxer, he had also become a kickboxing instructor. Whatever he took on, he drove himself to excel; yet his achievements seemed to go unrecognized by him. In spite of apparently high testosterone levels, he had trouble maintaining an erection during sex with his girlfriend. This made him feel inadequate. Why did he feel he was failing?

When we reviewed his sexual history, Lou disclosed that sexuality was rarely discussed at home and that his mother and stepfather were very modest about sex. His biological father had left when Lou was only two years old and maintained no contact with him. Lou's mother had regularly railed about how his father only cared about sex, "but not people." His mother eventually married an aggressive man who was abusive to both his wife and his stepson.

Learning from his mother's example, Lou had become convinced that sex was, at best, a necessary evil. He viewed his own body as something negative, the tangible form of what he called a man's "monstrous appetite." When with women, Lou generally felt apologetic and wanted to comfort them; when his relationships became more intimate, he became conflicted about his passionate sexual urges. And then, during sex, Lou grew increasingly unsure of himself, caught between pleasure and guilt. He equated his sexuality with selfishness: "I feel that women tolerate sex."

Afraid of his desire, Lou believed that any self-gratification in his sexual acts was taboo. Nor could he accept the notion that he, or any man, could be the object of a woman's desire; although women would tell him he was handsome, he was certain this was a mere courtesy. In the course of his treatment, Lou examined his depression and anger, his concern for his impact on women, and other fears in his relationships. Lou, true to his "good student" form, maintained a careful diary of his daily reflections. His notes reflected a boyish innocence that belied deep emotional struggle. On one day, he would note that sex was something to be enjoyed, as though he had discovered a new concept; the next day he was again describing the act as dehumanizing.

Over time, Lou began to recognize the psychological origins of his physical difficulties. His impotence unconsciously protected him from realizing his fear of hurting women. He learned that he had sublimated his anger, his intense struggles with his physicality manifesting themselves in his extreme athleticism. Fear had disengaged not only Lou's sexual functioning but also his connection to the True Self and his ability to establish a meaningful relationship.

With his trademark discipline, Lou worked hard to confront himself and the emotional shields that he had built to protect his mother. His impotence was only a symptom of the greater anxiety, phobia, and depression weighing on him.

Sexuality, as Lou's example shows, can serve as a key to one's whole identity. Lou's difficulty in keeping his heart open resulted from the impact of his mother's marital problems and his difficult experiences with men. His struggles with his love of self and love of others understandably affected his natural sexual urges and intimacy. But, in the end, his struggle with a sexual disorder gave him the opportunity to unify his expressions of eros and philia in the most intimate of relationships.

Expressing Our Sexual Desire

I have three key concepts for understanding the manifold ways our True Self struggles to express itself in our sexuality: the sexual self, the voices of sexuality, and the dance of sexuality.

The Sexual Self Our sexuality is best understood as a stage in our inner world on which we act out our fantasies, our desires, and our histories. The dramas we perform here speak of our affections and aggressions, and they communicate our innermost qualities of the True Self. We reveal our generosity and selfishness, and our sensitivity and carelessness. In our sexuality, we are more than physically undressed: we are psychologically naked.

Our emotions, wishes, desires, and personality manifest themselves in very particular and meaningful sexual actions. Our sexual dramas enact and reenact what we want and need, sometimes neurotically, sometimes healthily. Our sexual self, then, not only expresses our sexual concerns and fantasies, but also the multiple sides of our nature and character. With each relationship, each time our sexual self encounters someone new, a new and unique combination of personalities emerges.

Avodah Offit, in her book *The Sexual Self*,[1] expounds on this theme with the claim that personality disorder, or failure of the self, is played out in sexual behaviors. As character shapes sexuality and sexuality expresses personality, patterns in one area of the self tend to predict behaviors in another. Male narcissists typically blame their partners for sexual problems (how could they themselves be at fault?), while women with highly emotional styles have a tendency to dramatize interest in sex to the extent that they are often unable either to take initiative or achieve orgasm.

Questions of biology and gender and circumstances of culture and relationships equally affect the qualities of both our physical and psychological selves. By attuning to the sexual self, therefore, we identify how sexual struggles often reveal disconnects with our True Self.

The Voices of Sexuality   At the foundation of the sexual self rest the voices of sexuality. Sexual voices emerge, such as holding, kissing, and touching—derived from our sexual repertoire—that continue to expand throughout the course of our life. The sexual voices are metaphors in our head that reflect parts of our sexualities—drawing out ways of being sexual in one context versus another—which may draw out another voice or part of our sexualities. These voices are both conscious and unconscious and express all the facets of our personality. Each voice may represent a different part of life or a particular emotional need. Outwardly, these voices may manifest themselves in behaviors—in one context compulsive, childlike in another. Therefore, our sexual voices are connected to our various sexual attractions and communications.

By identifying our voices of sexuality, our particular sexual interests and desires, we may open a window to the range of different ways that we act and the different roles that we play. Moreover we gain new insights into our lives and so can stay away from conflicting views of our character. In *The Many Faces of Eros*,[2] Joyce McDougall provides an excellent discussion of how a damaged sense of self can inspire compulsive sexual pursuits. When a person fails to meet the task in sexual development, such as personal comfort or safety with pleasure, that person develops what McDougall calls a "neo-need." Haunted by the past and unfulfilled sexual needs, the individual falls into patterns of behavior referred to as "neo-sexuality," which may include fetishes or abusive sexual behavior. By this sexual extreme, the individual with a neo-sexuality attempts to reconcile the internal damage to the self through repetition to gain mastery.

Attuning ourselves to the voices of sexuality provides a vehicle for recognizing conflicts in our nature and resolving them before they master us. For example, I referred to how Lou spoke and wrote in his journal about the male sexual drive as a monstrous appetite—a sexual voice he feared and felt within. Once we identify the stronger, healthier sexual voices rooted in our positive self-concept, it becomes easier to confront our more negative and unhealthy expressions of self. Listening to different expressions of our sexuality, as did Lou, encourages us to recognize our sexual adaptations, good and bad. If we do not understand our sexual voices, we may not understand our emotional needs. Acknowledging our different sexual voices stands in sharp contrast with trying to shape our sexuality to meet the demands of one fixed voice, such as the dilemma felt to come out of the closet in the setting of super-hetero parents.

The Dance of Sexuality   A third aspect of our sexuality I call "the dance of sexuality." No, this is not the lambada or "dirty dancing." Where the sexual self and voices of sexuality concern internal dynamics of our sexuality (the ways we deal internally with sex), the dance of sexuality considers the unique elements of two people in a relationship, the interplay between the self and other through sexuality. The phrase "dance of sexuality" should capture both a sense of motion and the need for a partner in our sexuality. The dance metaphor also conveys both scripted steps and spontaneity as we share in loving that comes with pleasure and fun. By attuning to the dance of sexuality, we see how our individual needs emerge in sexuality, and we may tend to those needs that are rooted in our True Self.

"I Thought I Liked You"   Steve came into therapy with several sexual problems, including very low sexual desire. An athletic man in his early forties, Steve had had several relationships and a sexually active history with women since his college days. What, then, was wrong in his sexual desire?

Following a seven-year relationship that had ended, Steve had established a new relationship with Barbara, a woman in her mid-thirties with a history of unsuccessful relationships. Steve and Barbara were highly attracted to each other, but they found they had little sexual compatibility. Both Steve and Barbara had engaged in sex with other partners previous to their relationship. But Barbara's past partners had been rather dominant, while Steve was somewhat dependent and veered toward more egalitarian relationships. Simply put, they had different ways of dancing the sexual dance.

Steve was conflicted. Barbara was "fun, bright, and really out there," and he was fascinated by her beauty and gregariousness. But somehow a switch was flipped, as he put it, when they got into the bedroom. Steve presented Barbara as a strong, forceful woman who was quick to assign blame. Within a few weeks of starting the relationship, she had moved into Steve's home and, not long after, began telling him he was "not a real man." She castigated Steve for not initiating their sexual encounters, offering this as proof of his problems with expressing "masculine intimacy," as she put it. She said she was aroused only when a man "seized her," even if she denied interest. Although seductive, she had inhibited Steve's sexual response with criticism so extreme that he called it her "barrage of blasting." He found Barbara's demands and humiliation in their relationship utterly discouraging and never felt safe enough with her to initiate sex.

Steve was in a quandary: he discovered that Barbara's ridicule tapped into his boyhood days when he had felt trampled emotionally by an overpowering, demeaning father. He was shut down. At the same time, as Barbara perceived it, his lack of responsiveness was diminishing her sense of self. This connection would not work sexually because their emotional needs could not be met in sex. The relationship failed.

Can you step back for a moment and consider your own sexual responsiveness? To what extent are you present in the moment with your partner? To what extent are dynamics of your past emotional experiences affecting your encounter? Let's take a closer look at how the three aspects of sexuality that I have described come into play in the story of Gary and Brenda.

The Perfect Marriage　At first glance, couples and therapists alike are often baffled by marriages that begin with such promise but deteriorate into agony. In the following story about Gary and Brenda, we see a dance of sexuality that fails to embody a couple's individual sexual selves and their sexual voices. Given the number of elements that compose the dynamics of a marriage, it is not surprising that if these elements are not played in the same key, we end up with a cacophony rather than a symphony.

Gary walked into my office agitated and torn. At six feet two inches, the well-built and handsome twenty-seven-year-old training officer at a national military academy was both a congenial and an imposing man. Hardly pausing to introduce himself, he quickly presented the purpose of his visit:

> Ever since Brenda and I have been together, since my days at West Point, we've been on top. Brenda's beautiful; she's bright. And I always respected her because she did so well. And everyone said I couldn't possibly do better. When we were together we'd do all these things—from skiing to swimming, hiking. I loved it. She was always with me. She would take care of

me. I didn't know anything was wrong. I felt we were right where the action was, so I actually thought this must be it!

After this introduction, Gary arrived at the primary subject on his mind:

We've been married for six years now and in one week we'll have our first child. I love Brenda, but I'm in love with another woman!" This new woman, Cynthia, really makes me feel alive and complete. With her I feel things I never felt with Brenda. I love Brenda but it's over. I don't know what to do. I don't want to hurt Brenda.

I empathized with his agony, but I also felt thwarted by his apparent lack of responsibility and sensitivity. I was also deeply saddened for his unsuspecting wife.

"You hear what you're saying?" I asked.

Gary looked me in the eyes and for a minute said nothing. Then he sat back and started to share his situation: "You see, there once was another woman, but that was only one night. It isn't about sex. You know, I've never had the sex I have with Cynthia. It's unbelievable! It's really great!" Though Gary described his relationship with Cynthia as more than eroticism, he still wasn't clear about what was compelling him to abandon his marriage. I wondered what this sexual experience was doing for him that his other affair had not done: "What's different about being with Cynthia?" I asked. He replied:

I really talk about what's on my mind. One of the things I love most is my work. It means more than a lot to me to have training officers from around the country rely on me to learn how to motivate others, to teach them how to be their best. And I'm good at it! I know I'm good at it. Cynthia more than lets me be myself. She understands me.

As his voice rose with his last sentence, Gary began to describe some personal feelings that he had not shared before—even with himself. I heard a man discovering himself. From what he reported, Cynthia encouraged him to do what he believed in, while Brenda pushed him away from his personal passion. The affair wasn't only about being with another woman; it was about opening up to himself. The real struggle was only beginning.

Gary felt within himself that this was not just about sex—or about another woman. Gary and Brenda had been mired in a relationship founded on misperception. Even though married and physically naked, they related falsely, Brenda determining standards that Gary should meet, regardless of how true they were to himself, and Gary going along with a "package" that he perceived as socially—but not personally—desirable. She regularly minimized his work and suggested that he get a real job like being a lawyer. The risk, however, could not have been higher: a lost marriage that he had worked at for a decade; but Gary, however, was overwhelmed by the exhilaration of having a real life, a real self.

At our next session, as if simply by saying some of these things, Gary made the decision to break off all contact with Cynthia. Gary and Brenda now came in for couples counseling.

In the weeks that followed, I met Brenda, who was a high-powered attorney. Now I heard her minimize the significance of Gary's professional life, confirming his statement that he needed to get "a real job" like her father. But Gary could see what was happening, and he felt his rage build. He had lost what was vital and did not know how to express himself. He began to look for real, authentic answers to his problems—not just mirages to grasp at. In this crisis, he now found a way to awaken his True Self and to save his marriage.

As they began to understand their attraction to one another and to demystify the fantasy marriage that they had both portrayed, they began to better understand themselves. In therapy, they grew forward in understanding the differences between their fantasies and the reality of their marriage. Gary and Brenda began to discover their genuine qualities of the True Self in each other. Their passion was fuller and more fulfilling—as they embraced eros, philia, storge, and agape. They learned to support an exchange of love that was fluid, freeing them of their inhibitions, healing their incompleteness, and nurturing their growth.

REFLECTION ON SEXUAL HISTORY

Diaries are valuable for retracing our important experiences, our feelings, memories, and thoughts. For some it is poetry, and for others, art. Some, on the other hand, may simply jot down a few phrases that capture significant turning points. Reflect on your various sexual thoughts, feelings, experiences, or dreams. Can you identify your sexual self, your sexual voices, and the sexual drives in your life? What significance do they hold with your development? Do you see how these different expressions of desire may crystallize experiences that both encapsulate and cut off the expression of your True Self?

To help you get started with your diary, identify how the three key concepts that we have considered factor into your life.

		SEXUAL THOUGHT OR BEHAVIOR	MEANING OR ORIGIN
SEXUAL	1.		
SELF	2.		
	3.		
VOICES OF	1.		
SEXUALITY	2.		
	3.		
DANCE OF	1.		
SEXUALITY	2.		
	3.		

REFLECTION ON YOUR SEXUALITIES

Think about the experience of love and sexuality in your relationships. Identify the ways in which sexual self, voices of sexuality, and the dance of sexuality are played out in your relationships. Do you feel comfortable about these experiences of your sexuality? Do you feel that your full sexual needs and feelings express your True Self or something else? Please define what "something else" means to you.

	TRUE SELF	"SOMETHING ELSE"
SEXUAL SELF		
VOICES OF SEXUALITY		
DANCE OF SEXUALITY		

In Chapter 5, we will look at love and passion in our family and our work, and we will also see how we negotiate our love of self as we express our talents and balance our personal and professional relationships. To open our heart, we must feel that we can freely express our passion without suppressing our True Self.

5

⌘

HARNESSING YOUR TALENTS

Hide not your talents, they for use were made.
What's a sun-dial in the shade?
— Benjamin Franklin

Climbing up the craggy mountainside, immersed in the pristine atmosphere of the sacred monasteries of Mount Athos, my college friend and I hurried along, jumping over huge rocks. We knew that the sounding of the symendron meant that the main gates to the monasteries would soon be bolted shut for the night. The symendron is a wooden block instrument struck with a hollow wooden drumstick that sounds out the beat of the Greek word *talanta*, meaning "talents":

Ta-ta-lan-ta
Ta-ta-lan-ta
Ta-ta
Ta-ta
Ta-ta-lan-ta

As monks are called into the monastery at the end of the day, the continuous rhythm of the instrument asks them: "Your talents, your talents, what have you done this day with your talents?"

At first glance, it may seem a bit silly for a monk—always so deep in the solitude of spiritual devotion—to contemplate how he had spent his day. Hasn't the monk already committed to a vocation? Isn't his routine already established? Aren't his talents and his use of them obvious? Of course, the questions probe much deeper. They ask: "How have your unique abilities, rooted in the True Self, taken hold today? Have you planted seeds according to your calling and nurtured them well?" In Chapter 5, we, too, will answer the symendron as we learn how to express our talents through the True Self by balancing our love for self (in developing our talents) with our love for others (in developing our commitments).

Our fulfillment is inevitably defined by how we pursue our talents and execute our vocation. We need to develop our talents in accordance with the intrinsic gifts of our True Self. Unfortunately, accomplishments sometimes come at the cost of devastating defeats in our personal life. Our connection to the True Self, therefore, is a pivotal guide for us when handling choices surrounding our achievements and goals. The stories and exercises in this chapter present challenges that we must confront as we simultaneously develop love of self and love of others—balancing the passion of our work with our passion in relationships.

Often we do not consider how our work can condition our relations to both ourselves and others. Our talents are often thought of as things that we must develop independently. Yet we always live out and share our talents in relation to others; they directly affect those in our intimate circle as well as others in the wider world. In this chapter, we meet a woman making decisions of global importance while maintaining that her greatest fulfillment in life has been raising her children; and we meet a man who feels reluctance to have children because he realizes that this choice will take time away from his work in music. Yet another story concerns a man who, together with his wife, knew that they would never choose to have children. What principles and lessons connect these disparate stories? How can we be both self-loving and attentive to others as we develop our talents? Will our interests in our talented selves and the need of others always compete?

Discovering Our Talent

Maria came to see me with a problem of integrating her talents into a full and rewarding life. At twenty-eight years old, Maria had studied music for many years and had already performed at the Metropolitan Opera. Although her professional career was moving along very well, she had a history of depression and had struggled considerably in her personal relationships. None of this, however, led her to therapy; in fact, she came to me unconcerned about her personal life, claiming to feel "much clearer" about herself than she ever had before.

Maria explained that she had recently experienced a religious awakening and that her newfound faith had granted her a deeper understanding of life and how to resolve her problems. She was coming to see me, she continued, because she feared that her talent as an opera singer "drew too much attention" to her. She felt that it was "too egotistical" to have people pay money to hear her and that she should use her talent to serve God. Her religious commitments seemed to be at odds with her artistic career.

I learned that Maria had struggled in feeling fulfilled or finding meaningful relationships; she now felt that she was succeeding in breaking self-destructive cycles in her relationships by sharing her faith with those she loved. There appeared to me to be an "all or nothing" dependency in her approach to religion: Maria regarded anything less than strict observance, for herself and others, as a betrayal of her faith. It was this total commitment that had generated her present crisis. According to her faith, God commanded, "Do not become self-focused." For Maria, studying her art and perfecting her skills felt like total self-absorption. Her talents and her career suddenly competed very strongly with her faith.

Rather than arriving at an overly simple solution that could undo years of passion, labor, and achievement, Maria and I slowly reconsidered the multiple factors that she feared threatened her relationship with God. In doing so, we were able to find a balance that allowed her to pursue her skills while still honoring her religion. She realized that her singing ability was a gift of God that she could serve as a connection with others; she felt lifted out of the morass of her depression.

Our work—especially when we consider it an art—is a beloved, if not sacred, aspect of our lives. Work often becomes a passion, tightly linked to our identity. Our talents are unique gifts that achieve their fullest expression when we manifest them in our True Self. As we align our talents with our True Self and balance them with our commitments, fulfillment naturally grows. For many like Maria, the struggle between finding this balance is not simple. Self, others, or God can seem to demand too much or even all of our attention, throwing our critical connections out of alignment. However, Maria learned to recognize the significance of her independent relationships with self, others, and God rather than being consumed by any one of these; she engaged in all her critical connections.

In our highly competitive society, the demands of pursuing our talents often clash with the responsibilities of family life. As two-income homes have become the norm, and women and men have increasingly begun to share family responsibilities, we all have had to assess the value and meaning of our choices and our commitments to work and to our personal life. This search calls us to look at the use of our talents in a deeper, more heartfelt way.

None of our choices for personal and professional life are inherently right or wrong. They are often guided, however, by unconscious motivations, in addition to the more obvious forces of the physical and social pressures under which we find ourselves. For example, in the pursuit of our goals, our decisions cannot be based solely on what appears attractive, the approval of confidants, or even our own knowledge and needs. Our best guide comes from checking in with our True Self and our critical connections. By considering our decisions against the following criteria, we can make certain our choices enhance our True Self and critical connections and that we are making the right choices:

True Self

+ spontaneity
+ reasoning
+ creativity
+ free will
+ discernment
+ spirituality
+ love

Critical Connections

+ Self: self-knowledge
+ Others: attending to those affected
+ God: prayer and personal engagement

Balancing Self and Others

In this third millennium, men and women alike are equally confronted with the challenge of finding their own relevance in both their personal and professional life. The options for both sexes have never been so numerous: "Will I be Mom?" "Do I follow the pattern of affluent women in my upscale suburb, putting aside my career, and stay home to raise my family, sacrificing my own interests?" "Will I be the professional that my college loans remind me I worked so hard to become, acquiring the things I dreamt about having and the magazine lifestyle that defines 'success'?" "Does a man have to work rather than be at home raising children?" "What kind of a father do I want to be?"

For most today, passion appropriately describes both our labors and our love. While our achievements often increase our freedom and control, genuine freedom does not occur in meeting the old definitions of success. Freedom comes from making critical connections according to our talents that balance our strong, interpersonal relationships. Let's look more closely at how the elements of our critical connections help us choose wisely and lead us toward fulfillment in making those choices.

Making Connections

Relationships account for the most wonderful as well as most frustrating experiences in our life. Since we are naturally driven to relate to others, establishing meaningful and fulfilling relationships will always be critical to our success and satisfaction. What are relationships? What criteria do we need to assess whether our relationships are genuine? I believe the following elements provide the criteria for strong interpersonal connections in the various levels of our personal and professional relationships:

+ self-awareness
+ authenticity
+ attunement
+ attention to personal characteristics
+ willingness to establish a new space

Self-Awareness, as we have described, allows us to distinguish our feelings, needs, and motives in a relationship. The possession of self-awareness includes recognizing that our own feelings, values, and thoughts may not be the same for others. The degree to which we can honestly distinguish our own needs, motives, and perspectives from those of others establishes the foundation for real connection in a relationship. Mary Lou Retton left her happy home as a teenager to commit to gymnastics, persevering against overwhelming competition. Even her own physical limitations did not constrain her passion. Instead she followed her dream and cultivated her own sense of self. She loved her family but confronted this very hard decision about her aspirations and training with honesty and resolve.

Authenticity requires recognizing the validity of each other's values, beliefs, and convictions. This opens the door to genuine communication. An ability to express ourselves authentically establishes the tone in relationships. We need to say to ourselves, "How do I see myself? Do I also recognize and truly see you?" Openness refers to the degree to which we provide others access to ourselves. So we ask, "Can I be vulnerable? Can I ask for something? Can I manage rejection? Can I accept the trust of another? Will they come through for me?" Tom Hanks's ability to hear his daughter's apprehension and to honestly respond about how "things would be different" in his second marriage reassured her because she felt that he heard the depth of her question and responded openly to her doubts. She felt he could sit with her pain—not deny it or dismiss it, but feel it with her. Authenticity conveys our commitments—when we are authentic, we reach out and embrace with heart, mind, and soul.

Attunement means that we attend and extend in our relationships. Our ability to empathize is thus felt in our connection with others. Lack of attunement often means a lack of depth; the other does not feel understood. By attending—expressing care and concern through empathy, verbally and nonverbally—we convey interest in a person as an individual. By contrast, you may recall Bette Davis describing her father as wanting children to be seen but not heard, conveying his lack of attunement.

Our attention to personal characteristics helps us to recognize how our individual similarities and differences affect, resonate, and enhance our connections. Recognizing our personal characteristics allows us to develop and sustain authentic exchange—to understand why we are drawn to some and have difficulty with others. An example may be in how our vulnerability with another permits that person to take a risk and become vulnerable with us.

Willingness to establish a new space means we enter a new shared space, sharing our history and exploring the truth of our motives. We need to recognize that every new relationship offers opportunity through its uniquely shared space, a special exchange. This may occur even in a professional relationship. For example, a doctor may relate to a patient in different ways: the doctor may not even engage the patient personally at all; or the doctor may invite the patient to explain his or her own problems, thereby helping the doctor to understand the many factors that affect well-being, creating a genuine contact.

As you can see, our relationships are based on reciprocity and quality of connectedness. A better relationship results when we move beyond our own perspectives and progress toward shared considerations.

The Iron Woman with a Heart of Gold

As time approached for me to meet Jeane Kirkpatrick, appointed by President Ronald Reagan in 1982 as the first woman to serve as U.S. Ambassador to the United Nations, I confess that my excitement was mingled with a touch of trepidation. On the one hand, Kirkpatrick and her team were critically acclaimed for restoring the United States' voice in the UN. On the other hand, I felt intimidated by Kirkpatrick's portrayal in the media as "hypercritical," "a boxer of the mind," and "the iron woman." Though I was aware that media characterizations often fall short of reality, I could not help but feel anxious when Kirkpatrick began to grill me on the rationale for my study. "Do you see universal challenges for people in the workplace? Are there common elements for all of us irrespective of our individual talents?" she asked. Satisfied by my answers, she sat back and prepared to open up. Our discussion quickly turned to Kirkpatrick's early life:

> I never really thought that I would be married or have a family. These were the most amazing surprises to me. From youth I read and studied. I felt consumed by ideas. Books about ideas filled my thoughts. I wanted to remain true to this passion, which was so expansive and purposeful. However, once I met my husband, I also found a true companion in life. I love to be with him. So, now there were two great loves, only to be followed by another: becoming a mother.

The woman of iron, it seemed, was nothing of the sort. She was elated when describing how "a very special man" had asked her to marry him and became even more animated when describing the joy she experienced as she cared for her children:

> My academic career was fully engaged; however, I couldn't think of compromising the opportunity of motherhood. It was never a question. So I took an extended leave of absence to raise my family. It was marvelous! Totally magical, joyful, wholesome. Totally delicious! Nothing in life can compare. To give birth is a wonderful experience! It is by far the best part of being a woman. It is remarkable! Fantastic! No words are adequate to describe it. I only wish that I could further maximize these moments of being a mother, to exploit the very seconds of sharing life with my sons. It is so sensual—and it is the very essence of life.

There was no mistaking the importance of Kirkpatrick's husband and children in her life or the visceral passion she felt for them. I began to wonder if the overly harsh portrayal of her by the media was driven by the fear of a woman both brilliant and self-aware, or if the public had simply never known the more sensitive Kirkpatrick. For here was a woman who had clearly welcomed the highest development of her own talent as well as the responsibility of a fully engaged family life. Kirkpatrick exhibited courage, strength, and knowledge of what both personal and professional life offered. Of course, her abilities did not make her immune to uncertainty, but they did allow her to honestly face her dislikes and limitations:

> I love life and prefer it to work. Being with my family and friends, traveling all over the world . . . reading good books and dining and entertaining. Being cooped up in this office for the very long days that are required of me as ambassador is isolating and a sacrifice.

When her days of child rearing were almost behind her in the early 1980s, President Reagan called Kirkpatrick back to the professional world. For her work at the UN, she was awarded the Medal of Freedom, our nation's highest civilian honor, in addition to many awards from around the globe.

As I listened to the familiar recounting of the Iron Woman's service to the UN and her surprise account of the nurturing mother, my wonder grew as to whether these two women were really the same. Did Kirkpatrick experience her political appointment as a part of her True Self? When executing her duties as ambassador, had she drawn on her own sense of right and wrong? The more I delved into this question, the more I discovered that Kirkpatrick displayed the kind of dedication we hope for in all leaders. In spite of her professional success, she never lost grasp of her self or her values and beliefs. She instead adhered to her True Self and made herself a more compelling and effective politican.

Years after we had first spoken, I had the opportunity to resume our talks. Still thoughtful and decorous in her response, Kirkpatrick had nonetheless changed since I had last known her; the agony of her husband's passing two years prior was still fresh in her mind. Her husband had been her closest companion and genuine friend: "My life is lonely; I'm coming back to activity slowly." Knowing her to have been fulfilled both from her family and from her career, Kirkpatrick would have to adjust to her life without these connections.

Distance was apparent, however, between Kirkpatrick and her children. The profound closeness of the mother-son bonds she had described years earlier had diminished over time, and she told me of her differences with one son, who had become a Buddhist monk. She reflected:

> I don't think that the parent-child role is ever very even. Each [of my sons] is very deeply and very appropriately involved in his own life and his own family. I'm part of their lives, but in a somewhat marginal way.

Kirkpatrick saw her own professional commitments as the cause of her drifting apart from her sons:

> I think that the more task oriented one is, the more detached [one becomes] from others. There, I said it. I think at every time in my life that I have worked very hard to finish a book, I did it at a cost of some other part in

my life—for the years that my children were growing up, I did it. There would be more time with them if I had given less priority to finishing books.

Even when we are well intentioned in the beginning, we must monitor our critical connections.

Kirkpatrick has retained a constructive, accepting, and active attitude toward life. She continues to integrate her skills and attune herself to changes, always striving to express the values of her True Self in her work and in her private life. In her article "Making Sense," Kirkpatrick detailed these principles that have helped her make good choices and find understanding in her life:

> I shall probably never feel I have found certain answers. No one can entirely escape conditioning . . . yet our choices are not relative. We never operate from a tabula rasa. Our common nature provides the grounds on which we can make sense of our past and deal with those in remote places.
>
> I believe that commitments give meaning to life—commitments to family, country, friends, work, students of civilized behavior, God—and that a meaningful life requires making fulfilling commitments. Not intelligence, nor beauty, nor talent, nor charm is as important as character. Strong, loving, reasonable parents help, but, finally, character is each person's own achievement. People of good character are at peace with themselves, while those who lie, cheat, steal—who are indolent and self-indulgent—suffer in the here and now.
>
> The Greeks . . . understood that an ordered soul is a prerequisite to a good life. But it is not enough. The Greeks also believed that a good life is one which utilizes and develops to the maximum one's human and individual qualities. I believe it, too. Living life to the hilt, developing one's energies—learning, listening, talking, reading, writing, creating, seeing, feeling, sharing, traveling, cooking, eating, cramming into life as many experiences as possible—is my recipe for a good life.

Kirkpatrick knows she doesn't need "absolute answers" to live a life connected to her gifts, values, others, and God. "An authentic life," she says, "is one that is lived with integrity—that is not in conflict with oneself."

Kirkpatrick's story illustrates some of the benefits and pitfalls of striving to achieve balance between the personal and professional. She delighted in her family life and felt passionate about the professional opportunities she was afforded. Though she thrived in both spheres, it appeared that her ability to maintain a balance slipped away over time.

Kirkpatrick's passion in her work came from doing what she loved most. She was fulfilled through her work as she pursued the voyage of her True Self and realized the extraordinary demands of her vocations. If there is anything that is "ironlike" about her, it is her resolve to do her best and keep striving. Others, however, are wary about taking on family responsibilities with their already demanding professions, as this next profile illustrates.

Success in the Fast Lane

Keith Lockhart stood dressed in his tuxedo, vigorously waving his baton, stretching high on his toes, dipping deeply, as if magnetically drawing the music out from all 120 pieces of the Boston Pops. Only its third conductor ever, Lockhart seemed an unlikely choice to follow in the prestigious footsteps of Arthur Fiedler and John Williams when he was elected to the position in the mid-1990s. At only thirty-five years of age, his achievement was the result of incredible commitment, passion, and discipline.

There is no question that music is everything for Keith. Unassuming, friendly, and forthright, he openly admitted to me that he is "more comfortable out on that stage than in any other place in my life"—personal relationships included. The requirements and rewards of music provide Lockhart with the very structure of his identify. Music is the medium through which he connects intellectually and spiritually with others, and it is the door that grants him access to his True Self.

I've always been amazed by the emotive connection that I feel with music, and the way that it transports me. I don't feel that with too many things in the world. I've always been such a fan of language, too, and [feel moved] hearing, say, Lear's dying speech. But straight to the heart, the shiver down the spine, the lump below my heart I get from music—those are magical things.

Lockhart has had his musical passion since childhood. His parents, he claims, placed no pressure at all on him to perform. "Music intrinsically led me to pursue it for what it gave to me—physical and emotional passion," Lockhart said. He feels riveted by the challenge of interpreting the great musical masterpieces and delights in the opportunities that are open to him with the Pops to combine classical music with other genres.

So integral is Lockhart's musical career to his life that he cites it as a primary cause of his separation from his first wife, whom he married when he was twenty-two. The turning point in the marriage came when he recognized that many of the difficulties he and his wife were experiencing related to his new-found musical direction.

Lockhart's example shows us that pursuing talents of the True Self does not always deeply engage other spheres along with it. Lockhart explained that studying to be a conductor took up "too much time and energy" and he was not "willing to compromise" with his first wife, who delayed her own ambitions in order to support his. "She wasn't fulfilled," Lockhart admits, citing the flaw of their union: "There was no balance in the relationship." Realizing this finally made him aware of the acute difficulties he would face trying to balance the joy he felt from his talent with the love he wanted from a family. "In music," he notes, "it is difficult to separate yourself from your career because your career is so closely tied to your creativity and your passions." That passion includes his need to work to the best of his ability, an effort that demands "self-confidence, self-analysis, and self-criticism"—in sum, an enormous focus on the self, with not much energy left for anyone else.

Lockhart's musical commitments are consuming, but he would not dream of giving up any of them. In addition to the Boston Pops, which could itself be considered a full-time job, Keith also serves as conductor of the Utah Symphony Orchestra in Salt Lake City. In between these jobs, he occupies himself with projects in music education, recording contracts, and guest conducting spots, not to mention numerous public appearances. Considering the incredible demands of his career, Lockhart was fortunate to find a woman compatible with his all-consuming passion. His second wife, Lucia, is first violinist of the Boston Symphony Orchestra and shares his unflagging devotion to career and perfectionism. Their similar interests and personalities have permitted a great understanding of each other in their day-to-day routines—a clear example of his growth in attunement.

Seeking contentment within his marriage and wanting to remain true to his own needs, Lockhart is indifferent to the conventional dictates of society and its images of family life. Throughout our interviews over the past few years, he insisted that parenthood was not a priority for him:

> Maybe that's selfish, but I don't know why having space for children in your life is any more valid than having space for music in your life. Frankly, [parenting is] something that anybody can do—and not everybody does it well.

Finding "great happiness" in chasing demanding yet profoundly fulfilling goals, Keith unabashedly saw himself as having no time for anything other than music, declaring he has "only begun to scratch the surface" of his career's potential. In his life, he is first and foremost a conductor.

But in Lockhart we see an important truth: the convictions one brings to developing one's talents are not the same as—or necessarily fully compatible with—the convictions one brings to interpersonal relationships. Everyone's paradigm does not require marriage and a family. At one of our last meetings together, Lockhart informed me that Lucia was expecting their first child. He acknowledged that it was love for his wife and "true commitment" to their relationship that was leading him into the role of fatherhood.

Our passion in personal and professional pursuits and fulfilling connections through the True Self do not, as Lockhart's story suggests, require children. Others, as we see in the next story, show clear resolve about child rearing and career from the onset.

An Entertainer at Heart

Unlike some of the people we have considered, Jay Leno was not abandoned or deprived as a child. He came from a good home, learning good values from good parents; he witnessed the struggles of his parents and appreciated everything they did for him. Nonetheless, like many of us, he experienced some struggles without the tools he needed to sort them out.

Like any child, Jay wanted his mother's attention. Though he believes she wanted to respond to him, Jay's mother suffered from depression, and her attention was difficult to get. Inspired by a desire to bring his mother happiness and to be noticed, Jay performed for her, clowning around in his attempt to meet her needs. "She was really happy and had fun with her friends when I told jokes. I felt that she would notice me when I made her laugh." Jay learned something from this experience that continues to influence him: to receive people's love and support, you first have to give them what they want.

What people want, Jay discovered, was entertainment; in return for making people laugh, he received their recognition. The clean, friendly comedy that earned him the good attention of his parents soon became his trademark. Like most of us, Jay probably could have cultivated any number of talents; particular environments draw out our skills and make us "naturals" at particular careers. While the desire to please others is no doubt an admirable quality, relationships based on the question not of "who you are" but "what you do for me" may leave a person without feelings of genuine connection or personal value. As entertainers in both our personal and professional lives, we can be great pleasers while remaining severed from our True Self. When driven to get an emotional response, in fact, balanced relationships are hard to attain.

Frequently environmental factors contribute to our line of work and the particular talents we develop. Usually we are not surprised that most cowboys grow up in the Southwest rather than on the East Coast; that therapists, for various reasons, were good listeners from a young age; and that people in certain professions pass the torch from one generation to the next.

I recall one of my physician friends playing with his two-year-old and looking at him with amazement, saying, "Wow, look at your hands! Those are surgeon's hands. You're going to grow up and become a great surgeon one day." Attentive to his father's observation, the boy walked off, staring at his fingers, mesmerized and wearing a big smile on his face. Such emotional pretunings drive us to our professional fields. But regardless of the factors that lead us to our careers, our task is to make sure that our work taps our talents so that we can draw on our True Self.

Jay readily admits, "I have a hard time answering questions about who I am or what I really feel. I just do what I do." Like Jay, many of us can go on with our professional lives, failing to question what motivates us and knowing how our motives might make us happier. Sometimes we only think of the needs of those whom our work serves. When we do this, we are less connected to our True Self and are often unable to connect with the True Self of another. Before I began my interview, Jay's staff warned me, "He's very nice, and you will like what he says—but you will never get to know him." Jay may have known while choosing his highly reinforcing career path that it could afford him only transient, one-way interactions with others, but it does not appear that this emotional cost bothers him. Each of our professions carries emotional cost. What do we do in our search for recognition? How are our needs for recognition met in our job? To what extent do we go to get the attention we need or want from others? While we may struggle to balance our talent with our relationships, our resolve to satisfy both will lead us toward more fulfilling goals than simple rationalized ambition, pointing out our idiosyncrasies and encouraging new freedom.

So how does Leno fare in the test of marriage, the most intimate critical connection between two people? Is he the same person he tries to be in public, or is he more self-revealing at home? Jay has been married to his wife Mavis for more than fifteen years. Jay says that their romance began at a nightclub in Los Angeles, where Jay performed. Mavis knew just when to laugh. Significantly, then, it was precisely her appreciation for the timing and delivery of his jokes that Jay admits attracted him to Mavis and forged the couple's first connection. Highly self-effacing, Jay portrays himself as extraordinarily indifferent to the degree of his accomplishment as a comedian. His manner toward his work is matter-of-fact, speaking of his humor as though it were a product he put on the market and not a piece of himself he offered to the world. But his reaction to Mavis suggests to us just how important entertainment is to his sense of self-worth.

Speaking of his decision not to have children, Leno simply stated, "It's something that Mavis and I agree about. Some people want a family; we don't." None of us makes such personal choices casually.

While Leno describes his marriage as deeply intimate, often Mavis will travel alone, with Jay joining her for only a day or two, if at all. The couple enjoy very different personalities, interests, and hobbies. Some of the so-called creature comforts feel very unnatural for Jay:

Fifteen dollars for a sandwich in a fancy restaurant! I don't need that. Sitting down and waiting for a waiter—that doesn't make sense to me. I get my own sandwich, wash my own clothes; I don't need servants waiting on me. No, no, no. Get your hands off of me. I hate massages. Never. I eat my meals standing up.

While Jay does not seem bothered by this divide between his own interests and those of his wife, he also does not wish to comment on it:

My job is to make my wife happy: whatever she wants, that's what I do. When you say fulfillment, I'm not even sure I know what you mean. It doesn't come up. Mavis was in the Caribbean; then she went to Europe today: she and her mom. Whatever she wants. I have no interest in that. It always makes me laugh when people say, "We have this...." Yeah. Great. I'm glad that makes you happy. You know how hard it is to find love in the world. If you can find it anywhere, God bless you!

Today, Leno shields himself and others from his emotions ("No one ever knows what I feel about a topic; it's just business"), always saying the "right things" and avoiding detection. He does not admit to directly confronting his emotions. Nor does he wish today to pursue his feelings. After all, he asks, "Things went pretty well for me, didn't they?"

In Kirkpatrick, Lockhart, and Leno, we see the profound impact of our early development in our connection to our talents and the costs our talents impose in any connections with others. We see how our careers and the decisions we make in our relationships often keep us playing the same roles, experiencing the same emotional concerns we knew in our earliest experiences of conflict and comfort. We see how our engagement of the True Self and the engagement of our critical connections, discovered through our work and talents, can alter our established patterns at work and at home. And we see how finding authenticity in our work and our relations expands our journey and brings us greater fulfillment. While the demands of maintaining both a career and intimacy can be enormous, facing the challenge allows us the possibility of moving not only vertically through life, continuing established patterns from the past, but horizontally as well, learning new ways of being and growing in the present.

In sum, I call the turning-point relationships—the decision to have a child, to rearrange work schedules, for example—moments of "potential for action." I think every relationship has the potential for action, in which our self, others, and God are present and waiting for us to ignite them. To a great extent, the potential for action depends on our willingness to risk, to trust, to be spontaneous, and to share our thoughts and feelings. These moments in a relationship are the building blocks for deepening our connections. If we seize this potential for action, our reciprocal sharing leads to greater understanding and connectedness. The more we seize on such opportunities, the deeper our relationships grow.

Seizing these moments provides a setting for authentic exchange to occur. The potential for action leads to the beginning of a new, deepened relationship—a new beginning for both participants. The more we take interest, share in attuned ways, touch each other's world, and meet each other's True Self, the deeper our self-awareness grows as well. Something beyond us becomes part of us.

Ta-Talanta

How do you answer the beat of the symendron? What are your talents? Do you use them? In this book, we share the stories of people who have achieved high acclaim in their respective professions. However, we all wrestle with the same question of fulfillment. While these individuals have passionately pursued their talents, they have learned that particular qualities are essential that make their talents fulfilling. Often these people refer to the following seven qualities that they find helpful in pursuing their passions and being responsible within a relationship:

1. *Decisiveness:* You will know what to pursue when it becomes clear for you. Much like finding your match for life, you may consider various options. Sometimes you may date someone for a long time and realize that this is the love of your life; sometimes you know without much information at all. The process is idiosyncratic, coming not only from your head, but also from your heart and soul—and sometimes it's luck. As Bette Davis discovered, "It's not the people who want a relationship that find it; it's often just meeting the right one."

2. *Self-awareness:* Each of us is unique. But we are also quite similar. Your characteristics are often like those of others in your field. Recognize your traits; know your strengths and weaknesses; and see how these match with the field you are interested in. Lucille Ball, for example, had to establish reasonable boundaries that would allow her to follow her passion for acting when she found herself in a painful marriage.

3. *Community:* Support your interest with a community of people who work in your area. Find mentors who understand both you and your work. Develop friendships with peers who work in your field.

Tom Hanks, for instance, discovered his potential and found support through his community of actors in high school.

4. *Discipline*: Rarely are individuals who excel in their fields jacks-of-all-trades; generally, those who excel are masters of one. They are experts because they give everything they have to their passion. Jay Leno says, "I wake up and I'm right at work on the next monologue. Every minute, I give to my jokes, going above and beyond the expectations. I'm trying to improve and rise to that next level."

5. *Enthusiasm*: Fully embrace your talent. Many people do things for extrinsic reasons, such as money or prestige. And while these incentives are necessary, they do not lead to fulfillment. Mary Lou Retton remembers, "Sure, I worked hard, and there were many lonely nights; but I loved getting better at what I was doing."

6. *Meaningfulness*: If you do not believe that what you are doing is valuable, then you cannot sufficiently answer the questions, What are you doing with your talents? Do your talents connect you with others? Do they help you share and give? Keith Lockhart described his musical talents as spiritual, allowing him to communicate his most elevated experiences in the universal language of music.

7. *True Self*: The insights of those people who share their stories here are abundant in True Self qualities. Those qualities were present in their lives. The elements of fulfillment were goals, which they greatly sought. As Kirkpatrick stated, "An ordered soul is a prerequisite to a good life, which develops one's human and individual qualities."

PASSION, TALENT, LIFESTYLE

We may wish to pursue a particular field but find that we are not adequately talented for it. Or we may be gifted (talented) in a certain field but may not wish to pursue it. Or the relational and personal costs may outweigh what we are willing to sacrifice.

In the first column, rank (from most to least), the five careers about which you feel most passionate. In the second column, rank the five careers about which you feel most talented. In the third column, drawing on the first two columns, rank the careers in terms of their compatibility with your desired lifestyle.

	PASSION	TALENT	LIFESTYLE
1.			
2.			
3.			
4.			
5.			

To what extent do your career choices line up in the areas of passion, talent, and lifestyle? Do you see the significance of the connection in these areas for your passion, talent, and lifestyle?

ASSESSING YOUR QUALITIES IN CAREER FULFILLMENT

Assess the extent to which you have developed the seven qualities that were identified by leaders in their fields as significant for finding fulfillment in their career.

	Low		Average		High
1. DECISIVENESS	1	2	3	4	5
2. SELF-AWARENESS	1	2	3	4	5
3. COMMUNITY	1	2	3	4	5
4. DISCIPLINE	1	2	3	4	5

	Low	Average	High
	Low	Average	High
5. ENTHUSIASM	1	2	3	4	5
6. MEANINGFULNESS	1	2	3	4	5
7. TRUE SELF	1	2	3	4	5

Does your career engage these qualities within you? Do you think another field would? Have you ever evaluated the extent to which your position draws out your passions and gives you fulfillment?

6

❧

CREATING INTIMACY

All intimacies are based on differences.
—HENRY JAMES

WHILE MOST OF US DISTINGUISH right from wrong and desire to do what is right, events affect us and may compromise our good intentions. Relationships that have caused us suffering or tested our resilience may leave us feeling jaded, skeptical, and untrusting. Entering a new relationship may seem daunting, and the potential to reexperience pain too ominous to risk. How can we correct the damage inflicted on us in our most injurious experiences? And what happens when we discover that both we and our partner have brought to the relationship wounds that are slow to heal and scars that refuse to fade? Can we ever recover and begin life once more?

By creating intimacy in our relationships, a connection of trust experienced physically, emotionally, and spiritually, we establish the connections essential for healing and wellness. By creating intimacy, we can change and open up the pathways of our critical connections; we can feel and know the qualities of the True Self; we can create a fulfilling family and social life; and we can ultimately open our hearts. Let us consider significant elements of intimacy in various aspects of life as we look to create intimacy in our lives.

Intimacy in the Family:
Critical Moments and Opportunities

Our first intimate encounters are in our families. For many, the word *family* conjures up feelings of warmth and comfort; for others, it brings up feelings of emptiness. The feelings associated with this word are often loaded.

What impact does our family have on our lives? If our early familial experiences were fraught with difficulties, can we ever move beyond them? Are there, in fact, "critical moments" and opportunities in youth that we must successfully meet in order to be healthy adults?

Critical Moments   In a noted experiment, Austrian ethnologist Konrad Lorenz demonstrated the importance of a "critical period" in the baby gosling's life, explaining that instinctual behavior is governed by a kind of biological timetable. Lorenz showed that if he himself took the place of the mother goose in daily care during this critical period of early infancy, the gosling became permanently attached to him. When its mother returned, the gosling rejected her, not having made an original attachment with her.

What can we learn from these experiments? Scientists generally maintain that there is no true psychological equivalent, no "critical period," for humans—that there is no instinctual code or specific event in which human babies become attached to their caretakers. Yet human infants do parallel other species in forming bonds through their primary relationship with parents. Because of the significance of these critical attachments, I refer to our human bonds as "critical moments" for establishing connections and relationships. These attachments, or specific emotional bonds, stem from critical moments in our development. I illustrated this point when I mentioned playing with my infant daughter by tickling her and imitating her every move. The questions for parents to consider are: What are the processes through which attachments are formed? And what happens when there are no attachments? Our encounters with our children must embody fulfillment and provide satisfaction, comfort, and well-being. These encounters are essential for a healthy child. Deprivation in fundamental relationships can lead to impairment of interpersonal skills. Children deprived of nurturing and personal human bonds during their first two years are particularly challenged to make human attachments in later childhood.

By caressing, nurturing, comforting, and protecting our children, we provide them with a sense of security and safety. For example, through bottle-feeding, bonding is established. Bonding is also expressed through language and interaction. Between six and eight months of age, a newborn smiles for the mother as the baby associates her with the pleasures that she provides. Although the actual process is not completely understood, we do know that when these experiences are missed, emotional problems are likely to surface, including a lack of trust for others.

When critical moments are absent, emotional damage can occur. Studies of abused children find that the abusers were frequently victims of abuse themselves. Parental relationships are often marred by criticism, rejection, and physical punishment. They retain this childhood dynamic, in a sense, as they describe marital discord, emotional unavailability, and physical brutality from their spouses.

While it is not a prevailing norm in our society, two parents are really needed to make sure the kind of safety and nurturing I describe is fully available to a child. Girls who grow up in the absence of a father often have difficulty adjusting to adult interaction with males. Likewise, because of a boy's desire to be like his father, a son is surely influenced by the warmth of the father-son relationship.

We see that even if there is no simple critical period for humans, there are indeed several "critical moments" of attachment with parents in childhood and adolescence. In fact, when we lack physical and emotional bonding—basic touch and care—we often become ill. We are shaped—and sometimes distorted—by our experiences. In my clinical work, the marks caused by traumatic critical moments tend to dominate therapeutic sessions. It is easy to identify cases where this occurs, but rather difficult to get the patient to work through their memories and overcome the trauma.

Put simply, the questions we must all ask are: What kind of connection are we to establish with our children? How are we to love them? How are we to make the most of the opportunities that we have with them? How can we provide them with the love that they desperately need during the critical moments of their lives? In the following story, we learn several answers to those questions and the results of effectively meeting critical moments in our children's development.

Our ability or failure to pursue and repair these connections may ultimately stem from the family, as we see in the example of Dominick, a child of isolation and disconnection.

Becoming a Man   Although only fifteen years old, Dominick appeared to be in his twenties. The epitome of Italian machismo, the tall youth swaggered into my office, dressed entirely in black, from his leather jacket to his shoes. His demeanor suggested a conscious effort to appear callous and invulnerable. When I asked him to tell me about himself, lifting his eyebrows, he smirked and replied, "I'm Italian"—as if by those two words he gave a complete personal profile. Upon further prompting, he informed me that one of his favorite things to do was to start fights: to "take on" older guys and beat them up.

As I went through my preliminary background inquiries, I observed Dominick's keen recollection for details as he recounted some of his favorite adventures in vandalism. When I asked him about his procedure for breaking into a car, Dominick became vigorous and intense. Clenching his fists and exhibiting an unusual mixture of hostility and delight, he explained how he slashed apart dashboards to remove radios. He probably would never have been caught, he pointed out, had it not been for his accomplice setting off an alarm.

Dominick was so articulate that I decided to conduct a series of psychological tests to evaluate him more precisely. His verbal IQ score was close to 140—comparable to those gifted students at the best universities. I noted as well that Dominick showed great enthusiasm whenever he successfully answered a question. In fact, during the tests, his comfort improved significantly as he began to laugh and engage with me. In spite of his abilities, he had never done well in school and had repeatedly got into trouble.

In a family meeting, I saw Dominick's mother doting on him, insisting that her son was a good boy and denying his criminal activity. Meanwhile, Dominick's father was distant, insisting that if his son had done something wrong, he should be duly punished. I could not help but notice the contrast, and I began to see that Dominick was a product of a confused set of parenting signals. I asked Dominick's father how he related to his children. "Well," he said, "I talk to my daughters, but I don't believe in father-son talk. Guys should talk to girls—not to guys." As I gently pressed the father about more conventionally masculine activities, such as tossing a football together or going to a game, the father reflected, "I don't do that stuff; and he doesn't like it anyway." To this Dominick blurted out, "Did you ever ask me?" His father said scornfully, "Shut up! Who's talking to you anyway? If it wasn't for you, we wouldn't even have to be here."

As Dominick recoiled, I could feel the tension in his gut. His fury and aggression were a plea for his father's love. Dominick's story was not just that of a rebellious teen; it was also the story of a son who was trying desperately to become a man—a tough man like his dad— but he had to figure out how to do it his own way. While Dominick presented himself as oppositional, what was more salient about him was the lack of attachment, connection, and intimacy he felt at home.

While I could relate to having a strict and, at times, even frightening father, I could not imagine having an indifferent one. Relationships are a learned behavior, and we tend to understand best and to frequently repeat our earliest interactions. If we later recognize in ourselves problems caused by our early development, it is our responsibility to address them. Over the years, my patients who have confronted their childhood difficulties have generally improved their relationships with their parents and increased the vitality of their connections.

In the months of therapy that followed, Dominick accepted my offer to try to get him admitted to a school for the gifted. For the first time in his life, he felt enthusiastic about going to school and began to approach authorities as people he could learn from, rather than fear and wish to destroy.

I have identified with Dominick because of my own adolescence, though I was able to confront my father in my teens about the distress I felt in my childhood. To my surprise, he listened. The more he listened, the more I shared, and an intimate relationship developed. When we feel safe with others, we can enter their world, which may otherwise seem foreign. With my father, I began to watch the television shows he enjoyed about art, nature, and war. This became the special space where we would connect. I would learn about his earlier experiences, and I began to understand what was once his private world. Fathers and sons especially have difficulty, but need to overcome societal expectations that prevent recognition and development of the True Self—as well as substantive growth in their critical connections.

The "Cost" of a Visit from the Tooth Fairy   At seven years old, my son Anthony was showing more than his usual enthusiasm at losing a tooth. In addition to tugging at the tooth until it loosened, he announced that the tooth fairy should increase her normal gift of a silver dollar because he was getting older. In fact, he envisioned the possibility of more money or even some Yugio trading cards, a serious hobby with his friends at school and a sure item for connection with the new guys at hockey.

In spite of Anthony's earnest wishes, the tooth fairy remained steadfast, and her mysterious visit to retrieve his tooth earned him the same silver dollar it had earned in the past. The next morning, Anthony nonchalantly reported his discovery. While he lacked the excitement and wonderment he had shown following his finds after previous lost teeth, he said that he appreciated that the tooth fairy came—as if trying to convince himself.

That evening, however, after our children had gone to bed, Anthony came into the living room and asked if he could speak with me for a few moments: "Dad, I wanted to run something by you. I was thinking about writing a letter to the tooth fairy." Continuing with his very deliberate plan, he explained, "I thought that I'd thank her for her visit and that I'd leave the silver dollar under the pillow with a note saying that she could leave $1,000,000 and not have to come back ever again, so she could have more time to visit other kids. Or, she could leave 5,000 valuable Yugio cards, or $500,000 and 2,500 cards. What do you think?"

Astonished by his proposition, I felt disturbed by his expectations yet impressed by his ingenuity. As I tried to collect myself to respond to this curve ball, I joked, "It sounds like you think your teeth are pretty valuable." Then I gave an opinion: "Anthony, I'm concerned with your response to this gift. It sounds like you're really not satisfied. What do you think?"

While I thought that this question would suffice and he'd be off to bed, he responded, "Well, did you ever even ask her for something when you were a little boy? Have you ever talked with her about the possibility of other choices?" To both of these I answered no. Yet I repeated my concern and said we would speak in the morning.

As the one who turns in last every night, and thus the tooth fairy's envoy, I wanted to reassure myself that my counsel was effective. So I checked under Anthony's pillow before turning out the lights. Saddened and shocked, I found a letter alongside the new silver dollar:

To the tooth fairy:

Because you're very busy I wanted to ask to trade your silver dollar for one last trip to my house. This way we'll both be happy and you can use your time for your other visits. Please select one for my silver dollar and your last trip here for me—

1. Give me a $1,000,000 check.
2. Give me 5,000 Yu-gi-oh cards.
3. Give me a $500,000 check and 2,500 Yu-gi-oh cards.

Thank you for reading. I know you are busy.

Love, Anthony

P.S. I'm sorry for this late notice.

This was one of those moments when I felt the need "to sleep on it," so I exchanged the letter for his tooth and went to bed.

I missed Anthony's early morning rise. My wife, however, who was taking him to a 6 A.M. hockey game, told me she had found him dressed in his hockey gear at 5 A.M. and sleeping on the floor at my side of the bed, hoping that I would wake so that he could speak with me before they left. On the ride to the game, she later told me she found Anthony strikingly stoic and said she thought there was "some kind of male thing going on," because after telling her what had happened, Anthony did not express as many feelings as he usually did. When concluding the story, she recounted, "He simply said, 'I took a risk and I lost—and that's cool!'" at which point they both burst into laughter. While I was concerned about his pushing the envelope, my wife reminded me that our son was also exploring his limits and in fact had used ingenuity which should not be punished. Moreover, she suggested that the tooth fairy might write a letter to put things in perspective.

Still daunted by Anthony's behavior, I shared my concerns with him. The following letter on behalf of the infamous caretaker of teeth was composed and left under his pillow:

Dearest Anthony,

I never bring BIG MONEY when I visit after you lose your teeth—I just leave a token or two to share my JOY to celebrate as you become older. The kind of money that you want, you can only earn fairly by using your very special mind, heart, and soul, and this you will accomplish in due time. Let me know if you want me to visit when you lose teeth again. You are a special boy. I know that you will understand how to use your gifts and especially to find this JOY that you have today.

Love,

Your Angel

The next morning, Anthony was amazed by the letter. He said that he understood and "really like that she signed it, 'Your Angel'"; it made him feel connected to her and reassured him that he still had this special friend that cared about him.

As we progress in life, there is still much in us that remains from our childhood. As we may have told our parents where they went wrong when we came of age, quite reasonably our children will someday point out our mistakes too. When in doubt, the counsel of our partner and our relationship with God are the directions toward which we should turn. While we seek certainty in what we do, we need perspective of who we are. Most often it is not individual human errors that get us into trouble but rather the impact of the larger paradigm we follow that causes difficulty and distraction.

Single-Minded and Focused on Truth

Shirley Chisholm was a woman who knew her own will. She knew who she was, what she wanted, and was determined to keep fighting for her causes no matter what. Retired now, and still writing, forty years ago she faced formidable opposition in her pursuit of her professional ambitions. It was her confidence in her own capabilities, however, that enabled her to achieve personal fulfillment. Her ability to focus on great causes undoubtedly came from the strong sources of love and nurturing she had in her background.

By 1946, when Chisholm was barely in her twenties, the die had already been cast for her future career and the many difficult battles to come. An activist against racism since college, Shirley entered local politics head-on, confronting the white-male political system of her native Brooklyn and demanding to know why the city's garbage service did not extend to black neighborhoods. It was not long before Chisholm developed a reputation for fearlessness in taking on the toughest issues in politics—from civil liberties and women's rights to homelessness and the Vietnam War. Chisholm had unyielding determination, and in 1963 this champion of the downtrodden became the first black woman to be elected to the United States Congress. Later, in another first, Chisholm was a serious contender for the Democratic nomination in the 1972 presidential election, winning 152 delegates before withdrawing from the race.

I first met the congresswoman in the early 1980s. I was surprised by the difference between my expectations and the woman who greeted me. Shirley Chisholm's reputation as an unpredictable maverick hardly prepared me for her peaceful and sensitive disposition. Then, a few years later, a professor at Mount Holyoke College, Chisholm's calm yet independent manner was apparent throughout our time together.

She attributed her self-confidence and stability to her childhood in Barbados, where she grew up with a strong attachment to her family and an unawareness that race could be a factor in others' judgment of her. Chisholm's maternal grandmother instilled in her the value of education, teaching her that it was her mind, and not her skin color, that ultimately mattered. Her grandmother clearly encouraged her, nurtured her, and assured her that she could realize her greatest dreams. Speaking of her grandmother, Chisholm said:

> She was the driving force in my life. I didn't appreciate her until I was about fourteen or fifteen. She used to say, "Child, you're somebody, you know! You got a brain. Boy, you're smart!" Hitting her forehead, she said, "It's up here. Once you have it up here, no one can take it from you. You don't want to be known because you're a pretty woman. It isn't black power, pink power, white power; it's brain power that counts in this world, Shirley."

With her grandmother's words resting deep within her, Shirley Chisholm gained the strength to always remain secure with herself and to persevere against any and all opposition:

> I just [focus] on my own agenda. I'm going towards my goal, my purposes, what I want to achieve. I look straight ahead and ask: Am I strong enough to withstand the insults, the humiliations, the misunderstandings, the snickering, the laughter, the stories that others would put on the street about me? People would ask, How can you take it? And I would always say, I take it because I'm not going to spend my creative energy getting mad.

Chisholm is a great example of the long-lasting effects of strong nurturance in childhood: her upbringing took her all the way to Congress. Untroubled by others' thoughts about her, she did not suffer the anxiety of rejection. She instead moved with a clear sense of what and who was guiding her. Chisholm's objectivity drew particularly on her reasoning and discernment (two True Self qualities), giving her a solid grasp of her own strengths and weaknesses and of the people in her life who mattered. In the face of the insistence of both blacks and whites that it was not her place to be in politics, Chisholm never doubted her ability to do what she did best: bringing the community together. Her clear sense of herself and of her relationships with close people in her life permitted her to deflect the detractors. As with her grandmother, there were voices in Chisholm's life that she listened to and that resounded deep within her and influenced her profoundly. Chisholm had many strong voices from her childhood to draw on in forging this path:

> My father was very proud of me. I was the eldest of four sisters, and my father told me that I had talent. He would take me with him to the meetings of Marcus Garvey [the black author]. So I was exposed to black history. [My black pride was] instilled during all those years when I was growing up.

A career in politics, then, seemed to be Chisholm's calling—a way to combine her leadership skills and vision with her passions and to extend her True Self toward others. Chisholm had acquired self love, developed philia, and felt connection through eros, storge, and agape. Moreover, Chisholm found in her work a connection to God, always viewing her success as a result of God's faith in her. Her courage was bound to her deep personal belief that her work was good, that it was driven by God's will:

> God would not have permitted Shirley Chisholm to come forth in this country to be the first black woman elected to Congress and the first black woman to run for president of this country if he did not know that she

had the stamina, the audacity, and the guts to withstand all the things that would befall her and still make her mark for her race. God tells me I can do these things. I feel his words: "Go ahead. Go for this goal. Give the best [you have] within yourself to give."

With the personal inspiration provided by her faith and the critical connections she shared with her father and grandmother, Chisholm felt called to endure in spite of external attacks. She was deeply aware of how such attacks had paralyzed her constituents. She understood their paralysis and their dysfunction because of the isolation and abuse they suffered. The certainty she felt about her ability to overcome her community's problems is summed up in her motto: "I deliver." While her self-confidence made her seem brash to her opponents and to some from her own camps, she was never self-aggrandizing. Chisholm's sense of identity is grounded in actual experience, a product of her work and her diligence. She is realistic in the faith she puts in herself, in others, and in God and recognizes that while she may be strong, she is not invincible.

This clarity and strength has enabled Chisholm to grow and to learn from her mistakes without staggering. Among the consequences of Shirley's dedication to her profession was the failure of her twenty-seven-year marriage to Conrad Chisholm. Although she had access to all the qualities of her True Self, competing tensions continued to exist. In her second marriage, however, Shirley chose her family over career, leaving politics when a serious accident left her new husband in a wheel-chair. Similarly, when two miscarriages deprived Chisholm of the chance to be a mother, she redirected her nurturing instincts, finding great fulfillment in her efforts to educate children.

Chisholm's self-awareness has helped her not only to understand herself, but also to recognize her role in the struggles of others; she even approached her adversaries with a caring attitude: "People are made up differently and [grow] up knowing things differently." Taking into consideration the "origins, background, and environment" of her detractors before reacting to their harsh or insensitive words, she summed up her understanding of others succinctly: "An individual is the sum total of the milieu in which he or she has been reared"—or, in other words, of the help they have had in connecting to self, others, and God.

As we relate this story of Shirley Chisholm to our search for unconditional love, we gain insight into just how vital and deep these connections to family background are. The independence and sense of self that carried this woman through life were not generated on their own, but were founded on her relationships with her grandmother, father, and God. Chisholm's experience of love gave her personal clarity and freedom. But her experience was hardly untouched by the challenges of resistance and hatred. Her love's genuineness and authenticity permitted her to retain focus, connections, and power—and to serve as a catalyst of change both in the internal connections of her family life and the external connections served by her mission.

How Love Makes Us Whole

Loving represents the culmination of all the sexual and erotic connections we have already discussed. As we have noted, our sexual self, the voices of our sexuality, and our sexual dance together communicate the nature of our sexuality. When these expressions are intimately and genuinely engaged with our heart, our sexual activities openly convey the feelings of our True Self, and we can begin to share authentic love. In this way, sexual relationships mean more than just physical connections; they also represent unions created in the presence of God's sacred trust. Thus, love is a connection that unites self, others, and God. It unifies our body, heart, and soul and finds no dissonance in eros, philia, storge, and agape.

When love, whether in its physical or emotional expressions, grows stale in a marriage, it is often because our relationship becomes a monotonous routine. Intimacy can become reduced to sex or to some other limited interaction, becoming rooted in only one part of the sexual self, only one sexual voice, or only one sexual dance. What, then, is the meaning of loving with the True Self?

+ Authentic loving requires that we bring all of our True Self to a relationship. We must approach our partner with a healthy acceptance and integration of our body, mind, and soul.

+ By participating in loving, we affirm our own True Self and that of our mate, encouraging a discovery and development of these two inner beings.

+ Our engagement in loving creates a "new space" in our relationships, where neither partner individually forms the base of the loving experience, but where we as a couple shape a new life—a oneness—in love.

+ The involvement of our whole being in loving results in a dynamic experience. Physical at one moment, emotional or spiritual the next, our sexual life gains a meaning that resonates from within and sustains us.

Intimacy in Marriage

One of the very special connections for union and exchange cross-culturally is marriage. Through situations both religious and civil, marriage confirms our most precious relationships with a sanctity and enduring bond, and provides the committed space in which this bond is lived. As we have witnessed in our lives and seen in some of the stories in this book, marriage is the deepest of friendships, bringing together the love of self, others, and God. It is the deepest human-to-human connection possible and therefore the hardest to master.

More than any other opportunity, our relationships with our spouse and our family invite us to participate in spiritual trusts where we may directly experience God's love. By spiritual trust I mean that God has entrusted us to nurture his love in our moments of intimacy—both as marriage partners and as parents.

To nurture something means to devote thought and energy to a task, to show commitment, patience, and care. While at the time of their wedding a couple may agree, "The two shall become one," no ritual alone will create a state of oneness between them. Such unity will only evolve over time, achieved through the process of entering another's world and attuning oneself to that person's soul. Doing so can be particularly difficult in a culture like ours, where we emphasize independence, each individual focusing on him- or herself and "looking out for number one." These are values that often leave us unprepared for spiritual unity and unable to conceptualize a relationship centered on the seamless unity of two people.

Oneness is the bond formed between two people's separate spheres of self, others, and God: a connection founded on a mentality of not "me" or "you," but "us"—"we-ness." And it is not something we can take for granted. Genuine intimacy, the power of a marital union, evolves from the wellspring of oneness; but it is our own efforts, not the act of getting married itself, that open for us this new space for sharing. As many often say, marriage is work. Without the true creation of "we," the tension between "you" and "me" will strain love and distort relationships.

I have a general theory about intimacy: you need to have the same or similar individual positive qualities to fuel a relationship and the opposite negative individual qualities to complement a relationship (and to avoid explosions). The intimacy in marriage is simultaneously eros, philia, and agape—erotic, friendly, and spiritual. A good marriage takes a physical attraction and a genuine friendship and entrusts both to God, forging unconditional love. If love is driven by individual, narcissistic interests, it is understandably headed for divorce. Intimacy means sharing in vulnerability so much that both parties can say, "I can let go of myself to discover myself in you, for I trust you, and I trust you with myself." Personally, I think this process is hard, and without God, I sometimes feel it would be impossible.

When you are in a good marriage, life's uncertainties seem immaterial; when you are having a child in a good marriage, life could not be better. What accounts for one's genuine connection with another? How is it that you can feel part of another? The answer may be understood by basing any intimate relationship on establishing genuine friendship.

Intimacy in Friendship

When I was a boy in Chicago, I often visited my grandparents. I was always excited about these trips, not least because my grandmother always had something new to teach me from the traditions of our Greek culture. On one such occasion, she turned to me in her caring and deliberate manner, her big brown eyes wide open, her voice serious as she counseled in her thick accent: "Always be nice to everyone, but be careful that you don't get hurt. If you find a true friend in your whole life, you will be very blessed. True friends are very hard to find."

I think I was eight years old when she told me this. At the time, I could not understand the skepticism of her advice. I thought that perhaps she had been hurt, and I felt sorry for her. As time passed, however, and friendships came and went, I learned the trust I shared with others was somewhat incomplete and saw a certain wisdom in her advice. I began to realize that you cannot be friends with everyone, because a true friendship requires significant responsibility, investment, and commitment.

By the time I entered college, I began to see another part of my grandmother's wisdom: not only did friendship require a great deal from me, but it also depended on the willingness of others. My eyes had opened to the physical and verbal cues that often define the boundaries of a relationship. At times the people I most wished to be with did not share the same desire to be close to me; at other times, I was the one to draw away from someone else. True friendships, there was no doubt, did not come easily.

I remember one older student who took a personal liking to me. He took me under his wing, helping me to get settled and remain disciplined in my studies. More than that, he became the brother I never had: he visited my home in Chicago, came on family trips, and celebrated with me all the fun of college.

As our friendship grew into its second year, I began to feel that he had always been the initiator in our relationship, and I felt guilty for not feeling the urge to put as much into it. I talked with him about this, and he, somewhat surprisingly to me, said that he understood. This lesson came back to me when I was about twenty and on retreat at the Spencer Abbey, a Trappist monastery. Hanging on the wall, there was a plaque with two overlapping circles with one circle divided.

I never forgot that plaque, nor have I ever been without that friend. The plaque made clear what I was experiencing in this relationship, which became for me a vivid, personal measure of true friendship. My friend had doubled my joys and divided my sorrows, and his actions manifested the definition of philia. I assessed all my other relationships according to this measure. How would I double other friends' joy? Divide their sorrow? As we said earlier, close relationships often help us see ourselves and our impact on others—helping us reexamine our actions and grow. I felt that this simple model offered criteria that helped me see what was needed in a friendship.

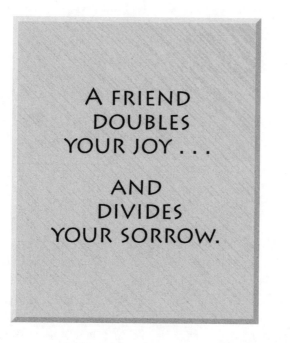

A FRIEND
DOUBLES
YOUR JOY . . .

AND
DIVIDES
YOUR SORROW.

Meaningful and sustaining friendships are those that resonate the qualities of the True Self. These relationships permit us to grow through our talents and in our understanding of others and the world.

WISH LIST FOR INTIMACY

Each of us has our particular needs for feeling comfortable in intimacy. Sometimes we neglect to identify them, much less share them with those closest to us. Identify the ten most important things that will help you feel safe with those who are intimate in your life (whether children, parents, friends, lovers, or spouse). After you have identified your needs, present your list in a caring manner to those you are intimate with, requesting that they provide you with their wish list as well.

1.

2.

3.

4.

5.

6.

7.

8.

9.

10.

INTIMATE GIFT LIST

Many times we interact with those with whom we love without recognizing that our intention does not convey what we actually feel: a man buys a woman that he cares for flowers, but she does not really like flowers that much. For him, the flowers are a meaningful gesture of care; for her, "flowers are OK" but hold no special value. Our intentions, whether positive or playful, may not have the impact that we intended. Think of the gifts that you would find very "special." Do those close to you know this list? Can you share it with them? Then identify ten items that you feel would appear on the gift list of someone you are intimate with. Ask that person to create his or her own list and then compare the two. How do the lists compare?

MY INTIMATE GIFT LIST	OTHER INTIMATE GIFT LIST
1.	1.
2.	2.
3.	3.
4.	4.
5.	5.
6.	6.
7.	7.
8.	8.
9.	9.
10.	10.

EMBRACING
YOUR SOUL

*In the attitude of silence, the soul finds the path in a clearer light,
and what is elusive and deceptive resolves itself into crystal clearness.
Our life is a long and arduous quest after Truth.*
—Mahatma Gandhi

We now come to the most important turn inward we will ever make:
embracing our soul. Our soul is who we most truly are, allowing for our
contact with God; it is the mast catching the wind and supporting our
sails so that we may travel with fluidity and direction. The soul invites us
to realize our values through our commitments. Alone, however, the soul's
services are limited. Just as sails lie motionless without the wind, the soul
without the Spirit prevents us from experiencing life fully. Charged with
the Spirit, the soul strengthens our connections to our self and to others
by infusing them with vitality. When we let our spirit-infused soul guide
our actions, we allow God to become our life's compass.

Certainly, capturing the Spirit in our sail may seem difficult. God
and our soul are connected to issues of religious faith. In this culture,
we are born into many different religious traditions. It is natural to question whether any one system of faith actually teaches the truth or
deserves our full conviction and commitment. How do we know if what
we believe is true? How do we know that we are on the authentic path?

How do we know that our compass is truly God? The answer to these questions is found in the feelings of wonder and awe we experience when we connect to the good, the emotional signals that alert us that our soul has encountered the Spirit. Through our soul, roused by the Spirit, we enliven the spirituality of our True Self and gain depth in its qualities. The further we remove ourselves from the experience of the soul, the more restricting of the qualities of the True Self. Many of our struggles with intimacy or fulfillment would end if we could embrace our soul.

Our culture is beginning to recognize that we cannot be fulfilled without finding the Spirit. Fields that previously ignored or even denied the existence of the soul, such as business or the hard sciences, are now joining in the search for the meaning that only the soul can provide. As our experiences of the True Self evolve, they dynamically reflect our multiple engagements with self, others, and God. However, we must realize that our knowledge of God and true coming of age occurs individually; such knowledge must be something personal and experiential, not based on cultural values, spiritualism, or intellectualism. We cannot merely speak of God; we must make direct contact.

As we begin Part III, ask yourself the following questions:

+ What role does knowledge of the soul play in the creation of my personal paradigm?
+ What is the difference between inauthentic religiosity and authentic religiosity?
+ How is my True Self strengthened through my direct connection with the Spirit?

Once we recognize the role of religion and spirituality in our personal experience of the soul, we must see those systems that may be stuck in traditionalism or pluralism, political correctness, or extremism and those that facilitate genuine spiritual growth. Religious and spiritual efforts do not always help us engage the Spirit. Since this essence is so vital a force for our lives, we must ensure through our actions and beliefs that what we feel, whether as part of a community or on our own, is truly the Spirit. We must each ask ourselves if we truly engage with the spirit in our lives. To embrace the soul, therefore, we must take conscious ownership of our spirituality and become navigators of our own voyage, accepting responsibility for the strength of our connections and gaining endurance and resilience through our commitment to the truth.

When we connect with God, we achieve perspective that allows us to reconcile some of life's paradoxical realities: that we are immensely important, yet totally insignificant; that however much we may grow in wisdom, we will still know nothing. When we take responsibility for our spiritual life, we will know that there is something greater than ourselves acting within us. By strengthening our awareness of our soul and establishing ties to our True Self and to others, we can finally find genuine fulfillment.

7

DISCOVERING YOUR TRUTH

*My religion consists of a humble admiration
of the illimitable superior spirit who reveals himself
in the slight details we are able to perceive
with our frail and feeble minds.*
—ALBERT EINSTEIN

ONE EVENING, BACK IN COLLEGE, a friend and I decided to take a break
from our studies and grab a bite to eat. The night was still as I drove, the
sky completely black. As we turned the corner, my headlights suddenly
shone on a young man walking into the middle of the street; he was naked
and desperately signaling for us to stop. When we did, he told us he
had been riding his bike when four men driving by in a car jumped him.
They made him take off his clothes, stole his bike and wallet, and left him
to fend for himself. As we drove him to a local hospital, my mind reeled
from everything I had just seen and heard. I found myself thinking, "I
sure hope someone would stop for me if I ever needed help."

So-called Good Samaritan tests have often been performed in sem-
inaries, schools, and street settings to see if people would go out of their
way to help someone in distress. Most of these experiments found that
the majority of people will lend their aid as long as they have the time;
a person in a hurry is less likely to stop (perhaps Scriptures would have

had a different story to tell if the man traveling from Samaria had come upon the man in need while running late for a business meeting).

While our actions do not solely depend on how much time we have, these experiments have a distinct relevance. Our reactions to those in need can tell us much about ourselves. At any given time we may be influenced by a range of motives, such as the desire to be helpful or the need to feel powerful. Throughout this chapter, we will be looking at moments, like my encounter with that desperate man, that test the capacity of our soul for benevolence and spiritual growth. By embracing our soul, we can better understand the impulses that drive us and thus find clearer and more meaningful relationships that include the True Self and God.

Chapter 7 explains the importance of the Spirit in finding fulfillment in all of our connections; clarifies the difference between authentic and inauthentic expressions of religion; and shows how commitment to God is the compass in life that points us toward truth.

We know truth when we develop our relationship to the Spirit. We are often told about the significance of our soul, but most cannot understand this message until we experience the power of the Spirit in our lives. Doing so ignites our values but also requires our discipline. Embracing our soul means committing to our beliefs and recognizing their significance: it is knowing God. Otherwise, we are without a compass to guide us and will likely drift aimlessly on our voyage.

Discovering our truth both grounds and deepens our criteria for understanding life. And it is through embracing our soul in relationship to our critical connections that we discover what is true. This dynamic leads us to fully live the qualities of the True Self through our critical connections.

But who decides what is true? What are the criteria by which truth may be pursued by those who have found more meaningful relations without a faith system? What is the difference between truth discovered with God and truth discovered without God? And why is it important that we know?

What Truth? Whose Truth?

Our personal beliefs about truth are the foundations on which we build faith. Truth is not simply imposed on us; we have a role to play in embracing it. Consider this story: A Christian woman sat in the pew at church, enthusiastically responding "Amen! Amen!" as the preacher read through each of the Ten Commandments. When the minister came to the commandment "Thou shalt not commit adultery," she paused, leaned over to the woman next to her, and crossly whispered, "Now he's beginning to meddle."

Embracing the soul requires unity with God. The woman described above participates selectively in her religious paradigm. She relates with God on her terms. She is engaged in and even excited about her faith—except where her faith requires her to do things that she does not fully agree with. The moment her officially defined truth interferes with her own preferences, she distances herself from that truth. I don't think any of us are immune to this tendency.

The True Self and the Spirit are mutually reinforcing. When we deny our innate responsiveness to the Spirit, we compromise our ability to engage the full potential of the True Self. We become distracted from genuine encounters with truth and favor alternatives that do not lead to fulfillment, such as occultism, so-called mind-expanding drugs, or astrology as a belief system. Though all of these are efforts to respond to and feel the Spirit, they are nonetheless distortions of our natural inclination toward a true encounter of the Spirit.

For many reasons, those who take their belief in God seriously tend to personally tailor their course of spirituality rather than wholeheartedly embrace their faith system. A recent study by the Pew Forum on Religion and Public Life reported that 87 percent of Americans view themselves as religious, yet only 57 percent participate regularly in worship and activities within their denominational tradition.[1] While some are steadfast in following the rituals and guidelines of their faith, others develop an eclectic direction to meet their spiritual needs. Still others prefer to commit to their own personal interpretation of God and religion outside of given practices. What do all of these different paths mean?

We must exercise discernment about our spiritual practice and be open to the personal investment spirituality requires. This is not a process of simply picking and choosing what is convenient for us, for the traditions in which we find ourselves are often sources offering great insight and truth. The great religions are great because they have stood the test of time and have met the spiritual needs of their adherents.

We cannot have it both ways; we cannot grow spiritually while totally controlling our commitment. If we establish our own criteria for our spiritual growth, do we lose that subordination of self to the Spirit? On the other hand, how can we expect to make spiritual progress on our own terms if we are only following ready-made paths?

Pursuit of the Truth

Religion, as many of us know, can either be a source of blessing or an instrument of abuse. We need only recall the infamous Salem witch trials to remind ourselves of the potential for abuse when power is mishandled by those with authority. Discovering our own path, then, entails distinguishing between authentic and inauthentic expressions of religiosity. On the opposite page, I have identified qualities that characterize inauthentic religion and authentic religion. Reviewing them will help you discern whether your religion is indeed a blessing that meets your spiritual needs.

We all know of incredibly smart, passionate people who have rejected all spiritual paths in the name of science, humanism, or self-reliance. They regard religious organizations as squashers of individual truths, or argue that the conflicts of faith are just part of the human will and desire to believe in something. Often I hear patients tell me of feeling stuck in front of a pulpit as a pastor delivers a sermon that seems to have nothing to do with their life. Their questions, then, lead them

Contrasting Inauthentic and Authentic Religiosity

Inauthentic Religiosity	Authentic Religiosity
1. Controls through an authoritative structure by fear and power.	1. Inspires and earns respect through concrete manifestations of spiritual truth.
2. Maintains control within leadership and a hierarchy of leaders who may not be accountable for their actions.	2. Is accountable to a broad power base that accepts responsibility for actions of all in the community.
3. Focuses on institutional objectives, and is not particularly introspective.	3. Contemplative and emphasizes contact with the Spirit of truth.
4. Serves group identity over individual interests.	4. Simultaneously promotes group identity and individual cultural awareness; encourages openness to differences.
5. Although it identifies universal objectives, it primarily seeks to protect the organization.	5. Protects everyone, especially the most vulnerable.
6. Holds narrow perspectives on spiritual problems, focusing attention on rote ritual and tradition.	6. Takes broad perspective when challenges arise.
7. Is dogmatic.	7. Is self-evaluative and evolving.
8. Promotes religious goals over direct experience of the Spirit.	8. Couples tradition with emphasis on direct experience of the Spirit.
9. Lacks attention to sexuality and other complex aspects of human life that relate to spirituality.	9. Establishes a holistic balance of all aspects of a human life.
10. Predominantly serves institution.	10. Predominantly serves intrinsic good.
11. Forwards positive goals but diffuse actions.	11. Is truth seeking in both words and actions.
12. Discusses but does not actually practice interrelation and communication among self, others, and God.	12. Demonstrates interrelation and effective communication among self, others, and God.

to ask, "How do I get out? And if I do, where do I go next?" Is religion just a matter of believers speaking a language different from that of nonbelievers? Are inauthentic religious practices defeating and discouraging the Spirit within?

The Journey of a Truth Seeker

In my own professional development, B. F. Skinner provided the principal challenge to my religious beliefs and my approach to psychology. Our first discussions, which began in the early 1970s, reflected our different histories and perspectives on human nature—both psychologically and spiritually. An experimental scientist and the father of strict behaviorism, Skinner believed that people are socially conditioned; a student of Greek Orthodox theology before turning to psychology, I saw God's influence in people's lives. Skinner had low expectations of religion; I had high expectations. He found no sustenance through faith in God; I found faith in God to provide both strength and nurturance. Suffice it to say we saw the world differently.

Skinner based the science of behaviorism on determinism, a view of human beings as programmed, predetermined, and without free will. As a college sophomore, I felt this perspective simply negated the role of religion and God; yet the behavioral methods he established opened connections with autistic children who, before his intervention, were essentially unreachable. Although his research yielded significant results, I felt a profound conflict between Skinner's findings and my beliefs. His truth, even as it denied God, certainly helped others. Was there a connection between the truth of science and the truth of faith? Were these mutually exclusive?

During that time, I learned that Skinner would be lecturing at Boston University. Seating some 700, the auditorium filled beyond capacity. As he approached the stage, religious protest groups picketed on one side, while Skinner devotees vigorously applauded on the other. Skinner was speaking on his book *Beyond Freedom and Dignity*, emphasizing that psychology needed to abandon notions of inner life, constructs of soul, and the like, to relate to modern scientific advances. He judged the methods of religion, philosophy, education, and government as futile prescientific disciplines. Even though I could not precisely articulate my dissatisfaction with his lecture, I felt that Skinner's perspective limited the range of human experience.

Later, I found words for my feelings and wrote him a brief note suggesting that his approach, which emphasized the "form" or mere behaviors in life, did not address the "content" or dynamics of those behaviors. I also requested some more information from him. To my surprise, he sent me a note recommending that we meet.

I was delighted to speak about the meaning of life with someone whose understanding of human experience differed so dramatically from my own. But just as I was poised to learn more, I began to feel that my own truth was at risk. This meeting symbolized a confrontation between "the truth" that I studied in psychology and "the truth" of faith that I had adopted throughout my life. I thought that Skinner might challenge my truth, but I also knew that our interaction might help me form answers to personal struggles; I believed that there could not be a conflict between the Spirit and truth.

Surpassing my wildest imagination, that first meeting between us began a relationship that lasted for the rest of Skinner's life. In the interviews I conducted with him over twenty-five years, I experienced B. F. Skinner as a truth-seeking scientist. He was an objective and reflective man with an unusual ability to persevere in his work, to express care for others, and to apply his theory to his own life. Although regimented in his life and restrained in his emotions, he portrayed himself and his work honestly, even refusing to edit our taped conversations for personal comments and private issues that casually entered our conversation, stating, "The comments may be painful but they are part of the record."

As I expected, foundations of our views of the world were quite different; but I also saw the deep affinities between them. At one juncture, I told Dr. Skinner that I found his approach to life and values spiritual. He appreciated that insight, describing the spiritual as an "elevated, positive experience" (although he did not believe in a personal God). He recognized the good and tried to live accordingly. Prior to our work, he said that he would not have viewed his concerns as spiritual ones. The word *spiritual* had previously had a mystical, silly ring for him because of his early religious experiences.

Skinner's beliefs were undoubtedly influenced by the religious lessons of his childhood. He is, in part, a case study of the deleterious effects inauthentic religiousity has on young children. Most of what he had learned from religion was fear: "Grandmother's threat of hell fire had pointed to the open lands" of temptation and sin and painted a negative, punitive image of human beings' formal relationship with God that Skinner expanded on in his autobiography, *Particulars of My Life*:

> The first religious teaching I can remember was at my Grandmother Skinner's. It was her desire that I should never tell a lie, and she attempted to fortify me against it by vividly describing the punishment for it. I remember being shown the coal fire in the heating stove and [being] told that little children who told lies were thrown in a place like that after they died.... Some time later I went to a magician's show, the final act of which concerned the appearance of a devil. I was terrified. I questioned my father as to whether a devil just like that threw little boys to Hell, and he assured me it was so. I suppose I have never recovered from that spiritual torture. Not long afterward I did tell a real lie to avoid punishment and that bothered me for years. I remember lying awake at night sobbing, refusing to tell my mother the trouble, refusing to kiss her goodnight. I can still feel the remorse, the terror, the despair of my young heart at the time.[2]

Yet Skinner did not simply dismiss religion altogether. In fact, as we spoke, he revealed how much his theories had been influenced by his view of a distant, punishing God:

> There was always a certain element of fear. I had a certain amount of fear of religion, I suppose. So that when I finally escaped, [there was] an ele-

ment of relief, although it took me a long time. I remember when I was a freshman in college, I was still somewhat . . . worried . . . about religion. I remember going to my professor and telling him that I had lost my faith. The fact that the biologist, whom I liked and admired very much, taught Sunday School bothered me.

I realized religion gave Skinner a negative image of God, which led him to exclude this disturbance from his concept of the truth. He told me:

> Religions work for their own aggrandizement—to strengthen the church and so on. And they use reinforcers of one kind or another to get obedience from their communicants.
>
> I believe that I have been basically anarchistic, antireligion, and antiindustry—in other words, antibureaucracy. I would like to see people behave well without having to have priests stand by, politicians stand by, or people collecting bills.

He felt frustrated by the institution's use of God as a tool for power and self-preservation. His suspicion of religion stemmed not from criticism of spirituality or spiritual philosophies but rather from the abuses of religion that he had personally witnessed. His frustration helped fuel his yearning to understand human behavior and to search for a better promise of hope.

In fact, that desire led him to propose the utopian philosophy in his fictional work, *Walden Two*. His experimental utopia put forth in *Walden Two* seemed to be Skinner's design for an alternative path toward a better life—a community based on serenity and freedom from negativity.

In his second autobiography, *A Matter of Consequences*,[3] Skinner openly acknowledged that his psychological argument—that people have no choice and no freedom—has its roots in Presbyterian theology. Skinner's emphasis on external control found a conspicuous parallel with the theology of Jonathan Edwards and with the discomfort he felt within the Presbyterian Church.

The psychologist accepted personal religious belief. He recognized them as a source of comfort or "of peace of mind" that helps people in times of need or provides them with answers to difficult questions. He observed: "It's very reinforcing for us to have a priest come when someone is dying." Like me, he valued religious emotional expression, which led me to conclude that the cause of our difference was really one of terminology and our different histories. Skinner—still associating spirituality with its callous depictions in his childhood—referred to the events and emotions I associated with religion and which I would call "spirituality" by the neutral term *feeling states*. Yet, though he may have called them by different names, Skinner sought and tapped experiences of his True Self that others found in their spirituality.

Our discussions surprised both of us: Skinner by the number of common issues we found between Christian theology and psychoanalysis; myself by Skinner's openness—however qualified—to spiritual possibilities. Committed to science, but recognizing its inherent limits, Skinner was open to assigning some causal force to the divine:

> I won't say that I'm an agnostic, since agnosticism maintains that one cannot know . . . and I'm not averse to the idea of some intelligence or some organizing force that set up the initial conditions of the universe in such a way that ultimately generated stars, planets, and life. It's easier to imagine the creation of intellectual force than a creation force that was able to create the Big Bang.

I had initially thought that Skinner rejected religion in favor of science and determinism; in reality, however, the Skinner I got to know was a man who had transformed his negative religious experience into a spirituality of a different form. During our weekly conversations over the last five years of his life, I also learned a great deal about tempering my own faith in religion and religious institutions. Just as he appreciated the opportunity to, as he said, "reflect on positive aspects of spirituality," so, too, did I learn more about the controlling and self-serving actions of religious systems that had so detrimentally affected him.

After some twenty years of our having exchanged so many thoughts and my having understood so much about Skinner's struggle with religion, we discussed a story about how faith guided people to do good works and find fulfillment. In the course of our discussion, I was stunned when now, he turned to me and said, "Religion can be used to reinforce good behavior, but what of the content? Well, yes, those questions remain concerning what has created the situation." Content! By this point, we had developed a language to grasp each other's experience.

One of the problems of religious communities, underscored and boldly documented by Skinner, is that in maintaining their structures and hierarchies, they can often lose sight of spirituality and the gifts of the Spirit: holiness, goodness, truth, love, justice—all of the virtues based in God. It is contradictory that religious institutions, intended to be sanctuaries for the preservation of the contract between God and humanity, can ultimately distance people from their spirituality. All too often, the authenticity of religion is exchanged for mere memory and ritual. We need to be discerning, especially as we inherit religious practices from other generations, to make sure our faith expresses our True Self, and that the True Self emanates this quality of spirituality in who we are and in our relationships.

Needing a Viable Faith   Attractive, charming, and effervescent, Connie was a valued chief resident at one of New York's teaching hospitals. Connie's professional life was marked by outstanding achievement. But her personal life was now affected by tragedy: her older sister Marie had committed suicide. The traumatic blow of her sister's death catapulted Connie into feelings of bereavement, guilt, and confusion. Confronting death shifted her outlook on life. A flood of questions came to the forefront. "What am I working for?" "What's the purpose of my marriage?" "Is money so important?" "Can my husband understand what I need?"

Connie and her sister grew up on a small farm in the South. Her family, Connie said, "embraced a very fundamental form of Roman Catholicism" and established standards "whereby the extended clan measured everyone's lives." Connie explained that she simply dismissed her parents' insular world and called their religious customs "silly" and "pure hypocrisy."

Watching her parents' display their religiosity at her sister's funeral, Connie felt both emotionally and spiritually detached. Just three months earlier, Connie had married a handsome stockbroker who, she said, was "concerned" about her crisis, but really was "preoccupied" with his own career. As she reflected about their relationship, Connie felt increasingly distressed that his professional life would get in the way of her emotional needs. These questions pushed her out of her safe world and into her true coming of age.

In our sessions, Connie not only confronted her feelings about her sister's suicide but began to understand the compromises that she had made in life, namely her authentic connections with her family and her husband. Professionally successful, she found herself desperate for genuine relationships.

Like many of us, Connie finally awoke to the disconnection, loneliness, and isolation that followed in the wake of her pursuit of "success." When she first started therapy, she quipped that her greatest achievement was "escaping her family," thinking that she had long ago freed herself from their oppressive and unrealistic emotional needs. She soon came to realize, however, that she still suffered from those needs which, unaddressed, derailed her from her True Self, especially her spirituality. Connie's disillusionment led her to seek out meaningful religious experiences. After visiting a number of religious communities, she introduced her husband to a church she called "home" — that embraced her need to grow in faith and the Spirit. In denying these connections, she had missed an important part of her life. For the rest of us, however, the process of healing need not be so dramatic and taxing, if only we start asking ourselves the right questions.

We cannot help but be prone to respond to promises that emphasize image over substance and substitute superficial connections for genuine intimacy. The lure of quick success, the dream of some shortcut to the key of life, and the appeal of fame attract us when we are looking for "a way out"; but such solutions obscure our real objective. Unless we discover our nature and learn how to create and maintain the direct relationships necessary for authentic fulfillment, we will, like

Connie, find ourselves unsatisfied, stagnant, or shut down. To find truth, we must discover our soul and fill it with the Spirit.

Trust in Faith We must trust that our beliefs are good. Just as when we were children we needed to trust our caretakers and depend on them, we likewise need to trust in our faith and discern between the truth of authentic faith and the falsehood of inauthentic faith.

I am reminded of the moving film *Brother Sun, Sister Moon* that retold the story of St. Francis of Assisi, the fourteenth-century Roman Catholic visionary.

An unusually sensitive and positive boy, Francis was drawn to Jesus's message of simplicity, poverty, and love, in which he found joy and meaning , which his mother affirmed. However, his efforts to implement his values created concern, not only within the religious culture in which he grew up, but also from his own father and the church leadership. Having pursued the Spirit above the established religious forms, and having provoked the religious authorities, Saint Francis was ridiculed, mocked, and condemned.

Francis pleaded his case before the pope. The humble, shabbily clothed Francis was given audience before the pope. Literally weighed down by the gold, pomp, and excess of the papacy during this time, the pope barely heard Francis's simple plea before Francis was led away by the papal curia and guards. But as if rekindling a flame long extinguished within the elderly pope's heart, the pope recalled Francis. Listening to Francis's request, the pope reflected on the Spirit that had escaped him for so long. Moved by the monk's simple yet profound faith, the pope embraced Francis and kissed his feet, sanctifying the truth that the monk had proclaimed. Saint Francis's mission was blessed, and he was encouraged to go forth and live as an example to others.

Our trust is earned by those who we count on. In the case of Saint Francis, it was his mother who encouraged his good intentions. Likewise, our trust is given to those we count on for positive support. Negative experiences of trust and love, on the other hand, not only deaden our ability to find the Spirit, but also inhibit our understanding of how to begin.

Truths and The Truth   Standing up for truth can be painful. Many creative people have been laughed at for believing in their dreams: Thomas A. Edison, the Wright Brothers, and Alexander G. Bell are only a few notable examples. As these exemplary individuals prove, however, defying those who may criticize or reject you and pursuing what is personally meaningful is one of life's most difficult and rewarding challenges.

The question remains of whether the truth of science or other systems (which may become their own religions) can deny the truth of God. There are evident distinctions between them, as they are different truths. It is precisely Skinner's version of scientific truth that challenged my own beliefs in college and led to our relationship of some twenty-five years, during which we tried to sort out whether the truth of science denies the truth of God. It is my belief that the truth of God as ultimate truth contains all truths.

Speaking to Different Truths

In 1977, Rosalyn Sussman Yalow became America's first woman to win the Nobel Prize in medicine. Yalow discovered the procedure known as RIA, or radioimmunoassay, which enabled the first accurate measurement of biological and chemical substances in bodily fluids. This technique is still used today in most medical laboratories and is regarded as a vital discovery in clinical medicine.

Such scientific achievements require persistent commitment to research in the face of failures and setbacks and the tenacity to keep fighting for truths despite encountering resistance. For a woman to have done all this in a male-dominated field must have required an even greater struggle. When I first met Yalow, I hoped to discover the convictions that had motivated her to reach such incredible heights.

As we spoke, Yalow largely attributed her success to her own independence: "I always thought of myself as very strong. I never felt the need to be like anyone else. I don't feel dependent on anybody." The Nobel

Laureate was proud of her own self-confidence and her ability to assert herself even if it meant bucking tradition and standing alone. I was interested to understand how Yalow understood faith and science, and I was surprised by her response. Yalow saw no reason in our discussions to analyze religion, believing it to be a world entirely separate from and irrelevant to science. She told me:

> I have no religious drive behind me. Science attempts to learn everything through experimentation and interpretation. Religion says you must accept on faith. I have no role [in a conversation] of this kind. I believe, as a result, in an organized way of thinking about things.

Having grown up in a Jewish home, Yalow did not scorn the religion of her family; she merely felt that God had no place in her life. "Neither an atheist nor an agnostic," Yalow simply claimed that neither seemed to "resonate with her moods, and she never considered God or religion to be important." The scientist preferred a life of action over reflection. She lived by a paradigm in which scientific criteria alone directed her pursuit of truth. Yet while Yalow placed so much emphasis on her self-proclaimed individuality and professed to having no formal religious beliefs, she nevertheless credited her parents for instilling in her values derived from their Jewish heritage. Her mother encouraged her to get the good education that, as immigrants, she and her husband had been denied. Her father taught her that a woman could do anything a man could. The confidence and clarity that had carried Yalow throughout her career rested on the foundation of her parents' religious beliefs.

The impact of Yalow's early childhood religious experiences remained influential in her desire to give something back to others:

> I participate in religion for my husband. I'd say the most important principles that guide my life are willingness to do what I can for the world.... if we live only for ourselves, then we're just not being very nice.

Although she did not express her notions of moral responsibility within a conception of divine law, we can nonetheless see that Yalow understood the world in light of a meaningful framework. Science, essentially, had become her religion. Its methods and significance were immediate, clear, and viable, while religion seemed passive and ambiguous. She possessed a worldview that, like any religion, guided her in her understanding of self and her interaction with others. Both Skinner and Yalow found their need to pursue truth through science and had experiences in religion that did not engage their positive pursuit to know.

Yalow's science, then, is its own religion. As we observed in Skinner's story, the difference between science and religion can be found in the language and symbols used to express similar meaning and significance. Besides believing in herself, Yalow was devoted to her family and to her "professional children," the students to whom she was both mentor and mother. They are her congregation and her community of faith with whom she shares her quest to answer life's unanswerable questions. To those who seek to understand themselves and their world, Yalow offers the following precepts of her philosophy:

> My father-in-law would say that if God was able to create this world, he could create it with all the evidence you have. How do you know this world wasn't created yesterday, with everything in place? There's no answer to this. My answer to it isn't science. There is no way in which I can prove to him that this world was not created yesterday with everything in place. There is no meeting of minds on the scientific and religious views of the origin of the world.

In Yalow's paradigm, only scientific criteria are to be followed in the pursuit of truth. As she says, she is neither atheist nor agnostic; she simply "does not consider" God or religion. Her advice to those who seek to understand themselves and life is simple:

> Know who you are. Look ahead. Know what you want; and don't do things because they're conventional one way or another. Don't do it because the world thinks this is the way to do things. Examine yourself. And try and find out what it really is that you want.

Is there anything missing, then, from the paradigm that Yalow urges us to follow? From her exclusively scientific model of the path toward truth, she has accessed many qualities of her True Self: spontaneity, reasoning, creativity, free will—and even spirituality and love. Though she claims no faith or spiritual reflection, we see that spirituality is evident and active. Her spirituality is communicated in the depth of her values and is an alternative to conventional spirituality. Her love is apparent in the commitment, respect, and affection she feels for her family, for others, and for the world. Thus, values—like spirituality—can arise in lives in which the spirit is not explicitly valued.

Skinner's iconoclasm emerged from the experience of inauthentic religiosity; Yalow's indifference emerged out of the experimental pursuit of truth that she found outside of religious tradition. Paradigms will often contain particular elements of the Spirit and truth regardless of how we formulate them. Whether we realize it or not, we each settle on a paradigm that accounts for the Spirit and truth. However, the degree to which we recognize this and are able to deepen our connection to the critical connections and True Self remains critical for our fulfillment.

Claiming Your Truth

Many philosophies claim to hold the truth and that their God is the only God. But it is your life that you have to live every day. Drawing on your True Self, you must discover what is true. As with Skinner, your history may bring you closer to or further from religion or lead you to create one all your own. As with Yalow, the content of your truth may be apparent to you and an explicit acknowledgment of a spiritual sense, even though it does not fit with conventional religious beliefs. Often our experience of religiosity affects the extent to which we pursue our relationship with God.

Your truth and fulfillment are far too important to be neutral about critical connections. You must draw on your True Self and design your critical connection with God as your compass.

THE I DON'T KNOW EXERCISE

This exercise demonstrates that we all have fundamental belief systems and that regardless of their particularities, we enhance our lives when we take our beliefs and their implications seriously.

Get someone—perhaps yourself—to admit that they "don't know" about God or the truth. Ask the following questions of yourself or of someone else. Keep going until the questioned person must say, "I don't know." Then you have the opportunity to explore the basis of beliefs and to identify the source of authority in your (or your friend's) life.

- How do you think we got here?
- What was before that (or before us)?
- Before that?
- Do you believe in something greater than yourself?
- What is the basis of your belief in that thing you have named? Or is you belief based in the method by which you have named it or considered it (for example, a belief in intellectual reasoning, in human creativity)?
- How does your understanding of God and truth affect your life?

WHAT DO YOU KNOW EXERCISE

You probably have a belief system (regardless of whether it is acknowledged or implicit). How do you understand truth? God? Consider the following questions.

1. How do you define the truth?
2. How do you know that your truth is the truth?
3. Is your belief system personal? Applied? Practical? If not, how do you think this affects your relationship to your soul?
4. What qualities of the true self are expressed through your religion?
5. Does your religion nurture the qualities of the True Self?
6. Do you have a relationship with God?

8

⚜

CONNECTING WITH THE SPIRIT

In the beginning the faithful went out to light the fire,
*   and that was enough.*
The next generation did not go out to the place but lit a fire
*   and gave thanks.*
The third generation did not go out to the place, nor light
*   the fire, but offered a prayer.*
The fourth generation did not go out, nor light the fire,
*   nor say the prayer, but said, "We'll tell the story."*
The fifth generation did not go out, nor light the fire, nor say
*   the prayer, and told no story—but, intellectualizing,*
*   debated whether or not the original experience was an*
*   example of symbol or myth.*

—POPULAR HASSIDIC STORY

TO CONNECT WITH THE SPIRIT, we must light the fire! But how will
we get it started? Each successive generation in the story became
embroiled in the diminishing gestures of religious behavior instead of
the authentic religious experience—the very purpose of the activity.
We are entrusted by God to live life with integrity and respect, trans-
lating the power of Spirit into action. Acknowledging and experiencing that trust enables us to develop and commit to authentic living.

This trust can begin in childhood or can be found later in life. But both external and internal challenges to God's trust can make it difficult to connect to and hold on to the qualities of the True Self. When we trust, we integrate our actions with our values. We learn to link ourselves genuinely to others, and we begin to live in ways that sustain fulfillment and purpose.

In this chapter we will witness the power of authentic religiosity working in the lives of people whose missions remind us of what it is to live in touch with the True Self: They are Maya Angelou, whose story "A Child of God" teaches us that contact with the Spirit is a tangible, transforming force, not some mythical ideal, and Archbishop Anastasios, who revived a devastated nation.

In this chapter we will see how authentic religiosity preserves spirituality and how spirituality in turn expresses authentic religiosity; how authentic religiosity leads us to deep encounters with the Spirit; and how the Spirit leads us to embrace our soul.

The Spirit in Spirituality

Spirituality is the enlivening of the Spirit of God who is in our midst. Various cultures throughout history have captured the Spirit in language that literally sounds like the breath that the word implies: the onomatopoeia of *psycho* (in Greek), *ruach* (in Hebrew), vital force (*élan vital* in French). Yet the essence of the Spirit is such that it goes beyond our ability to capture it with language and intellect.

Our spirituality makes all of us clairvoyants, visionaries, and torchbearers bringing the light of our True Self into the world. By grabbing hold of our True Self, we take ownership of the power within.

What are the traits of genuine spirituality?

1. *Humility:* Ironically, such awesome power begets utter humility. Humility is the recognition that we are visitors on earth and that, as guests, we need to see ourselves and our posses-

sions in an unassuming and courteous manner. We must feel thankful for the gift of life and the opportunities it brings. We understand always that life is not only about us. Humble, we are not passive but aware, appreciative of and sensitive to all that surrounds us.

2. *Prophetic courage:* Prophetic courage is our affirmation to declare the truth. It is the moral strength to persevere in our beliefs. While humility encourages awareness of our demeanor, courage clarifies commitment to what we believe. Courage permits us to define ourselves in the face of opposition and to resist forces that might lead us to compromise our beliefs. Courage points us to our goal and to the revolutionary, transformative challenges of our beliefs.

3. *Holiness:* Spirituality transforms us by allowing us to participate in that which is sacred—that which is holy. We are designed to experience the divine. When we connect to God, the growth of our True Self leads us to fulfillment through awareness and conviction. In holiness we participate in the good, the truth, the absolute; we take part in the *mysterium tremendum*, in the awesome mystery. Coined by theologian Rudolf Otto, this term conveys the intensely positive mystery of ominous awe before God. Holiness is distinct from simple good feelings; in holiness, as a contact with God, we are transformed.

4. *Action:* Spirituality is not "spiritualism," a system of belief that diminishes the significance of our physical activity; rather it is a behavior that promotes active development of our whole person. Theology must be lived, otherwise it is poetry and philosophy. Theology separated from action is like medicine that stays bottled up: to be of use, it must be taken fully into our bodies. Spirituality as action is a conviction that connects physical life to the light of God.

5. *Love:* Our true union with God and others transforms us with new vision: *theoptia*—God-vision. Love is a quality of the True Self and uniquely expressed in spirituality. Love in spirituality

is more than being altruistic, selfless, and unconditional; it is ultimate fulfillment. Spiritual love breaks down barriers; it fills us with joy and liberates our soul to experience wholeness and to feel peace.

Our spirituality makes us torchbearers of an inner light. Alive in humility, prophetic courage, holiness, action, and love, we have full access to the qualities of our True Self.

Spiritual Development

All of the great world religions value contemplative paths to develop the spirit. Ken Wilbur's detailed examination of "integral psychology" integrates these disciplines with models of spirituality and psychology from cultures both ancient and modern, both Eastern and Western.[1] He found that all people who have kept the contemplative path open demonstrate basic parallels in spiritual experiences. The similarity among the saints' and spiritual persons' experience of spirituality and spiritual meditation confirms the immeasurable applicability of the saints' experiences. These lives, historically remote as they may seem, apply to our spiritual development.

As I attempted to make connections between spiritual and psychological studies, I examined the lives of several saints in the Eastern Orthodox Church and found that although they pursued independent spiritual journeys and described their own experiences of God in different terms, five distinct stages emerged that were common among all of them:

1. Image (personhood or potentiality)
2. Conversion (*metanoia*)
3. Purification (transformation)
4. Illumination (light)
5. Union (*theosis*)

How do these stages relate to your spiritual growth?

1. Image, personhood, or potential refers to the natural state in which we accept and cherish the qualities of the True Self. At birth, all of us begin at the same starting point with the potential to develop our innate qualities in the True Self.

2. Conversion, or *metanoia*, refers to the point at which one makes a conclusive commitment to God. We see how the qualities we possess may direct our lives. We recognize our relationship with self, others, and God and how this affects our life. This stage marks the threshold into true coming of age, where we commit to our critical connections, living in the True Self.

3. Purification, or transformation, is when spiritual exercises loosen our attachment to the world, leaving us to live in accordance with our principles and beliefs. In this stage we confront the roots of our difficulties and strengthen our life in virtues.

4. Illumination, or light, refers to a step in spiritual enlightenment that is described by those who are illuminated by the light of God. This transformative experience is not only mental or spiritual but also physical. The fourth-century Christian church father Saint Gregory of Nazianzus observed that alone we are like iron, cold and hard, but when brought before the fire of God's light, the iron glows, and we are illuminated. Likewise, when we are committed to living spiritually, we are illumined, speaking clearly, enlightened body, mind, and soul.

5. Union, or *theosis*, refers to a state of communion, participation, and intermingling with God. Another fourth-century theologian, Saint Gregory of Nyssa, explained that in our higher spiritual growth, we progress to *theosis*, deification, or union with God not as an end state, but as a continuous growing "from glory to glory." Our spiritual goal is this open engagement with God, which requires our receptivity and preparation.

The stages are not static but dynamic; we can move in and out of these levels.

The saints illuminate our understanding by demonstrating that life is fulfilled when it is sanctified—as are ours when we live fully according to our nature, or when we live out our True Self. The means are available to feel like a saint. The saints call us to look within, just as we have been learning to do throughout this book. The lessons these saints (and holy people from other traditions) teach us are cross-cultural and universally applicable. Through what I call theology of silence, we communicate with God in prayer, reflection, and meditation; we feel, understand, and experience our spiritual identity—the True Self. Saint Isaac the Syrian expounds on this:

> Enter early into this treasure-house that lies within you, and so you will see the treasure-house of heaven, for the two are the same, and there is but one single entry to them both. This ladder that leads you to the Kingdom is hidden within you, and is found in your soul. Dive into yourself, and in your soul you will discover the rungs by which to ascend.[2]

Spirituality is unique for each person and yet collective. Authentic spiritual progression is attuned to both our own particular emotional and spiritual needs and the objectives of our spiritual community. As the Spirit works within each of us, the effect of the Spirit unites us and fills us, bringing us together. This reflects both unity and diversity, a recognition of a universal goal reached through individual paths.

This dual cause of spiritual development honoring both the individual and the community is the major reason for the existence of religious institutions. But the work of spiritual development is often set aside, as reflected in Connie's family. Spiritual development is the essential issue of religious and spiritual communities; it involves very sensitive and personal matters and should not be muted or relegated to second place by the community's social and cultural concerns.

Why do I like reading about the lives of spiritual people? Because when they write about themselves, they make spirituality relevant, placing it within the trials of their sometimes sordid life experiences, details that pious biographers often mistakenly omit. There is a tendency to idealize the spiritual person, and though respect is certainly due, idealization narrows our perspective of spirituality and isolates it as something exceptional that someone else is supposed to do.

Personal reflections of truth seekers provide honest descriptions of their spiritual experiences and permit us to relate to their spiritual development and explore our own doubts, struggles, and progression. When we are developing spiritually, we may also feel crisis and uncertainty. Spirituality does not guarantee a life free of challenge, but it does give us the strength to overcome them. A saint's life is not static or perfect but shows pursuit of the connection with self, others, and God that is grounded in the True Self in view of challenge and adversity.

An institution can neglect the encouragement of spiritual growth even when it is a key part of the institution's mission by directing itself toward special groups, such as monks or those exclusively pursuing spiritual paths. While some may engage in spiritual growth by being cloistered off, forsaking community in the name of individuality leaves only one aspect of the institutional mission fulfilled. Spiritual development is essential work for each of us. While each responds differently, our spirituality must attend to actualizing the qualities of each believer's True Self and strengthening each person's critical connections.

To grow spiritually, we need to recognize that we possess spiritual power and to assess the expression of these qualities as intricately linked to spirituality. Are we actively developing the qualities of our True Self, or are these qualities engaged haphazardly, like a boat drifting in the winds? Do we develop the qualities of our True Self, the way a bodybuilder strengthens his or her muscles, or are our particular muscles (specific qualities of our True Self) atrophied?

Visualizing Your True Self Wheel

This exercise is based on the wheel that both steers your vessel through life's journeys and serves as the basis of drawing you into your True

Self. Use this visualization exercise to move into yourself more deeply.

First, go to a quiet and comfortable place. Slowly, take ten deep breaths. Close your eyes. With each breath, comfortably inhale and exhale. You will begin to feel more and more relaxed. Continue to take deep breaths throughout this exercise.

Next, imagine the wheel of your ship as your True Self. Is the wheel spinning quickly, spun by the environment? Is the wheel locked in place by damage to your ship: a broken hull, lack of wind? Or is it easy to move, steering your ship in the direction that you want to go? Think about the external activity of your daily life: the people you see, your workplace tasks, and other regular commitments. Feel the spin of that energy.

Moving inward, think about your spokes; they are your seven intrinsic gifts: spontaneity, reasoning, creativity, freedom, spirituality, discernment, and love. Redirect that energy that moves you through your daily life, gently bringing yourself closer toward your center. Each spoke draws from within you. Some of these spokes represent parts that you like; others, parts you may want to change. Keep your breathing easy and relaxed. Each of these spokes draws on your characteristics that people in your life experience. Scan your body for tension and release it each time you exhale. Looking at the spokes, you begin to notice that the speed of your wheel is slowing down.

As you move further into your center, imagine the center of your wheel as the core of your True Self: spontaneity, reasoning, creativity, freedom, spirituality, discernment, and love. You can see which seven qualities flow from your center. The center itself drives the rest of your ship. You can feel how the wheel is connected to the rest of your ship. If the center is loose and makes the wheel wabble, your True Self lacks influence on your heart and soul. If the center is firmly connected, then the True Self can guide you and direct your ship. Securing your wheel's connection to the ship, moving toward your True Self allows you to feel inner stillness. You feel at peace. Reflect on this reservoir of your person: what images do these qualities generate for you? Do you feel the wheel—your True Self—strongly connecting to the rest of your ship? Do you feel the conditions that surround you, including the weather (other people's influence), spinning the wheel around uncontrollably? Let yourself see these inner qualities that move you within. These images are within your reach—they are your True Self.

Growth and change come through attention to our feelings, thoughts, and actions. Any of these entrances can permit access to the qualities of our True Self. This is why we need to enter within and look. In peace, we need to listen and search. This practice of the theology of silence allows us to examine the inner workings of our vessel.

In our honest search, we ask not only about ourselves but also about how we have touched the lives of others. Has our spirit-to-spirit connection been warm and tender, or harsh and cold? Have we drawn others to us through the qualities of our True Self, or has something interfered?

The contemplative, reflective, prayerful path is not for a particular group of people; it is necessary for all of us. While we can work on the individual qualities of our True Self through attention to our specific thoughts, feelings, and actions, self-awareness gained through entering within permits us to reflect our thoughts, feelings, and actions. As we engage the qualities of our True Self, we can gain hold of our whole self: body, heart, and soul.

The Miracles All Around Us

The person who is spiritually attuned knows that God acts in the world. What do the spiritually attuned see? They exercise their capacity to discern the work of God (the supernatural) from physical phenomena (the natural). The term *miracle* is loosely used in medicine today to refer to results that are beyond scientific explanation or expectation. However, according to Webster's dictionary, the primary definition of a miracle is "an extraordinary event manifesting divine intervention in human affairs." Rationally, it makes sense that if our True Self is a manifestation of the divinity in our being, then we can believe in miracles and facilitate their action. It is not that we cannot believe in miracles, it is just that we need to be shown how.

Hundreds of scientific studies demonstrate the power of prayer[3] as well as how intrinsic religiosity decreases depression and increases optimism;[4,5] how religiosity is associated with significantly higher CD4+ counts (measures indicating improved immune functions); and how religion eases depression and lowers anxiety.[6] Science is confirming that religion and spirituality are antidotes to mental and physical illness. Medical schools today are requiring courses in religion and spirituality. The wedge between science and religion is removed as we permit ourselves to see the power of the spirit in our lives.

In addition, as scientists are building evidence of the power of prayer in healing, they report such incidents in greater frequency. Not only is prayer improving individual health, but interestingly, prayer for others who may not even know they are being prayed for has been shown to correlate with marked improvements in physical illnesses. Double-blind studies have confirmed the validity of these fascinating reports.[7]

Have you felt that God hears your prayers? Have you had personal religious experiences?

Many people I counsel eventually get to the subject of faith and religious experience. I am encouraged by how frequently patients confide in me their personal experiences with God and how deeply valued those contacts with God are for them. Many of us may experience "the nudge" from God. Rarely, however, do we hear of anything like Saint Paul's Damascus experience. The early Christian persecutor en route to Damascus describes in the New Testament (Acts 9) how he was thrown to the ground by lightning, blinded, and converted after the Lord spoke directly to him, saying, "I am Jesus who you are persecuting." While most of the miracles around us are not so dramatic, they are indeed potent—if we have eyes that see. A miracle occurs according to how prepared we are to catch the Spirit in our sail and use this contact to progress forward. A miracle happens when we seize and pursue this moment; not only can we respond to "the nudge," we must!

A Personal Story   When I returned home at age eighteen following my first several months at seminary, I learned that my sister's friend Darren had been brutally attacked. Darren had been left for dead; he was unconscious, with an uncertain prognosis for recovery.

When I entered the hospital room, Darren's mother was with the neurologist, who explained that he was unsure if Darren would come out of his coma, as two weeks had passed and there had been little improvement. Darren lay lifeless and thin, with no signs of progress.

I embraced Darren's mother, a very devout woman who was in tears, and asked her if she wanted to pray. We both knelt. I prayed from the depths of my heart privately asking God to heal Darren; I felt his mother's heartfelt plea and conviction that prayer could change things around.

I spoke with Darren's mother for a while and then left. The next day, my sister received a call early in the morning that Darren had awoken from the coma. He slowly recuperated, enduring years of physical therapy and rehabilitation, but eventually more than 90 percent of his functions returned.

Several years later, my sister went to visit Darren's mother, who was near death. She told my sister that she and I had once had a very special experience. She said, "When your brother and I prayed that Darren would be better, I knew that God heard us and answered." She told my sister that she was forever grateful for that moment and that she wanted me to know that "our special secret" was his life, a thought that comforted her as she was preparing to die. On occasions, God works through all of us if we let Him. When we do, we see Him in daily life.

I have met many people in my life who have believed in the power of prayer, but few have impressed me so much with their dynamic spirituality as the poet and author Maya Angelou.

Hearing the Caged Bird Sing

Maya Angelou, at age four, sat frightened and uncertain in a train car traveling halfway across the country. Her parents were separated, and neither alone had the time to parent their children attentively. So Maya found herself riding in a train, traveling toward her grandmother's house, accompanied by her brother, whom she admired and adored. "[Don't] worry," her brother said soothingly. "You're the second most intelligent person in the world. Things will always be okay for you because you can always use your brain to figure out any problems that come your way." The little girl asked, "How do you know I'm the second smartest person in the world?" to which "Because I'm the first!" was his confident reply. Knowing her brother to be very smart, Maya felt sure he must be right, and she settled back in the train car.

In 1970, she showed the public the strength of her spirit in *I Know Why the Caged Bird Sings*, her critically acclaimed chronicle of rape and suffering in her childhood. Guided now by a force much greater than her brother's wisdom, the imagery and sounds of Angelou's poetry communicate her ability to accept the beauty and ugliness of her past and to see how God enters into the darkness.

For Angelou, being connected to God means learning who we are and how to relate to others:

> I believe myself to be a child of God and it is incumbent on me, then, if I am a child of God, to see every other person as a child of God: that means the brutes, the bigots, the batterer, the braggart. That means that there's no place I can go alone. Even when I go inside myself, I don't go there alone. There's always "it" there before me. "It" is the God Spirit. "It" is already in there. So I believe there is no place that God is not.

Angelou's primary relationship is with God; her soul is her *raison d'etre*. The Spirit gives her strength not by telling her she is smart, but by teaching her to accept that there are things in the world she will never be able to explain. Angelou finds peace and strength by telling herself, "I understand nothing save I am a child of God." This is more than an understanding of the justice of God in the face of abuse. A direct relationship with God produces utter confidence and fortitude.

Angelou sees a connection to God as something much larger than any of the several religions she has studied and the Christianity she herself practices. She knows the truth of placing authentic personal spirituality above institutional affiliation. In formal religions, she explains, people get caught up in telling each other what to do and minding someone else's business.

> It's like Nero fiddling throughout [the] whole world, and the world's on fire. Why not be engaged in something about one's own self? One's own soul? One's own reason for being?

Angelou does not suggest that we think only of our personal concerns and refuse help to those who need it. Rather, she believes that we must ease demands and expectations of others in light of their struggles. We must have empathy for one another, rather than behaving as though we ourselves possess the truth and are beyond reproach.

Ultimately, this is the kind of generous strength Angelou gains from her faith. She does not use God as a justification for her behavior, nor as an explanation or excuse for the world—a mistake Angelou claims is made all too often: "I trust that a number of people adhere to religious doctrines because they are afraid to come face to face with God." God, she explains, is not something for people to hide behind; He is there to give us the courage to live a meaningful life.

We cannot, then, expect to simply turn to God and have all our problems go away. Just as the saints lived lives of great challenge, so, too, should we expect some hardship. Faith is not intended to make our life easy, but to reward our efforts by supporting us through whatever challenges we may face. To help me better understand this important message and the nature of our responsibility to grow in the spirit, Angelou was moved to sing a Gospel spiritual during our exchange. The song expressed perfectly the unadorned participatory nature of our relationship with God:

> Lord, don't move your mountain. Just give me strength to climb it.
> You don't have to move that stumbling block, but lead me,
>   Lord, around it.
> My way may not be easy. You never said it would be.

If my way gets too easy, I just might stray from
    Thee, so I'm asking you,
Lord, don't move your mountain, just give me strength to climb it.
You don't have to move that stumbling block, but lead me,
    Lord, around it.

"That's some deep stuff!" she ended.

As much as Angelou's faith tells her that God has power in the world, it tells her also that each person must decide his or her own fate. Though she declares we are born into various positions, situations, and environments, we are the ones who determine how we will traverse it:

A person has to decide, with whom shall I participate? Shall I participate with the murderer? The brute? The one who will belittle me and erase me from the face of the world? Or my cousin? Or that stranger who said, "Morning Ma'am!" He didn't owe me that. That was a gift. Who do you want to serve? Do you want to serve that bad element.... [or do you want to know] I'm doing the best I can?

In Angelou, we witness her direct access to the qualities of the True Self; moreover, she tells us that God is her compass. Angelou insists that we must take an active role and use our lives to learn. Doing so has allowed her to see something positive even in events such as her parents' divorce that has connected her, she feels, with her whole body. The writer's passion and confidence can be heard in her fiercely triumphant declaration, "Not even life has the right to wrestle you to the ground and put its hand on your throat and make you call uncle."

With this battle cry, however, comes a plea for authenticity. Angelou counsels that "the path of self-understanding lies within." This requires humility that, unlike modesty, bears no pretense; such truly spiritual humility helps us recognize that we are not always in control, and it highlights our limitations. Angelou's advice, then, is simply to stop and listen:

You know when you're sick before any doctor can diagnose you. You know yourself. Stop and, rather than allowing anyone else to defend you, first see yourself at whatever age you are, whatever state of health you are. Admit what you believe. Declare what you don't understand. Vow to be passionate, compassionate, humorous, generous. People have to want to be healed of whatever it is. You have to collaborate with healing.

What does Angelou, so in touch with her True Self, show us about true coming of age? Her understanding of herself as "a child of God" attests to her awareness that she is engaged with self, others, and God, fueling a trust that she is living in truth. From Angelou's words, one senses her freedom, her True Self, fully alive in its spontaneity, reasoning, creativity, free will, spirituality, discernment, and love. Her joy is life affirming:

> Why waste this precious gift exhibiting a timid mind? Nobody should whisper. Don't whine. It makes you ugly, and it rarely has any positive affect on that, the subject of your whining. Whining lets a brute know that a victim is in the neighborhood. Show me yourself! Know yourself!

At the same time, as she urges individuals to stand up for themselves, Angelou recognizes that no one can make it alone. The question, then, is who will accompany us on our journey: Our brother? God? Someone who will encourage us to listen to what we know is right, or someone who will lead us to ignore what we know is right? Where is our religious community leading us? When we ask ourselves who we are, the question that necessarily follows is: "Who do we bring along?"

The connection to our self, others, and God is eternal; it awaits only our recognition. At that moment, the dynamic that propels us—whether we call it drive, fate, desire, need—ignites the qualities of the True Self. In Maya Angelou's life, creativity came to the fore in her self-awareness of her role as an author, and as a person who could both touch and be touched by others. For her, this creativity combines all of these vital qualities; through writing she makes her choice of who she is and who she wants to be:

> I describe myself to myself and to God as a writer. So when I think or life makes me believe that God has forgotten my address, I say, "Lord, you remember me, Maya Angelou, the writer."

What will your key innate value be? How will you describe yourself to yourself? How will you present yourself to God?

Looking inward is where many begin and end the process of coming of age. For true coming of age, looking within is only the beginning; action comes next. Looking within allows us to see and take hold of the great potential contained within the divine spark always present in authentic moments. That spark is in ourselves, in religion, and in people the world over. We must find that authentic religiosity.

Spiritual Transformation Through Universal Vision

Prayer and contemplation are the most direct ways to authentic spirituality. Prayer is an exercise in strength, turning us into lightning rods of God's power. Though we may have witnessed the travesties committed in abuse of God's name, nonetheless we must not lose sight of the marvels that have been inspired by a true connection to God: awe-inspiring paintings and sculptures, reverent musical scores and architectural achievements, endless advances in science by people fascinated with the intricate complexities of God and our universe.

When we engage the spirit authentically in our faith through prayer, reflection, and meditation, we open our connection to others and God. We are connected with clarity and strength to the qualities of our True Self. Many of us engage this kind of faith as followers; a few, though, are leaders. Archbishop Anastasios Yannoulatos, head of the Greek Orthodox Church of Albania, was first sent to Albania in 1991, following the collapse of communism. Previously a missionary in East Africa, Anastasios had been forced to leave his duties there after suffering two severe attacks of malaria. Accepting his new assignment, he arrived in Albania to find 1,600 churches destroyed by forty-five years of communist rule, and 22 priests serving where once there had been 440. The archbishop realized that there would be far fewer resources to help him here than there had been on the mission he was leaving.

Looking back, he observed that the challenges he had faced in Africa "were only preparation for what I was about to begin."

Anastasios recalled for me his reaction to the daunting task he faced of helping to rebuild this ailing country. Seeing the despair in the faces of the Albanians he met, the humbled priest had wondered, "Who's going to help these people? Who's going to give them hope?"

> I knew that this was a test, which went something like: If you have faith, stay and struggle. If you don't, go home. I received my answer in prayer.

Rather than give up on himself and his ability to make a difference, Anastasios chose to remain in Albania and devote himself to its cause; as a result, he has led the Albanians to improvements that a decade ago were mere fantasies. While a victim himself of snipers, would-be assassins, and vociferous detractors, Anastasios's charitable offering has given so much to Albania that not only the people but the new leadership voted to overturn a 1994 referendum by the previous Albanian government to oust him. Although not an Albanian, nor a speaker of the language, Anastasios learned Albanian so that he could minister to his new flock. But the devastation caused by decades of communism, Anastasios explained, could only be reversed by the "interested response" of an inspired people. Where there were only 22 clergymen, there are now 129; hundreds of churches have been restored, rebuilt, or newly founded; and new clinics and roads have been constructed to help people meet their basic needs. "We are not here to play good Samaritans," Anastasios says, "but to live with them—share the risks they face and to show them that even in the worst of times, there is still hope."

This, Anastasios believes, is the aid that can be given by all religions and religious institutions, whatever their constituency. An outgrowth of prayer is action, "works." A spokesman for world peace and a former professor of history of world religion at the University of Athens, the priest has thoroughly explored the emphasis that major world religions place on peace and reconciliation. Having studied Buddhist, Hindu, Taoist,

Confucian, Islamic, Judaic, as well as Christian teachings, Anastasios advocates that the kind of harmony he has wrought for Albanian Christians cannot be achieved without respect and justice for all people.

Anastasios advised the same sort of respect to Americans as they entered Iraq in the wake of Saddam Hussein's regime. He recalled his own experience: "When I arrived in Albania, I was perceived to be a spy. The people were suspicious and hostile because they had lived in fear and oppression for so long." The secret to changing those attitudes, Anastasios explained, is respect—for democracy and for various religious beliefs. This route of leadership opens up the heart in places where cultures clash.

Following his credo, Anastasios joined hands with Albania's many Muslims in his ministry to demonstrate that religious communities can and must come together. He specifically reminded us Americans: "Islam has the possibility of becoming very aggressive or very moderate—like most religions, actually. The important thing is to prevent the people from falling into the hands of fanatics." Anastasios believes that in truly protecting freedom of religion—as in the case of Islam in Iraq—the world can go far toward eliminating feelings of hatred and mistrust. Strength through prayer is his example for each of us.

Maya Angelou moves quickly within her talents as author and poet, engaged in her critical connections, feeling God's presence: "I am a child of God." Because of his primary contact with God, Anastasios penetrates the bureaucracy of politics and religion, seeing direct service and caring for souls as his predominant task. Validity of religion lies within the Spirit, within our personal encounters with God. The genuine function and value of religion is to facilitate that contact. The religion of legitimate authority is derived from their facility and capability to serve as vehicles of the holy.

For Angelou and Anastasios what is important is authentic religiosity. We must each pursue the personal encounters that lead to our acquisition of the Spirit. We have seen that guidance and discipline to pursue such contact are found in genuine religious institutions. In their words, but even more so in their powerful actions, we see in Angelou and Anastasios discernment of what is tangential and what is significant for spirituality: for Angelou, laughter at the vanity of empty rituals; for Anastasios, a keen sense for using time and church organization for the good.

LIGHTING THE FIRE

The signs of the Spirit are humility, prophetic courage, holiness, action, and love. To engage the Spirit, we must make contact. Stop what you are doing now, enter a peaceful space, and using a meditative, contemplative, and prayerful position, tune in to your soul. Try to feel the presence of the Spirit.

How do you feel? What are your thoughts? Maintaining contact with the Spirit changes us. Such reflective engagement leaves the marks and signs of the Spirit. Identify incidents where you have experienced signs of the Spirit from your contacts:

HUMILITY

1.

2.

3.

ACTION

1.

2.

3.

PROPHETIC COURAGE

1.

2.

3.

LOVE

1.

2.

3.

HOLINESS

1.

2.

3.

OTHER SIGNS

1.

2.

3.

BEING TOUCHED BY MIRACLES

Have you ever experienced a miracle? Have you shared this with others? Sometimes people encounter a miracle but isolate this experience from their life. They find this unusual experience difficult to integrate into their daily life. However, such encounters provide opportunities to develop our spiritual life. Reflect on the following questions.

1. Have you ever experienced miracles?
2. Do you feel that you can be an instrument of the power of the spirit?
3. Do you try to tap this potential and serve as a vessel of God?
4. You are a lightening rod of the spirit: identify ways that you may strengthen your spirituality through contact with God.

9

❦

LIVING IN TRUTH

On the existence of God:
I don't need to believe. I know.
—C. G. JUNG

A FEW MONTHS BEFORE my doctoral exams, I received a twelve-page list of books I was supposed to know for my comprehensive exams. I felt overwhelmed. Looking for advice, I went to my advisor's office, hoping that he would tell me which books were most important. He instead repeated what I already knew—that I was responsible for the content of every book listed on those twelve pages. I panicked. With tunnel vision, I resigned myself to the library's study carrels for weeks. After continuous review, I emerged from the stacks on the day of the exam, my mind and body exhausted. Emotionally, I was drained; I felt I had learned nothing.

When I arrived to take my exam, I was escorted to an austere, wood-paneled room and left alone to write my answers. Sitting there apprehensively, I noticed a mosaic plaque hanging on the wall, inscribed with a message in Hebrew: "Where were you when I laid the foundation for the earth?" (Job 34:4). Suddenly, my work of the past few months no longer seemed overwhelming. Laying "the foundation for the earth" seemed a much bigger job than anything I had to endure, and the significance that I had placed on the entire process seemed out of proportion.

As important as this exam was, the verse reminded me that more important things exist in life. I realized that I had to let go of my self-doubting and just do my best. Taking a deep breath, I thanked God for giving me the perspective I had lost.

In the end, I did well on my exam. But most importantly, I understood that my academic hopes had to be in touch with my faith in God. Thankfully, the Hebrew inscription gave me a much-needed reminder to do my best and trust in the Spirit regardless of the outcome. For engaging the Spirit is the powerful cornerstone of living in truth.

Such truth is what Carl Jung, the founder of analytical psychology, referred to when a BBC interviewer asked him if he believed in God. The first part of his response disappointed me: "I don't need to believe"; but his follow-up was both shocking and inspiring: "I know." Jung's research on human experience led him to study cultures around the world, and he had come to this powerful conclusion. Jung's pursuit of knowledge brought him beyond scientific criteria to encounter the Spirit that moved differently among various cultures. In *Modern Man in Search of a Soul* (1933), Jung concludes:

> The living spirit grows and even outgrows its earlier forms of expression; it freely chooses the men in whom it lives and who proclaim it. This living spirit is eternally renewed and pursues its goal in manifold and inconceivable ways throughout the history of mankind. Measured against it, the names and forms which men have given it mean little enough; they are only the changing leaves and blossoms on the stems of the eternal tree.[1]

In this chapter, we will learn about living in truth from Archbishop Desmund Tutu, Mother Teresa, and Commander Eileen Collins—all leaders of different missions who are torchbearers of truth.

By taking action that reflects our beliefs, we reinforce our values. In following these lessons, we develop our authenticity. In my experience with the exam, the awareness of my control versus God's control was a more important question to answer than any academic question. In this chapter, we affirm that encountering God in all the great religions of the world manifests the Spirit and universal truth; explain how contact with the Spirit guides us toward living in truth; and show how truth will center our lives in the Spirit.

True Knowledge and True Growth

True knowledge, or knowledge based on the Spirit, is the understanding that brings fulfillment. It is not merely information or skills but direction for living in the truth—for knowing and living out the good. By engaging body, mind, and soul, we can combine our passions, thoughts, and spirit to transcend an otherwise narrow relationship with our self and God. True knowledge goes beyond idealism or utopian fantasy, as well as empiricism or the understanding of physical nature alone. If we focus only on one side of ourselves, we fail to engage and develop our full potential and thus fail to develop true knowledge.

True knowledge, then, is a dynamic of various dimensions: intellectual, moral, emotional, experiential, and philosophical; it relates to our very identity by calling on the qualities of the True Self. While we can separate its components, true knowledge connects our body, mind, and soul; without this wholeness our faith and religion are deficient.

To live your truth, you must first decide what you believe and then apply it to your life. Once you accomplish that, you can gain a new perspective to honestly evaluate yourself and your life, and you can begin to overcome personal fears, anxiety, depression, and uncertainties. To solve all those problems, we must link our faith to our daily life; in other words, our truth must be lived.

Are You Spiritual or Religious? When asked in a poll if they believe in God, 94 percent of Americans responded in the affirmative. Yet, only 59 percent of respondents believe that religion is important to their daily lives.[2] Often it seems easier to identify with spirituality than religion because of political, social, and moral conflicts found in religious organizations. Those who answer, "I'm spiritual, but not religious," may associate spirituality with positive values, connectedness, well-being, or qualities that reach beyond the formalized ritual experience they often associate with religion. Spirituality often refers to experiential encounters with God; it is vital to increasing our closeness to God. How so? Because spirituality provides a direct link between the True Self and God, whereas religion often accentuates ideas concerning believers and God through its hierarchy and doctrine. Because of this understanding, spirituality is a direct experience of something personal and unifying.

But as we distinguish the more individual, subjective qualities of spirituality from the more collective, collaborative qualities of religion, we must not miss the strength that lies in personally combining the two. Together, religion and spirituality confirm the importance of personal discipline to grow in truth while also reinforcing the vitality of our faith community. Through humility and self-awareness, each of us can affirm a universal, spiritual truth while seeing the potential of religion.

What is the difference between your own faith and the faith of others around you, both fellow congregants and those of other denominations? How do we learn to share our faith with others? And how do we learn about other cultures? I have often been struck by the different ways faith has been represented in various cultures throughout the ages. In paintings, for instance, the Christ child is often vividly portrayed as native to the culture in which it was painted: black in Africa, white in Europe, and red-skinned in North America. This diversity is an example of the institutional faith adapting to the culture, while the truth of each remains the same.

The Truths in Religions

All known societies have had religion, and all of these religions have spoken to believers' needs for meaning, resonating with each one's True Self. Each tradition seeks answers to questions about its unique needs. While their forms and doctrines are different, all religions primarily address the meaning of life, advising how to cope with our struggles while providing opportunity to connect with one another with an understanding of self as an experience of God. Although different religions express their ideas differently, we can nevertheless see important parallels. For example, Judeo-Christian religions make the connection of God's creation with the nature of the human person, starting with the first words of the Bible: "In the beginning . . . God created man in his own image . . . male and female he created them" (Genesis 1:1, 27). In Buddhism and Hinduism, there is no doctrine of the origin of the world because the traditions consider the world to be eternal, and humanity, divinity, and the world to be interconnected. The Koran reads, "God created you from dust, then from the little germ he divided you," similar to the Bible.[3]

Although all of these traditions describe their own beliefs as "the truth," within each individual claim on the truth there are many variations—not only between the major religions but within each of their different groups and sects. Indeed, in the United States, we have more than 250 denominations of Christianity, all professing the same basic belief in Christ as the savior but with considerable—and sometimes acrimonious—differences of opinion on particular issues.

Judeo-Christian religions see the person as a reflection of God, claiming that humans are made in his "image" and "likeness"; thus a person is able to know God. In Buddhist religions, instead of references to God, we find "the boundless Openness," where the divine is a pervading force. This idea meshes with Buddhism's image of the person as distinct from parts of nature and the world, animate and inanimate. To a Buddhist, a human is no more significant than a plant, as all life is interconnected. This interconnectedness also leads to another dimension of the Buddhist idea of no-self. The person is constantly in a state of flux, making the existence of a static self merely an illusion. Yet through enlightenment a human can achieve growth in consciousness that allows the person to be free from the worldly desires that prevent the person from truly experiencing the "boundless Openness" and seeing the interconnectedness of all beings. But again, there are multiple forms of Buddhism, each with a particular nuance of this truth.

Meanwhile, the human condition in Hindu philosophies is a "fallen state," and humans find redemption and enlightenment through the divine. In the Islamic tradition, humans are a bridge between earth and heaven perceived through harmony and beauty. In Islam, as in virtually all religions, God is truth; however, a Hindu view does not speak of rewards or punishments, or of a He-God communicating in local languages.

The dimensions of spontaneity, reasoning, creativity, free will, spirituality, discernment, and love are used in religion to describe human nature, though not necessarily with these particular words, nor with this particular emphasis. The binding similarities within almost all religions are the qualities of the True Self. While in Buddhism there is no such thing as the self, discernment is still a basic tool in Buddhist progression toward enlightenment. Thus, we can perceive in the many different constructions of faith—reflecting culture and semantic—a persistent agreement of what I have called the significance of the True Self and critical connections. The Christian says, "Love your neighbor as yourself" (Matthew 22:39); and in *The Story of Gotoma Buddhat* we read, "The first Perfection, of Generosity, was practiced and followed by for Bodhisattas" (Jayawickrama, 124).[4] The believer in Therevada Buddhism puts the same idea this way: "Before spreading loving kindness to others, a person must first come to feel what it is like to feel it for himself or herself, by coming to accept himself or herself fully, warts and all" (Harvey, 2000),[5] emphasizing the necessity for generosity and compassion—the two structures that hold life together.

In fact, Hinduism, which most authorities consider to be the world's oldest major religion, advocates that our paths unite us with the divine infinite. *Bhakti*, an "intense love of God," is a path where we adore God with all of his being, which pours into our other relationships and activities. Buddhism emerged in the context of Hinduism, where *karuna*, the Sanskrit word for "compassionate action," arose to describe what Siddhartha Gautama, the first Buddha, confirmed as the rational thing to do to end suffering.

Hinduism and Buddhism do not identify a single God, as do believers in Islam, Judaism, and Christianity; Hinduism is polytheistic, and

Buddhism avoids formal distinctions of differences between beings. Nonetheless, all describe truths about affirming the good and denying evil. In Islam, jihad, often mistranslated as "holy war," actually refers to trying to one's utmost, whether struggling against oneself to control base impulses or resisting Satan or aggressors—but not in the sense of aggression. The *Qur'an* explicitly states, "Let there be no compulsion in religion."

Of course, the true test of these similarities in philosophy comes when we consider the kinds of action the world's religions advocate. Would the results of the Good Samaritan test be different for a Muslim, Buddhist, Jew, or Christian? Would the result of such a measure of "good" behavior be different among the groups within each specific religion? Claims to truth are only as good as what that truth delivers. The triumphant claims of truth require an illuminating fire—the force that spurs on transformation and the good. Each religion has those who have made contact with the holy: prophets, saints, shamans, yogis, and gurus. Each religion also has its lapses, illustrated by skeptics like Marx, who called religion "the opiate of the masses," or Nietzsche, who called churches "tombs of dead Gods," or Skinner, who focused on the primary actions of religion as self-serving and pursuing control.

Finally, there is another key element binding all our beliefs. In all these religions, love is valued as the highest means of understanding. When given to others, love counters prejudice and hate. Love recognizes no doctrinal boundary; it cannot be the domain of any one religion, but rather must be the medium for reconciliation and unity. Love is the universal language for wanting the best for others. It is through love, therefore, that we can learn to accept others and affirm our differences. Love is peace—and thus the window to ultimate truth.

It seems to me that we should not assess the truth of others. The evidence is before us concerning how difficult it is for those within the same faith to concur on details of faith, how complex a task it is to fully know the almighty God, divine, holy, truth. I believe, however, recognizing the diversity of humanity, that the power to comprehend the essential message of God is transforming.

Bringing Heaven to Earth

Although a religion may claim to preserve God's authoritative message, human souls, not institutions, serve as vessels of its living truth. Through expressing our True Self, both religious leaders and believers alike communicate truth. Occasionally, there is someone whose very life communicates humility, courage, and love; this person serves as an example of living in truth. Desmond Tutu, an archbishop in the Anglican Church, is one such communicator.

Tutu learned at an early age the importance of maintaining spiritual connections in the fight for freedom. As a young boy, an influential Anglican priest and head of the antiapartheid movement inspired him to embrace an active life of spirituality. Tutu recalled that the priest's political activity, "flowing from a life of prayer," was intimately connected with his spiritual practice.

Appalled by the injustices facing blacks in South Africa, Tutu committed himself to transforming the country into a democratic and just society. Finding the situation in his homeland "an unacceptable blow against truth and the spirit," he loudly declared God's truth as key in the fight against apartheid.

The blatant injustice and violence against blacks in South Africa, "attacks against people for no other reason than the color of their skin," ran totally counter to his understanding of what is fair, good, and just. The oppression was so great, he said, "that if the only thing that we ever did was to say strongly to the people, 'please stop the violence,' we will be delivered to the kingdom of God in an incredible way."

Tutu's dream for world peace has driven him to ever-increasing engagement in world affairs. Working with the South African Council of Churches, a group of the World Council of Churches, the archbishop has been able to pursue his objectives of antiapartheid on an international platform. They include gaining civil rights for all, abolishing South Africa's racist passport laws, creating a common system of education, and ceasing forced deportation of native South Africans.

I asked the archbishop how he integrated his spiritual discipline with his day-to-day demands of responding to human crises. Tending to our spirit, Tutu said, is not a selfish retreat away from our neighbor's suffering. Rather it is the practice by which we are enabled to love more fully. He explained:

> The heart of our care is in our connection with God. The most important task is our relationship with God. While monks often leave the church to meditate and retain that connection, we in the world must also maintain that priority for God in our life—from there our truth emerges.

He continued stating that a direct relationship to God precedes our responsible commitment to others. He acknowledged the Christian concept that "we live in this world but not of this world," yet he does not entirely subscribe to living a spiritual life severed from physical reality—"particularly when the latter involves so much suffering." He does not wait for the future heaven to come, but rather seeks victory over oppression and injustice in the world as he encounters it. Tutu recalled that he had discovered a recurrent pattern in the scriptures:

> I reflect on this pattern ... found especially in the Gospels [of] how our Lord was operating, going off alone into the wilderness and onto a mountainside to pray and then returning ... doing good works, healing people, feeding people.

"Contemplation," according to Archbishop Tutu, "is crucial to action."

In spite of the good that the church can accomplish, Tutu is not uncritical of the institution. Firm in his beliefs, he is especially outraged by the church's silence in the face of oppression, which is often based on the "use and abuse of scriptures." It is unjust, he argues, for the church to turn its back on a significant portion of its congregation:

> We have inflicted on gay and lesbian couples the pain of having to live a lie or face brutal rejection if they [decide] to reveal their true selves. But oppression cuts both ways. Behind our "safe barriers" of self-righteousness,

we deprive ourselves of the rich gifts that lesbian and gay people have to contribute to the whole body of Christ.

Tutu also feels that the church should grant women greater access by allowing them to be ordained in the ministry. Considering the church's present situation, he says women would bring many talents to the church, enabling the church's message to serve a larger portion of the population. "Each one of us," he emphasizes, "is of infinite worth. We are all children of God with different gifts, different makeups. We belong in God's family."

I asked Tutu how he responded to those who argued against his views on biblical grounds. He confidently pointed out several scriptural references to the "proper place" of slaves and women, referenced by Saint Paul and Saint James:

> You can get lost in the details and lose the true picture of compassion and love. We have lost this transforming message of faith. The use of the Bible through picking and being selective in the passages that we use is a cause of considerable anguish. We need to be extremely careful how we do in fact use the Bible, [recognizing] that it isn't made up of proof texts which you pick and hold up as sticks with which to beat whoever you're arguing with.

Acutely aware of how such injustice damages an individual's experience of truth and the Spirit, Tutu believes that oppression runs contrary to the church's ultimate mission. Tutu suggests that we ask, "What are the essential truths that they are communicating?" According to the archbishop, when Jesus says, "If I be lifted up, all will draw near," he means that the mission of the church is "absolutely inclusive."

Inclusiveness is important to Tutu because he feels charged with "proclaiming the good news" to the entire world. To him, everyone is God's partner, regardless of religion, sexual orientation, sex, or race. We are all meant to join with him and change the injustices of society:

> Changing the ugliness of the world—its hatred, its jealousy, its hunger, its injustice, its oppression, its loneliness, its rivalry, its competitiveness, its grasping, its sickness, into their glorious counterparts so that there will

be laughter and joy, sharing and caring, justice and reconciliation, peace and compassion.

"Our connection with all others—whether they do or do not recognize the image of God within them," Tutu says, is based on the same principle that God exists in all people. His belief in God demands acceptance of others. We do not hold God hostage. "God," he reminds us, "has the whole truth about God."

Proclaiming the Spirit

Religious traditions and their practitioners disseminate universal truth by preaching and demonstrating their beliefs. We would do well to listen to them. Often, we disregard the words of people outside our own group, thinking that their claims must be irrelevant to our own lives and communities. You can find universal truth in many different spiritual messages; truth, as I have said previously, is not limited to one denomination or another. Universal truth resonates clearly with all, awakening qualities of our True Self and our innate understanding of the good. These messages, brought by individuals living as one with the Spirit, are powerful enough to reach even the most hardened hearts.

During India's civil unrest, Mahatma Gandhi is said to have received a tormented Indian man who admitted to several war crimes—including brutally beating to death Moslem children. Gandhi asked why he had done so, and the weeping man replied that Moslems had killed his wife and son. The tormented man asked Gandhi what he should do. Gandhi responded, "Find a Moslem boy who has lost his parents and raise him as your own." Adding to that, he said, "However, while keeping him as your son, raise him as a Moslem."

Proclaiming the truth—the universal truth—is Archbishop Tutu's charge for life. Others such as Mahatma Ghandi and Mother Teresa have shared this same message. With Mother Teresa, I witnessed how one speaks directly to their truth.

In 1982, Mother Teresa was invited to Harvard University to address the student body and faculty. Upon taking the podium, Mother Teresa prayed from her heart to grant the truth that she personally knew to those in the audience:

> Dear Jesus, help us to spread your fragrance everywhere we go. Flood our souls with your spirit and life. Penetrate and possess our whole being so utterly that all our lives may only be a radiance of yours. Shine through us and be so in us that every person we should come in contact with may feel your presence in our soul. Let them look up and see no longer us, but only Jesus.

Disregarding the cultural, political, and religious differences among the spectators, she did not waver in proclaiming her message and beliefs. She did not, for instance, touch upon the themes of some of the speeches before hers regarding individual rights. Instead, Mother Teresa prayed that the Spirit be with all and shine forth as a beacon to guide them to the truth of God. For her, in a time of worldwide fear, pain, and suffering, it was more important to educate students about being good people, about aiding others through their intelligence and sharing the message of God through their actions than it was to give them intellectual reasons for doing so.

On that day, it was as if Mother Teresa had shifted the audience into another reality. Her message was profound. She directly addressed those in the audience who might disagree with her belief in God. Creating an open invitation of acceptance and love, she said:

> We all long; we all want. Even the disbeliever wants to love God in some way or another. And where is God? How do we love God, whom we don't see? To make it easy for us, to help us love, he makes himself the hungry one, the naked one, the homeless one. And you will, I'm sure, ask me, "Where is that hunger in our country?" Yes, there is hunger. Maybe not the hunger for a piece of bread, but there is a terrible hunger for love. There is a terrible hunger for the word of God.

Using the stirring image of Jesus as the face of the world's suffering, hungry, and homeless, she proclaimed her universal truth: that the most important need in our life is to be loved. And the word of God, she said, was an avenue leading to this love.

Continuing, Mother Teresa discussed her first mission trip to Mexico and the extreme poverty she encountered there. Interestingly, though, the people living in the small villages and towns, she said, were less concerned with acquiring material goods, such as food or clothing, than they were with learning about God. In her view, these people who suffered physical deprivation found their dignity, self-respect, and purity through God's love and shelter. Poverty to Mother Teresa was not just a financial issue, but also a personal and social problem, causing feelings of rejection and loneliness. Giving an example of the need for the poor to feel acceptance, she recounted a visit she had taken to London:

> I [will] never forget. One day, I was walking down the streets of London, and I saw a man sitting there. He looked so sad, so lonely. So I went right up to him . . . and I shook his hand. My hands are always very warm. And he looked up at me and he said, "Oooh, after such a long time I feel the warmth of a human hand." That little action was so small and yet it brought a radiating smile on a face that had forgotten to smile, who had forgotten what is the warmth of a human hand.

Invited to Harvard to speak about her human rights work, Mother Teresa knew that she could not speak to the real truth underlying her work without declaring her faith: the spiritual awareness and dignity she brought to the world's poor. Although her message was centered more on spirituality than Archbishop Tutu's message, they both affirmed action in this world as physical manifestations of the Spirit.

In the end, I felt she raised even more subtle points. She made all of us in the audience, people who are typically in the position to minister to others as "teachers, ministers, or privileged Americans," feel among those in need. Who are the truly hungry? she led us to ask. We all hunger for love. Who are the truly naked? We all lose our dignity at certain times. Who are the homeless? We all feel rejection and loneliness when we lose our critical connections. Mother Teresa's message not only touched on the difficult challenge of committing one's life to God, but also touched on finding strength, universal truths, and reconnection to our True Self through the Spirit.

On that day, we were asked to be open to a universal truth, profoundly expressed by an iconic believer. From that moment, after hearing Mother Teresa's resonant truth, I knew that I had to speak my truth as well. How do we take the truth of faith and live it? Are mere ritual and discipline and doctrine enough? By now it should be clear that these rituals are not enough; but how do we wrap ourselves around our spirituality and our truth and possess them as our own?

Living Your Faith

Although some identify themselves as spiritual by being in the presence of ministers, saints, and holy people, this behavior is akin to calling ourselves athletes because we are spectators of sports. We are not to be spectators of life—we are to fully participate in it. The stories of Anastasios, Angelou, Tutu, and Mother Teresa show us how real spiritual athletes stay disciplined and take physical action in concert with the holy. In all cases, their particular religious beliefs appear to be of less consequence than the testimony of their truth.

Prayer and Double Messages   When my older daughter and son entered preschool, one of their earliest reports of peer pressure and cultural pressure involved being corrected when they waited for the class to pray before eating lunch. When my son and daughter asked their teacher about why the class did not pray before meals, they were simply told: "We don't pray at school; you pray at home."

As my three-year-old daughter reported the story and her younger brother nodded in agreement, I could not help but feel that their meaningful experiences of prayer were being negated, and that a void was forming in their hearts. Although I understood the purpose of the rule at school, the message sent to them was that our society is one that does not pray. My wife and I decided to take this experience as an opportunity to discuss with our children the differences of others and the importance of being yourself. While I knew that it would be difficult for my children to pray at meals in their school setting, I also knew that they would be challenged to apply their beliefs. A few days later, my daughter stated that she still prayed quietly in her heart at lunchtime. Over the years, our children have found alternative solutions to respond to the problem of praying in public, such as "praying anyway," closing their eyes, and "thinking about God." In my son's case, his humorous alternative is to "say 'Thank God' out loud" because, as he put it, "They don't know who I'm talking to anyway."

Taking a few moments for prayer before meals has always been a valued ritual in our family. Faith provides the chance to step back from whatever else occupies us and to reconnect, joining hands to symbolize the meeting of our bodies, minds, and souls, thanking God for His bountiful blessings. Mealtime prayer is a chance to unite as a family and to connect with God and one another in a moment of faithful meditation on a particular thought or concern.

On a recent occasion, my son's eight-year-old friend visited and joined us for dinner. As usual, we prayed before the meal. Though his friend did not join in holding hands with the rest of us, nor understand exactly what we were doing, my son tried to coach him. When the boy came for dinner again a few weeks later, he seemed totally prepared, with his hands folded in prayer, ready to participate according to the symbols of his own faith.

Through each of these incidents, the children's sensitivity to and need for direction regarding faith struck me. In teaching them, I myself learned that faith needs guidance. While as adults we may understand the difficulties of practicing our beliefs in public settings, we do not need to defer to those rules as if the options were all or nothing. We need to consider alternative ways of maintaining our valuable critical connections and proudly declaring our life in the Spirit—just as my children did, and just as Mother Teresa did.

Penetrating the Heavens,
Secure in God's Presence

We all have dreams and goals that sometimes seem like fantasies. While we know that sheer determination and hard work help us achieve, support in our struggle eases the difficulty we encounter. When that support resonates from deep within our True Self, we have more confidence in our abilities and ourselves. Astronaut Eileen Collins is an excellent example of a person who used her True Self to her advantage. Blasting off into outer space in 1999, Collins became the first woman to command a space shuttle flight.

When I first met Commander Collins, we spoke about her quest to become an astronaut. She explained that she had failed her first eye exam for pilot training. This incident seemed to close the door on her dream; pilots are required to have perfect eyesight. Luckily, though, her colonel at the time realized her capabilities and offered her another chance to take the test. As if the event had happened just yesterday, she recounted her preparations for the exam:

> For two weeks, I pampered my eyes by performing exercises, taking vitamins, sleeping, and eating so many carrots that my hands literally turned orange. I returned, passing the exam without any problems. That was the biggest break in my career.

But though Collins had satisfied the requirements, she was unable to fly combat fighter jets as she had hoped. In the 1980s, the military maintained a strict policy of not allowing women to fly in combat. Ironically, Collins became a flight instructor and trained the very same pilots she was unable to join on military operations. Pursuing a career in a field dominated by men, Collins tapped her inner strength and immersed herself in flying to prove that women could fly in combat alongside men. She believed that the system would eventually change, and she was right!

Although flying is certainly one of her passions, Collins conveyed a clear set of priorities in her life, saying, "My family always came first.

I've always put my family as number one." This commitment arises from her own experiences at home as a child. Even though her parents separated when she was very young because of "differences," the pair never legally divorced and remained close friends. Collins has always had a meaningful relationship with both of them. She describes their support for her as unconditional:

> My mother would always say things like "I love you no matter what happens." My father would say, "I'll always be there." My mother would say, "I want you to talk to me about what happens. Talk to me before you talk to your friends." She'd really get specific: "If you want to have a cigarette, have it here with me, right now, in the house."

Although Collins's parents were unable to financially support her dream of flying or fund her college education, their encouragement provided a secure basis for her to etch out her future and remain centered. She had learned to focus on positives, rather than negatives, and to use her energy constructively. Her religious community confirmed this type of focus as well.

The next time I spoke with her, the issue of space exploration had taken on a more pressing dimension: the space shuttle Columbia tragedy had just occurred. As a spokesperson for NASA and the commander for upcoming missions, Collins expressed to me her confidence in the space program. At first I was surprised how anyone, much less a parent, could grasp such certainty after having seen colleagues and friends die in service of a mission. The more we spoke, however, I understood that Collins's philosophy of living is deeply rooted in her knowledge that some things are beyond her control. To distinguish between what she can affect and what she cannot, she turns to prayer. In this way, she wastes no time and energy worrying over what might happen, but instead focuses on making the program better and safer.

Reflecting on the Columbia disaster, she simply stated:

> We lost a crew, but we also lost seven individual friends. The loss of one friend is hard enough, but the loss of seven friends.... you think through

your relationship with each one of those people, things that you said to them and things that they said to you. And you think about their life, and the wonderful things they did as individuals.

You have to think [also] about what the loss of the shuttle is doing to our space program. Nothing is perfect. We don't live in a perfect world, and the shuttle program isn't perfect. But the point is we need to focus on how close to perfect we can make things and to [let go of] things over which we have little control.

In these comments we see that Collins does not ignore death; rather she is able to find comfort and direction through her strong engagement with God. Unlike B. F. Skinner and Roslyn Yalow, who pursued advancements within science through a lens skeptical of religion, Collins believes that science and religion are complementary to each other. She explained:

God wants us to explore. Otherwise, why would he give us the universe and technology? I don't see any conflict in faith and science. I have a very strong faith in God. That's a major part of who I am.

For Collins, faith is a gift from God and an important part of her identity. She recognizes its importance in her own life and believes it to be fundamental for anyone else's life. After all Collins has been through, it truly bothers her to see individuals suffering. She resonates the sensitivity we heard in Mother Teresa in this regard:

I know now how much my faith has helped me. I have some very specific things that have happened to me that are very interesting. It's just amazing how prayer works if you really have faith. It gives [you] the strength to help others and the world. It's a feeling of confidence that you get through prayer that's hard to describe. I think God has a plan for everybody. And sometimes your plan is not God's plan. I think the answer is to turn your life [over] to God and say, "God, I'm praying that whatever your plan is for me that I can do it well."

Collins is a wonderful example of how faith provides formative values and leads to truth. She believes that she does her flying for the good of humankind. Collins' spiritual life is not blind; it results from the challenge of reconciling scientific paradigms with various religious perspectives. She uses religious traditions to nourish her spirit, and she does not get bogged down by the rules or the system. Instead, she never loses sight of the heavens, committing to the purposes and values that uplift, direct, and fulfill her personal spirit.

We too must add this kind of resolve to our spirituality and our religion, and in so doing, we must thoroughly embrace the change. Our faith and our religion must reflect our active spirituality; then can we grow and move forward.

Living Faith Examination— How Do You Live Your Truth?

Mother Teresa identified actions that demonstrate the intensity of our faith, such as clothing the naked, housing the homeless, and feeding the hungry in both body and spirit.

First, list the five activities that demonstrate your faith in action and note how regularly you express these activities:

Action	Frequency
1.	1.
2.	2.
3.	3.
4.	4.
5.	5.

Second, identify five principles that you believe in, stating how often and in what ways you demonstrate these beliefs.

	BELIEF	ACTION	FREQUENCY
1.			
2.			
3.			
4.			
5.			

LIVING YOUR FAITH

List the ways in which you practice your faith.

		RATING
1.		_____
2.		_____
3.		_____
4.		_____
5.		_____

On a scale of 1 to 10, indicate which of these practices bring you closer to living your faith and a connection with self, others, and God. Can you identify other acts inside or outside your tradition that strengthen your spirituality?

PART IV

INTEGRATING YOUR LIFE

The art of making art is putting it together.
—STEPHEN SONDHEIM

JUGGLING THE DETAILS of our daily lives is one of the most difficult efforts we face. Whether it is writing a report, getting the kids to school on time, keeping in touch with our extended family, or just remembering what to put on the grocery list—how well we manage our situations makes all the difference. Our experience is analogous to shipbuilding, in which types of wood and methods of joinery unite in the hands of an experienced builder to create a first-rate seafaring experience. Just like the shipbuilder, we bring together our heart, soul, and True Self toward building our own personal masterpiece, our true coming of age.

But where do we start? How can we integrate our True Self, heart, and soul, considering all of today's competing demands, deadlines, and constraints? We begin by understanding who we are, evaluating our personal commitments in relationships, and recognizing our connection with our soul. Equipped with an invigorated self-awareness and informed perspective, we are then able to take possession of and responsibility for our True Self. These tasks can be difficult, however, for a fog clouds our view when we focus too much on any one of these factors—

self, relationships, or beliefs—and neglect the others. Accepting struggles and challenges as part of life prepares us to deal with them and create a clear horizon.

True coming of age is an ongoing process. By staying centered on our True Self and maintaining critical connections, we can continue to reap the benefits of our true coming of age. This does not mean that we will be free of tasks and demands, but rather that we will have clarity as we approach them. In other words, by being oriented in our True Self and engaging in our critical connections, we have built a sturdy vessel to travel the ocean of life. We are ready to encounter rough water and storms and the beauty and adventures of our voyage.

To aid you in your task of shipbuilding, we must ask:

1. Do I understand my self and my history?
2. Have I worked on the parts of my self that need repair?
3. While building the boat for my life's journey, have I only focused on one piece? Is it the hull (my heart), the mast (my soul), the rudder (my True Self), or the wind (the Spirit) that guides my ship?
4. Rather than build my vessel, have I decided to remain on land essentially dry-docked, pursuing unrewarding activities?
5. Do I follow the maps of others or my own?
6. Are those people surrounding me positive influences for my voyage, or do they take me off course?
7. Do I have a working compass? Have I sought direction from truth and the Spirit?
8. Have I fought the wind (Spirit) because it seems invisible, incomprehensible, or nonexistent?
9. Do I dare to travel in unfamiliar waters outside my birthplace and home, or am I locked into traveling only near my current locale?
10. Finally, do I truly desire to create authentic connections between my self, heart, and soul while on this voyage, so that I can invigorate and renew my life?

By genuinely responding to these questions, we will feel a triple dynamic at work in our lives: the physical, the emotional, and the spiritual. No longer stuck or lost, those who answer yes immerse themselves in the vitality of spontaneity, reasoning, creativity, free will, spirituality, discernment, and love. We are now open to a life lived through truth.

By centering on truth in these ways, we experience "oneness" with God and others and gain a higher sense of purpose in our lives. This in turn aids us in connecting to our True Self and accessing our intrinsic gifts. At the same time, we open our hearts to greater emotional connection in relationships. It is here, at this moment, that we can embrace both our own soul and another's. True coming of age thus becomes self-renewing.

As you read Part IV, ask yourself these questions:

+ How do my work, relationships, and beliefs get redefined when I engage my True Self?
+ How does truth affect my character and my values?
+ How can I create authentic moments finding the truth, knowledge, balance, and peace that lead me to my fulfillment?

10

❧

MAKING CRITICAL CONNECTIONS

What we're all striving for is authenticity,
a spirit-to-spirit connection.
—Oprah Winfrey

IN THE LATE 1980s my mother and I went to Greece. Reveling in both the ancient and modern Greek culture that surrounded us, we felt our senses refreshed and energized. The scent of crystal seas enchanted us; the sight of monuments and museums inspired us; and foods and drinks tasted more flavorful than I had ever imagined.

Leisure appeared to rule Greek society. In contrast to workaholic Americans, the Greeks seemed to be proud of working very little. We overhead one conversation, for instance, between a young female lawyer and her dentist friend. After exchanging a few common pleasantries, they happily discussed working only ten to fifteen hours per week. Later, while traveling on a bus, we heard a middle-aged man sharing with a fellow passenger that he only worked twenty hours each week because "life is too short." The message of these Greeks seemed to be that "work is work" and not as important as enjoying life to the fullest.

This notion was foreign to me. I commented to my mother that it seemed strange that professionals would take such satisfaction in limiting their commitments to work. I realized how immersed I had become in the American work ethic. To me, as to many Americans, a person's worth is directly linked to his or her labors. But in Greece the attitude is very different. As in many other warm-weather cultures, the Greeks promote recreational and leisure activities; and through this perspective I began to see that life really was too short.

In this book, we have read of great achievers, many of whom attribute a large portion of their success to one prominent factor, such as "drive" (Bette Davis), "determination" (Tom Hanks), or "hard work" (Mary Lou Retton). Working with tremendous dedication, these achievers may be considered rarities—not for their talents or gifts, but for their willingness to go the extra mile in their respective endeavors. Yet many of the highly successful individuals admit they have overworked themselves, driving themselves into anxiety and distress.

How do we know when we might be overdoing it, or going too far? Is the sacrifice of other parts of our life—family intimacy, leisure time, play—worth achieving our goals? Is there a way to be successful without losing a piece of ourselves in the process?

This perspective should not just pertain to work life. Working the right job with reasonable commitment is intimately connected to the quest to help us understand who we are and develop our critical connections. In this chapter, we will examine how an intense focus on our work can unconsciously lead us to neglect our lives, resulting in destructive patterns in our spirit-to-spirit connections; show the importance of the True Self in correcting and rebuilding our critical connections with others when they are damaged by our work; and learn yet another way how critical connections enable us to maintain a balanced body, heart, and soul.

A Father, a Son, and the Spirit

Bringing a child into this world is probably our greatest privilege in life. Through this one act we participate with God in the greatest creation possible: the making of a new human life. Words cannot describe this miracle as we usher a child through life on a road of endless possibilities. At the same time, the child we create is also one of our greatest responsibilities. Entrusted by God, parents will guide their children toward their futures. The bonds we forge with our children help them find truth, and fully embrace their own unique True Self.

Ron Howard's parents guided him to acting stardom. Born in 1954 in a small town in Oklahoma, Howard, the son of two actors, began appearing in movies when he was only eighteen months old. His first real part came at the age of four, when he played Opie on the *Andy Griffith Show*. Later, as a young man, he starred in the popular *Happy Days* sitcom; and now as an adult, he directs movies, including the critically acclaimed *Apollo 13* and *A Beautiful Mind*. Meanwhile, the redheaded, freckled-faced star has remained an icon of the wholesome American boy, the man with the heart of a child. How, though, has this been possible? How has Howard retained this air of innocence, constantly inspiring the love and trust of others, after a lifetime in such an aggressive and competitive industry? How has he managed to successfully negotiate the many hazards of his career, and what does his example mean for us?

His warm persona is not a product of Hollywood image making: I found Ron every bit as gracious and unassuming as I could hope. Extremely grateful for the stability in his life, Howard credits his parents for giving him support and encouragement to handle the inevitable bumps of life. As a result, Howard has a strong grasp on the importance of parenting, knowing that good parenting helps a child handle life's surprises and upsets:

> I've always said, I don't ever have to worry about anyone doing a television movie about my life so far. There's not enough conflict, and that's a real blessing. You still have to negotiate disappointments and cope with circumstances which are less than ideal, and even a little threatening. And that's I think what parenting is supposed to be all about. It's preparing children not so much to excel—that's kind of up to them—but to learn how to cope. To learn how to be reasonable problem solvers, because no one's exempt from those curve balls.

While most of us know Ron's sensitive demeanor through his frequent conversations with his screen father, Sheriff Andy Taylor, he notes that it was his connection to his own father that provided the model for his portrayal of Opie:

> My father was the one who was always there. He taught me as we went along. It wasn't just the acting; I learned as I saw him direct plays. He ran an improv group out of our house. I would watch him write, and I would help him a little bit. [I would] pitch ideas with him, things like that. He was really creatively engaged, [but] he wasn't having tremendous success in writing and acting. He had enough success that you could see that there was [a] reward. He was a remarkable man.

It is clear from Ron's words how his relationship with his father nurtured his creativity and supported his discovery of his True Self. The relationship with his father demonstrated a critical connection that can be found in sharing creativity, spontaneity, discipline, and spirituality. Through his loving mentoring, Ron's father taught him how to approach life:

> [My father] is a very mature, very wise guy; great problem solver—good common sense—just fundamentally incredibly sound thinking. He's a pretty selfless guy, but again, he doesn't wear that as some sort of a badge. No martyr complex there at all. He's just out there doing the best he can.

To explain his father's dedication, Ron told me a touching story of how his father helped him prepare for an important audition when he was only three:

> My dad got a friend to come over and hold some tin cans on a broomstick over my head and create some distraction so that I would learn to concentrate on the other actor and not be distracted by other things going on overhead. So we did that; I got the part.

His father's support afforded Ron countless positive, authentic moments in his youth that had a wonderful impact on him.

This does not mean, though, that every experience with his father was fun, for as Howard found out, good parenting comes in many forms. Howard recounted one particularly significant lesson he learned one day on the set of *The Andy Griffith Show*. Not feeling much like the adorable, popular tyke he was supposed to be, Ron became cranky during one of his scenes. His father picked him up, spanked him, and told him that people were working and that he needed to be responsible. While Ron may not have enjoyed the experience at the time, today he knows that his father's loving firmness taught him how to have perspective of himself and others.

Ron's mother also ensured that her son developed skills for finding happiness. Her unwavering love and optimism made his home feel permanently safe and secure. Together, Ron's parents were actively involved in their children's daily activities. And though others found Ron's parents to be very protective, Ron felt that they showed him what it meant to be part of a committed family. Howard understands and appreciates what his parents did for him and his art. By instilling in Ron a firm set of values that would help him live a good life, his parents let him control his own behavior. The self-awareness they imparted to him gave him the maturity and freedom to make his own decisions when Howard was only a teenager:

> When I started the tenth grade, it was very important to me to be a part of the high school experience, and I really wanted to play high school basketball. And to do that I started turning down work, and it was the first time in my life that I was really turning things down. But I also knew that I had to show up every day at basketball practice if I was going to be on the team. So I took this one semester and I didn't go on any auditions. Once the season was over, I was free to go on auditions, and I started going to auditions and not getting any work. There [I was], at about fifteen and sixteen, for the first time experiencing rejection—and shocked by how much I missed [working].

His ambitions to be both distinctive and normal frustrated Ron, and he reacted with a foresight unknown to most teenagers:

As a result of that experience, a couple of things happened: One, I decided I wanted to be a film director. I realized that I loved the business, was probably not going to be a professional athlete, and that I really resented waiting around the phone and being given jobs or staring at the phone and waiting to be given work. So I wanted to be proactive about my career and try to create my own creative opportunities.

Howard realized these creative opportunities through an activity quite different from his acting career:

[Later I] started coaching in the kids' basketball league and baseball, consciously because I thought it would be good for me to learn how to work with people. I enjoyed it. I loved the sport, but also in the back of my mind I thought, this is actually pretty good practice for me, pretty good training for a director.

Ron made his choices purposefully. He knew that it was important to him to live a normal teenage life, and so he committed himself wholeheartedly to his school basketball team. Had he not done so, he may not have realized just how integral his work in television was to his sense of well-being—and he also may have regretted never exploring the high school experience. Likewise, when he realized the frustration of waiting for an audition, he did not abandon himself to a feeling of helplessness; he had the strength to listen to the direction given to him and has followed this direction through years of work to a new and more personally rewarding career path. In knowing his passion and recognizing his priorities, Howard made choices that combined his interests and satisfied his desires. He is an excellent example of putting it all together.

Ron's self-awareness and ability to integrate his different needs and desires extends to his relationships with others, where he has also enjoyed remarkable foresight and good fortune. Though eager to have a complete high school experience, Ron did not date much in his youth. By the beginning of high school, he had already met the girl he knew was right for him. As he put it,

There was simply no reason to search any further. [I fell] in love in high school with this incredible girl [who] I trusted completely. That trust has just been the foundation of our relationship all these years; it's never wavered. I don't know, I had just incredible laser focus. Something was really right. So that usual two- or three-year period of adolescent angst and frustration just sort of melted away.

We see how Ron's parents set him on a course of honest self-assessment that has benefited his future relationships. Howard's self-awareness, confidence, and clarity of purpose are assets in both interpersonal and professional relations; and these hallmarks of a genuine connection to the True Self shine through brilliantly in his collaborative style, facilitating the creative process and helping to bridge his crew members' various styles of interaction, thus making differing goals compatible:

[My] work became much better when I learned how to listen. As a very young director, I so feared losing control of the crew or the actors that I was far more rigid than I am today. And somewhere along the line, I really learned to open up and be willing to say, "I don't know, what do you think?"

Howard learned that there would always be times when he would disagree with one of the actors, writers, cinematographers, or other talented people with whom he worked every day. He also discovered that in spite of this, they could still cooperate—that accepting someone else's suggestions would not compromise his own objectives as a storyteller. In fact, in such a collaborative art as film, compromise is absolutely necessary.

As Howard learned, work does not have to just "coexist" with family values. For work, when handled correctly, can reinforce family life. In Howard's experience the balance between self and others gains an even greater resonance when we are with someone we care about deeply and whose goals we share. This is the experience Howard has had as his family has grown.

In 1970, Ron's wife Cheryl, having had some trouble conceiving, was confined to her bed during her second trimester. Ron suddenly found himself running the household and caring for his wife, feeling more responsible for his family than he had ever felt before. A self-proclaimed "slob who had never really helped much with the chores," Howard confessed to feeling somewhat "cramped" when he was required to take on this extra work: "I stopped watching hours and hours of sports every week. My recreational time largely ceased being my own. I made an adjustment that for me it was going to be really 'work and family.' . . . I chafed under that a little bit." Ultimately, however, it was through this experience that Howard says he really grew up and became a man. He knew his priorities and felt gratified in changing his life. Though in the short term this may not have been an easy decision, he knew that in the long run this was what he should and wanted to do. Like most couples, he and Cheryl have endured plenty of challenges since this turning point, but because of Ron's ongoing attention to his critical connections and, as he puts it, seeing the best in people, he is able to maintain his True Self while helping those around him find and cultivate their own.

I asked Ron about his understanding of God. Ron gave a typically reflective answer, one that draws out the importance of placing the spirit over institutions, as we discussed in the last chapter:

> I believe in God—and feel pretty spiritually sensitive—but not in any formalized way. I haven't heard any doctrine that I believe represents more than just sort of an inkling of what God might want for us. To me, formal religions are human interpretation and therefore deeply flawed, not really worth dying for and fighting for. I appreciate the patterns in various doctrines, and that's what intrigues me the most. I had a great meeting with Joseph Campbell talking about mythology, which is the same thing as religion in a lot of ways.

Ron's beliefs are as much about the search for the spirit as they are about direct experiences of the Spirit itself. He is a classic searcher, using his art in a quest for spiritual meaning:

> I believe that there is something built into our DNA which is part of our evolution, that leads us to reach, to be moral, to quest. Yet I have no idea where

God resides. I believe that we have a responsibility to make moral choices and that we are defined by those choices. I think that there's a reason that we sense right from wrong and that a majority of people have a shared sense of right and wrong. And I think that in that intuition lies the path.

Ron summarizes himself, his moral life, and his place in Hollywood this way:

> I feel good about myself. How do you feel about yourself when you look at yourself in the mirror? If you live your life with that as a guiding principle it works: because I think I have a strong sense of what is right or wrong. And I recognize that you're not going to be liked all that time.
>
> It's not about being liked or even pleasing people. Although I am a people pleaser by nature, that's not necessarily the goal. Sometimes you have to do some hard things, but if you can look at yourself in the mirror and believe in it, then that's sort of the guideline.

While simply growing up invites us to make connections within ourselves, others, and God and to draw on our True Self, how well we accomplish this is often not tested until life throws us a curve ball, as we see in the story of the first woman to sit on America's highest judiciary.

Solid Family: Sturdy Judge

Justice Sandra Day O'Connor was the first woman appointed to the Supreme Court, accepting Ronald Reagan's nomination in 1981. Yet long before that historic moment, O'Connor felt the warmth of her parents' love and support throughout her childhood. The eldest of three children, she grew up in the 1930s and 1940s on a 155,000-acre ranch in Arizona that required the attention of the entire family all the time. She recounted:

> Ranch life is utterly different from urban life. The family is together day and night. There are no "office hours." I probably spent more time with my parents than most young children.

This solid foundation at home provided a secure setting for nurturing her personal capacity for reasoning and discernment. Her humility, her desire to interpret the law fairly, and her strong work ethic are certainly rooted in her upbringing. Growing up on a ranch, she quickly learned the value of sacrifice, commitment, and discipline. By closely identifying with hard work and with her family's values, she became the conscientious judge she is today. Following a highly focused direction in life with great success, she dedicated herself to the study of law, married the man she loved, raised three sons, and served as an appellate judge. Seated before Congress during her confirmation hearing, she was asked by one representative, "How do you want to be remembered?" To this she replied, "I hope it says, 'Here lies a good judge.'"

One of O'Connor's first missions as a Supreme Court justice was, strangely enough, to establish an early-morning aerobics class for herself and her colleagues. O'Connor recognized the huge amount of stress entailed in her work and also knew that exercise could reduce stress. As she matter-of-factly stated,

> I do continuous work. It's been very challenging—unlimited anxiety. It is so busy that I'll have a bite at my desk for lunch. And I also take work home. There is simply no time left after work at this Court for other activities.

One might wonder what drives O'Connor to such a hectic lifestyle. Like Ron Howard, O'Connor derives great satisfaction from her work, demanding as it may be at times. Describing her motivation as something related to a need for self-respect, she said:

> No doubt we are all motivated in part by a desire to have self-respect. Part of gaining self-respect is the respect of others. As a trial court judge, I enjoyed trying to resolve some practical problems. No one ever went away feeling that I hadn't heard and listened to them.

Motivated to gain respect among her colleagues, peers, and the American public, O'Connor finds it extremely satisfying to help others with their problems. Quoting Teddy Roosevelt, she described happiness as "work worth doing." She further explained, "I enjoy helping others, doing things that tend to help others who need help. All in all, I am happiest when I am busy. I spend my days in action."

Many of us work hard and exercise, yet do not find life as invigorating as O'Connor. When I asked about her religious affiliations, she chose to limit her comments to the principles that guide her life, and she summarized their meaning this way:

> Helping others is the gift of life. One can't do that by being self-centered. I suppose that the universal principle is that one has to develop the self. Eventually, we have to develop a consensus with others, rather than the self alone. Life has meaning to the extent we try to leave it a little better than we found it.

Since our initial interviews in 1982 and 1983, O'Connor has faced considerable challenges, including the deaths of both her parents and her own breast cancer surgery. In remission now for nine years, O'Connor shares her experience with me:

> The postoperative period was depressing; I felt very weak [and] very emotional. I was hearing things I didn't want to hear. It was a real tough time. It makes me value each and every day . . . more than ever before. It was shocking to be told that my disease was cancer. Thankfully I had work to do and could keep my mind off my medical concerns. That helped me enormously.

Although O'Connor's relentless work ethic helped her maintain a positive attitude through her struggle, it did not keep her from acknowledging the severity of the disease. In fact, her willingness to face the seriousness of her illness enlivened within her a sense of life's fragility and a call to make each moment count. She recalls:

> I discovered something else, however. It was a sense that life after all is finite. When as an adult you are faced with the potential end of your life, I think that at least for me it gave me an awareness more than I previously had of the pleasure of enjoying each day.

It was an awareness, as we will see, that enriched the Justice's connection to others and her feeling of responsibility toward them. Part of her commitment to make each day count requires her to make each of her encounters meaningful:"Think about your relations and contacts with other people and how people make those beneficial to the world. These were the things that I learned from that experience." O'Connor's commitment to make such encounters meaningful arose in face of a horrible illness. Our connection to others, however, may not always require such a crisis.

O'Connor reminded me that although her battles with breast cancer enlivened her connections to others, her childhood also gave her a foundation for understanding her responsibility to the community around her. She emphasizes, therefore, the need for communities to educate people on their responsibilities toward others. Yet unfortunately, many today are unable to sense their connections to others:

> We have families that are seriously broken or defective or troubled in a variety of ways, and many young children today who don't have a home environment that is conducive to learning values of the kind that I think might be beneficial or worthwhile.

Unlike her childhood on an Arizona ranch, in which she was constantly reminded of how much each family member depended on one another, children today find themselves in a highly individualistic culture, and often feel little responsibility toward others:

> There are high levels of unemployment. Schools tend to be large and difficult experiences for children. Responsibility, being honest, being careful, these are the things that young people today sadly don't experience. Our nation has become so urbanized that children grow up with no family responsibilities.

We do not, therefore, have to face a crisis to become more authentic in our connections to others. We should rather educate both ourselves and others in ways that promote greater awareness of our connections and responsibilities toward each other. This heightened awareness, as Justice O'Connor's experience shows, gives us the ability to make each day and each encounter of our lives meaningful.

Howard and O'Connor both grew up in homes that led them to develop qualities of the True Self. By establishing deep connections with their families and strong, positive self-awareness, they were able to build strong relationships with others, which in turn benefited their careers. Like Howard and O'Connor, we, too can connect directly to others through the True Self. These high achievers found their truest mission in helping and collaborating with others. Both describe their connections to God as less vocal, though as genuine spiritual interests in their lives. They are propelled by their desire to lead a fulfilling life.

The Drive to Be Fulfilled

Whatever our occupation or relationships, each of us is driven to do things well, to get things done, and to achieve a feeling of efficacy. It is in our nature, psychologist Robert White explained, that we are also driven to be competent. Psychologist Alfred Adler pushed the notion further, claiming that our goal is to strive for completion—though recognizing this is approached differently by various people.

As each of us strives individually toward mastering our field of interest, we also enlist the help of others. Since we want to be competent ourselves, we are more likely to befriend or be attracted to others who possess the competence we lack. For Adler, the striving for completion is innate and involves a range of levels: from self-esteem, power, and self-aggrandizement to Jung's concept of striving for unity and self-realization.

Feelings of competency, however, are not as simple to obtain as pride in a sports team. The truth is that many of us do not feel adequate or competent because, unlike Howard and O'Connor, we have not received assurance from others throughout our lives. Failing to recognize that we can and should depend on support from others, many of us attempt to travel emotionally and spiritually alone. Often, our survival instincts give us the impression that this is possible. Sometimes this takes the form of overworking and the belief that through our overproductivity, we will find the competence and adequacy we crave. When addressing these problems, the true prescription lies in rebuilding critical connections— that is, reconstructing healthy dependencies on others and God that have inevitably been severed in compulsive, unhealthy behavior. Healthy dependencies, however, are necessary to meet our emotional and spiritual needs and to develop our True Self.

Our primary dependency should be on God, a special link that works in conjunction with our relationship to self and others. In fact, we can trust God more than we can trust anyone else, including ourselves. How many times have we said, "I'll never do that again" and then proceed to do it anyway? Or maybe we've said, "I can't do that," but then find that we can. We change our minds, and this can be good; but we are ultimately not sure of many things. God's standard is unchanging, and for that reason, it is the model we must use within the core of our True Self.

We can form healthy relationships with people when we trust God as our core dependency. We are dependent by nature, from the womb to old age. If we do not find good relationships on which we can reasonably depend, we will often unconsciously create other, unhealthy dependencies. If our natural yearning for good is combined with negative dependencies, the result is often devastating confusion where we are unable to strengthen ourselves and grow further.

Our Natural Drive to Do Right

The family is the natural place where healthy forms of dependency are learned. Indeed, if they are not learned there, they are very likely not learned at all. While we may tumble into life, we do not have to tumble through it. Most of us never truly leave our homes, for we continue to re-create the patterns that we learned there—healthy or disastrous— at school, at work, and in our own homes.

We begin life as innocents, with everything we require for happiness inside us, needing only love and nurturing of our critical connections to bring it out. In closing, I am reminded of the story of a family who were expecting their second child. The parents were concerned that their oldest child, Jimmy, who was five years old, might have mixed feelings about welcoming their new member. Yet Jimmy had begun expressing considerable interest in getting a chance to talk to the new baby before it was even born.

Concerned about the oddity of his request and also wanting to protect the relationship between Jimmy and the new baby, the parents promised their son that he would be "the first person in the room after the birth." On the joyful morning, Jimmy's parents, as promised, had him come into the delivery room minutes after his new sister was born. Jimmy ran into the room, very excited, and said to the baby with total innocence, "Baby, tell me about God; I'm beginning to forget."

Jimmy knew something most of us have long ago forgotten: We, too, must strive to keep our contacts vigorous and alive. Instead of getting stuck in our patterns of diversions to our critical connection, we need to keep open our direct connection to God. While we may feel reluctant to face the unknown, to trust someone new, or to try a new activity, like Jimmy, we must engage life with a childlike innocence, not allowing its complexities to overshadow our critical connections.

In marriage, I have learned that one of life's greatest gifts is feeling comfortable enough to express my vulnerabilities to my wife. With her I can safely acknowledge that I do not have all the answers or do not really want to do something. My wife and I share in the critical connection that allows my world to open up. This same connection occurs when we unite in prayer or share our lives with others. Hard work will often bring us the rewards we seek, but we must not miss those rewards by being beaten down in the process. We need to keep our objectives and our means for achieving them in balance. As we have seen in this chapter, to be honestly fulfilled in life, we need to pursue our dreams while actively maintaining our critical connections.

THE REEVALUATION RETREAT:
TAKE ONE TWICE A YEAR

This exercise can help you open your heart and embrace your soul. Based on the qualities of our True Self, critical connections help us to strengthen our self-awareness, clarify our dependencies, and establish a process for regular self-evaluation. To discover that our connection to God is the only lasting source that we can count on, we often need to gain distance from and perspective on our life. People sometimes talk about going on retreats to gain a deeper sense of self-awareness; retreats may also provide us with an excellent way to stop the whirl-wind of life and regroup.

Your retreat should:

- provide peace and opportunity for personal reflection and prayer
- create an internal dialogue that enhances your self-awareness and movement toward wholeness
- shape your self and provide a clear evaluation for your course
- facilitate personal encounters with a higher power that create feelings of connectedness

Providing Peace   First, you will need plenty of uninterrupted quiet time during your retreat. Peace is one of the greatest gifts in life, and it is our spiritual center because it gives us the opportunity to see ourselves. Peace is the absence of anxiety, the presence of clear-mindedness, and the spirit of calm and joy. Those with a clear sense of themselves work from their centered self, immersed in peace. When we are centered in ourselves, we feel security, certainty, and power that emanates from within. Without peace, we often feel overwhelmed by choices and do not know where we are going. As the Mad Hatter told Alice in *Alice in Wonderland*, "If you're confused, any direction will do."

Creating Internal Dialogue   You can then move toward consistency and centeredness as you integrate your beliefs and activities. You must start by looking at your self. To perform a self-analysis, you need to create an internal dialogue. An internal dialogue emerges in quiet solitude and allows us to hear our inner voice. We then become self-aware and capable of taking responsibility for our lives.

Shaping the Self   Now you need to reevaluate your path, plan, and relationships. Through monitoring the True Self, we shape our convictions and directions, deciding what we need to do in our lives. Authentic living means functioning from within, not finding our direction by reacting to or being directed by others.

Encountering a Higher Power   You then need to find your place in creation and establish a link with the universal life force that many of us call God. Movement toward authenticity without a source of moral and spiritual values is, at best, indirect. Without God, truth comes as a mere reflection. God permeates all creation, and a meaningful retreat will lead to the filling of your life with the living God. Through spiritual listening, you can connect with the source of your soul. This may be accomplished through contact with nature, religious worship, or meditation. Retreats can be designed within a formal religious structure, but they can also take you on your own itinerary to the mountains or to the seashore, as long as you get away from your daily world.

Once you select your form of retreat, make the most of it. A retreat provides a context for refueling and gaining control of your direction. However we do it, we need to turn off the noise in order to hear the voice within. It does not matter whether your retreat takes place on the sacred sands of Mount Sinai or in your own home. If the setting and the props provide what you need to do the work, repeat it regularly. Whether you are single or married, living with a large family or living alone, retreats should separate you from your usual acquaintances while still placing you around people you trust. They should be scheduled twice a year to offer you regular opportunities to disengage from forces that take you in divergent directions.

11

⚛

FORMING YOUR CHARACTER

Be conscious of your thoughts; they become your words.
Contemplate your words; they become your actions.
Take care of your actions; they become habits.
Convert your habits; they become your character.
Be aware of your character; it becomes your destiny.
—AUTHOR UNKNOWN

NOT LONG AGO, I attended a special church service held by the Rainbow Coalition in Chicago. Hundreds of people had gathered together to praise God and hear numerous religious and political leaders give speeches in support of the organization. Between speeches, members of the congregation sang hymns and inspirational songs. During one such intermission, a five-year-old boy walked on stage to sing a popular ballad.

As the audience awaited his performance, the boy stood at the microphone and scanned the enormous crowd before him. As he attempted to sing the song, "The Wind Beneath My Wings," the sheer size of the crowd combined with the excitement in the room slowly drained his courage. He became so self-conscious and intimidated that his voice began to quiver. Although I felt the congregation watching him with increased support, his legs were buckling under the weight of the crowd's stare. Not knowing what to do, he began looking around, as if seeking a place to hide.

An older minister walked over, placed his arm around the child, and softly began to sing the words with him. With his support, the boy stopped shaking, and his voice slowly grew stronger. By the time he had reached the last stanza of the song, the boy was belting out the words, filling the church with overwhelming emotion. The congregants, teary-eyed at what they had just witnessed, rose with thundering applause as he finished. It was as if the song's message had come alive before our very eyes.

How we face our successes and failures has an enormous impact—either positive or negative—on the formation of our character. We all need support and a warm arm to help us through life's challenges. Healthy support freely given leads us to affirm our natural talents and to find our authentic inner character.

In this chapter, we will learn how to distinguish between portraying a character and actually developing our own self. We will learn how to build our character and nurture it by engaging the values we derive from our critical connections.

Being a Character and Having Character

Fictional characters have been around as long as recorded history. Serving as the heroes, heroines, and villains of treasured legends and intriguing myths, these characters are often designed to teach important lessons about the development of integrity. A greedy character is punished; a patient one is rewarded; and sometimes all must bow to the power of the gods. These characters still capture our imagination today, and their struggles do more than just show us how our life can be restricted or opened up by the qualities we possess. Their choices also reflect our own flaws and serve as models for overcoming them.

You may remember the powerful Hercules of Greek mythology, the strongest man who ever lived. His very name has become synonymous with fitness, power, and strength. Hercules, however, also had some character flaws: in stark contrast to his strong physique, his internal character had weaknesses. Although courageous and strong willed in the face of physical challenges, Hercules had difficulty making moral judgments. Love for wine and women were among his greatest weaknesses.

Hercules demonstrates how we may sometimes develop one side of our lives while neglecting our other dimensions. Although a model of physical strength, Hercules was not connected to the range of his intrinsic gifts and their role in his relationships. He mightily developed the power of Zeus, the god living within him, yet he remained one-sided, more a caricature than a person with character. Hercules is symbolic of the fact that we have the power of God inside us, but, like Hercules, we may not embrace it.

Another character, Oedipus, shows us that we do not have complete control over our lives, no matter how much we may desire it. Oedipus visited the Oracle at Delphi, where he was told that he would kill his father and marry his mother. Understandably, he tried to change his fate, so he moved far away from his family. Little did he know, however, that the parents who had brought him up were not his biological parents; his real parents now lived in the region to which he had fled. In the end, Oedipus proved the oracle true, killing his father and marrying his mother, without knowing their real relationship to him. When he learned the truth, he was so grief stricken that he gouged out his own eyes.

But the story of Oedipus carries another message: that we cannot solve our dilemmas through rational action alone. Oedipus thought that he could overcome forces he did not fully understand. Trying to overcome things that were beyond his control through rational action, Oedipus typifies our reluctance to recognize human limits.

Myths such as these, which are found in all cultures, highlight the virtues and vices within each of us. They should serve as our guides and inspiration. Sometimes, however, instead of viewing them as valuable lessons or cautionary tales, we unwittingly mimic the flaws of the characters and fail to look at their deeper messages—in the same way that we sometimes blindly imitate famous people of our own time. We may even permit ourselves to be stereotyped, falling into social categories or affiliating ourselves with certain groups. Many of us can probably remember people from school branded "a ditz," "a brain," "a jock," or simply "a cool dude." If we simply stop and consider how far our own reputations can be from the complex reality of our lives, we know that such images fail to convey the character of the real person. Both judging others through limited character traits and allowing ourselves to be so categorized covers up the True Self. One who tries to live up to a stereotype abandons the True Self and masquerades as another person.

Moreover, if we allow others to stereotype us, we will become characters and not shape our character. Let me illustrate this process through a historical figure who comes down to us almost entirely through myth. Xanthippe, wife of the eminent philosopher Socrates, became unfairly portrayed. Xanthippe developed an image as a nagging shrew who constantly griped and failed to understand her husband. In historical accounts, she was always depicted as a spouse who belittled her mate, continually dissatisfied and forever complaining. But the opposite was probably true: Xanthippe was not a horrific person but was likely one of the most progressive and understanding women of her time. Although it is true that her husband was an extraordinary thinker, Socrates was uncannily unconventional and noncommittal. Whether Xanthippe's reputation was created by those who misunderstood her actions or by a begrudging local historian, her character has been unfairly connected with men whose egos lead them to feel that they are like Socrates and also have nagging, ungrateful wives.

Many of the well-known individuals I have interviewed have had their characters portrayed wrongly through the years, just as Xanthippe experienced. Remember the story of Ambassador Jeane Kirkpatrick, who had been dubbed the "iron lady," or Ron Howard as "Opie." Famous people (and especially actors who play certain characters) are often victims of such misrepresentation. Lucille Ball was regarded as "merciless and impossible to please" when she became president of Desilu Studios; Bette Davis was thought to be "incorrigible and flippant." By contrast, male actors tend to be given strikingly positive characteristics: Tom Hanks is said to be a "solid, wonderful guy"; and Ron Howard cannot seem to escape his image of being "the boy next door."

Rather than stereotypes or broad characterizations, I believe that we all want an honest appraisal of our well-intentioned efforts. To do less is to stifle our person and our character, regardless of whether the judgments are good or bad. In the end, the most accurate measure of character is our long-term behavior. And as we shall see, some find that the best way to know the genuine character of a person is to see how they respond to adversity.

We have seen that imposing a characterization on a person is damaging. What we seek—even for those who are professional actors—is not to be type cast in our life, but to have the opportunity to claim our true identity. To do this, all of us must establish our true character through our True Self.

What Is Character?

Our character comprises the attributes that come out in our actions and distinguish our person. Each of us has different gifts and a different personality. On the basis of these gifts, we each express particular virtues, and through these virtues our particular character is formed. Thus, we each develop our True Self with different virtues. Some virtues that both nurture the True Self and give expression to our character include:

compassion	empathy
confidence	equality
consideration	fairness
courage	faith
determination	holiness
discipline	honesty

hope
integrity
loyalty
optimism

perseverance
responsibility
strength
wisdom

How Do We Build Character?

Even though it often involves following the lessons and examples of ethics, our character first needs to spring from inside ourself. Developing character means discovering the qualities of our True Self, nurturing those qualities, and integrating virtue with our talents. This lifelong process involves the interconnections of our history, our personality, and the innate qualities of our True Self with values we want to bring into our life.

When I visited the monasteries of Mount Athos in Greece, I noticed that the monks there had taped little axioms and scriptural passages on the walls, at the doorways, and by book shelves as reminders, prompts, and lessons to help them reach their goals. The monks are, strangely enough, a bit like B. F. Skinner: they design their environment to guide their behavior; and with prompts to reinforce their actions, they recognize how the world affects them. Do you place prompts in your environment to affect you?

While education and external prompts can help shape character, they alone do not constitute it. Many of us live in serene environments yet remain oblivious to the natural beauty and calm surrounding us. In addition to a good setting, character formation requires good behavior, good thoughts, good feelings, and the Spirit to nurture them. We can hear an inspiring story and be open to the idea of good character, but implementing those qualities in our life requires something else—enactment. We have all been through enough schooling and counseling to know that external lessons alone cannot fully transform our feelings or behaviors, just as a sermon does not always make us act differently or change our ways.

What we see when we are growing up influences our development. We reflect the atmosphere and attitudes of our environment. One man who I was counseling left his job to become a high school teacher. He had always wanted to teach and was enthusiastic and excited by his new career. Following his retraining, classes, and exams, he began teaching science and math. However, so distressed was he by his students' poor attitude and their lack of interest and cooperation that he resigned after six months. He was shocked by the students' lack of manners and respect. By contrast, another patient, a substitute teacher in another town, absolutely loved his teaching experience. The school emphasized respect and values and not just the classroom lessons. Both teachers and students realized that they were benefiting from the environment they all worked to create.

Identifying models that have good character, recognizing good character, and establishing rules that affirm the respect of (and for) each individual are at the foundation of character building. Models of good character are found in literature and in both ancient and modern heroes and heroines. Sometimes, however, it can be difficult to select good models in a sea of lost ships that can surround us. One evening I was watching an early-evening sitcom with my young children. The show opened with a little boy being sarcastic (with the intention of being humorous), commenting about who his single parent was sleeping with. As I quickly changed the channel, my kids asked, "What's so funny?" The modeled moral confusion and sarcasm was supposed to make you laugh. I believe the antidote to moral confusion is reading, watching, talking about, and building good character.

We can exercise our strength of good character especially by calling on the qualities of our True Self. Sandra Day O'Connor commented about how modern life leaves us so independent rather than interdependent—essentially how it leaves us with a self that does not know how to connect with others. We can often change our world. For example it's often fascinating to engage people that you do not really know. On the other hand, if you do not say hello or are not particularly pleasant, you may never know who they are. A smile, a kind gesture, a pleasant statement can turn these isolated individuals into meaningful connections. By extending ourselves positively toward others, more often than not we open up new opportunities for growth and exchange.

In our homes, we must establish standards of behavior to build good character. Do we have rules of respect for one another? My grand-mother would regularly counsel, "If you do not have respect, you do not have anything." Truer words have never been spoken. Because if we do not have respect, we cannot really listen, we cannot really care, and we cannot really learn how to love.

Character building, acts of kindness, and goodness make every-one feel safe and able to grow. And just as schools may have rules to offer structure that help everyone, they should celebrate everyone as well. Part of character building is having fun. Celebrations reinforce the bond of the community at home, school, or work. Enjoyment is both a by-product and a goal of character building.

Better Than Good Enough

What is it that we can do to assist our development of good charac-ter? In psychology, efforts to release parents from the demands of per-fectionism sometimes draw on Donald Winnicott's notion of the "good-enough mother" and acknowledge that although we cannot be perfect, if we try our best "we will do good enough." The idea of being good enough is realistic and relieves the well-intentioned parent of the destructiveness of doing it perfectly.

Nonetheless, there has always been something about this phrase that felt lacking to me—not in the context given by Winnicott (who would never support mediocrity), but in the implication of the catch phrase: "Do what you can, and don't sweat it." I think that to sympa-thetically conclude that our best is necessarily good enough, we first need to have a definition of our best and what is good. Particularly in the task of guiding our children in their character, we need to assess our effectiveness by looking at our results.

Clearly, how parents relate to others often carries the greatest messages to our kids. We may say to our children, "Don't do as I do, but do as I say." But we must accept that our actions have the most lasting impact on the formation of our children's character.

Possessing Integrity

Character development is intricately related to those who nurture us. As so many often remark, our parents show up in our own adult selves. Thus, it is not surprising that from the way Diane Sawyer describes her parents, we can understand some of her own character: she calls her father a "lighthouse" who weathered storms, shining forth as a beacon through the fog, giving direction to those in his midst; and she describes her mother as "sheer rocket fuel," giving her children vitality and energy for achieving goals beyond their imagined boundaries. Diane Sawyer is the harbinger who greets Americans every morning in ABC's news magazine. She is a beacon for identifying injustice with her investigative reports. In her we can clearly see the influence of her parents.

Sawyer grew up in rural Kentucky, near Glasgow, with her parents and two sisters. Her father was a lawyer and her mother a schoolteacher. Their family attended, and was "extremely involved" in the local Methodist church that her father had helped establish. She described her Scottish-Irish background as a significant factor in the family's dynamics, characterizing her cultural ancestors as a "spiritually and physically wiry people." Among them were pioneers who had crossed the Cumberland Gap into Kentucky and whose determination came down through the generations. But in reference to the more immediate impact of her upbringing, Sawyer sees herself as "the product of parents who believed in the perfectibility of children."

The parents sought every opportunity for their children. With her mother's encouragement, Sawyer's father began working in the "big city," moving the entire family out of their small hometown and into urban life. Sawyer attended Wellesley, a rigorous women's college near Boston and graduated in 1967. After her father's death in a car accident, Sawyer returned to Kentucky and worked at WLKY-TV in Louisville for three years.

In 1970, she took an administrative position in the press office of Richard Nixon's White House, a position that became quite dicey once the Watergate scandal broke. After the allegations arose and made headlines, Sawyer decided to remain on Nixon's staff throughout the ordeal, until his resignation. Sawyer explained her loyalty this way:

> If I would have abandoned him then, I just don't know how I could have felt honorable. And it was just my way of saying, we're all human, and in this moment, I'm not going to run away.

Many in Washington disapproved of Sawyer's decision, and her association with the president nearly ruined her burgeoning journalism career. For her, though, it was a matter of individual conscience, of "being able to live with what I'd done" if she had "left in the president's greatest time of need." While history or hindsight may not have vindicated Nixon, we gain a glimpse of Sawyer's character—her honor, loyalty, and integrity. She attributed her decision to her father's strong belief in maintaining one's honor. He taught her as a child not to let "any opportunity override a sense of duty."

After Nixon's resignation, Sawyer even assisted him in completing his memoirs, feeling it her duty to get the historical record correct after Watergate. Clearly, Sawyer does not run scared when the world closes around her. She discerns the situation from within, potentially risking her future to do what is right.

Sawyer then moved into journalism, joining *CBS News* as a reporter in their Washington bureau. Her personal standards of presenting the audience with the unblemished facts helped her ascend quickly into the world of television journalism, eventually becoming one of the highest paid and most respected women in the industry.

Even with all of her successes, professional accolades, and broadcasting awards, Sawyer has remained a very modest person, refraining from self-promotion and deflecting attention away from herself, preferring to highlight the issues she has covered. The integrity of her work is based on the facts; for her a job well done is one in which she avoids bias and is able to enhance public awareness. Personal satisfaction springs from these moral basics.

When I asked Sawyer how she deals with her own feelings about the injustices she reports, she candidly said that sometimes she can barely stand them. Faced regularly with the challenge of accepting whatever impact she can have on the terrible situations she sees, Sawyer says she resolves to "go for the biggest change you can make. And knowing that you have other changes to make, you've then got to move on and do the next thing."

Sawyer's professional involvement has, of course, come with some trade-offs. So focused on her career, Sawyer did not marry until she was forty-two and a well established member of *60 Minutes*. Her husband, film director Mike Nichols, had already been married twice and had children. This family life opened the door for Sawyer to experience parenting without actually having children herself. When I asked if she had ever felt a biological and emotional need to have her own children or if she carried any regrets, she openly remarked: "Everybody thinks it's so mysterious not to have your own children. But if you don't marry until you're forty-two ... lots of other factors come into play. If I had married when I was thirty, I probably would have them." Moreover, she did not want to add strain to her husband's already established family. She said of her step-children, "I love them so much, and I want them to be happy. I don't want them to think I'm taking their father away."

In all, Sawyer seems to have achieved that elusive melding of professional and personal life, even if it came a little later in her life.

Sawyer lists her priorities as family, love, and work, and she describes her desires this way: "I think that what I want, and what I hope I want, are the same thing. I mean family; I mean laughter. The random pleasures of every phone call and every moment spent together."

Such "random pleasures" come from a sense that she and her spouse have a duty to continually surprise one another: "We spook each other all the time. I'm so present in the room [and] to everything that's going on in the room. He's a dreamer; he's just so trusting. I can do the concrete; he can do what we're really living for."

Arising, then, from her parent's strong influence, Sawyer's character—marked by honor, loyalty, and integrity—is deeply rooted in her commitment to both her family and to her profession. The strong base she developed in childhood has led her to handle all stories, regardless of the different emotions they raise within her. She sees the light, and she knows where she's headed. The "rocket fuel" inherited from her mother fills her with a reserve of great energy and power. Though unassuming, she has great confidence and a solid sense of purpose in life, built from integrity and a respect for her personal history.

Having Character and Being Real

We often want to ask, "Am I good or am I bad? Am I an angel or a devil?" The truth is that we do not fall into either of these extremes, because as Diane Sawyer remarked to me, "we're all human." The defining moment for character is neither simple nor singular: we define our character over and over again every time we place (or do not place) ourselves at risk to uphold a principle. According to the dynamic definition of character, we could call Sawyer empathetic and loyal for risking her future welfare by continuing to work for Richard Nixon during the Watergate scandal. This risk took character.

We should remember that even those people we place up on a pedestal have both positive and negative qualities. They are real, not ideal, just like the rest of us. The ways we often have of knowing such people—magnifying their strengths and weaknesses, believing that their flaws are the reason for their fall—are too simple and are insufficient models for assessing our True Self. We must avoid total idealization and total denigration of ourselves, because both can harm us.

Psychologists describe a phenomenon called the "halo effect," wherein a person is viewed by society through the lens of one outstanding trait or quality. Experiments, for example, show that people tend to credit an attractive person with intelligence, grace, and other admirable qualities. We see this sort of character by association everyday in the media. For example, the prowess of a famous baseball player gets transferred to the particular shoes he wears; or a political figure's opinion about a subject is accepted as authoritative and factual. We know that no correlation exits between these associations, but the glow of the halo leads us to generalize the actual facts.

The Golden Girl

Jessica Savitch, the first woman anchor for *NBC News*, is one person who experienced this halo effect. In the early 1980s, Savitch paved the way for women to enter broadcasting, a field that had been traditionally dominated by men. I first met with Jessica in 1980. In an atmosphere of uncertainty about the role of women in the media, Savitch's physical attributes were a bigger issue than they should have been. She described her feelings about the halo effect like this:

> No matter what I do, no matter how many awards I get for reporting, people will always say first that I'm a "petite blonde" and second a "network reporter." I have distinguished myself as a reporter, but it makes no difference overall. It makes a difference to me, and I think it makes a difference to the viewers. But it's a put-down to viewers to say that they would watch somebody just because she's some blonde lady on TV.

For years, Savitch brought millions of Americans the news; she became a familiar face in the American household. But tragedy struck in 1983 when she was drowned in an automobile accident. Both before and after her accident, Jessica's character was idealized and distorted; her story reflects the important difference between having a character and being a character.

Savitch hoped her work would show the industry that women were capable of taking on the most prominent positions. These actions defined her character, but the stereotypes she faced were many and strong:

> In our modern society, with regard to men, you have a choice. If you do your job well, then it means you are decisive; it means you have opinions and a plan of action and you lead. All of those things are described as positive things for men. When you take the same adjectives and you apply them to a woman, what do you call her? "Tough!" You call the men "decisive," "bright," "masterful." You call the women "tough." I don't think I'm any tougher than any male in the business; probably less so. I don't see myself as personally tough at all. But I must display, in this position, those qualities which are usually in this society applied to men. "She's tough!" He's "aggressive" yet "terrific."

Like so many other successful and powerful women we have seen, Savitch endured a double standard. A thoughtful and loving person, Savitch was sensitive to her critics but kept a healthy distance from them.

During one of my visits to interview Savitch, I watched off-camera as she presented a one-minute news update. She seemed strong, totally in control, with a strong sense of poise and delivery. She ended the segment with a humorous aside and her usual tender smile. What made her words so striking was that only moments before, Savitch had been emotionally recalling the tragic events of her husband Donald's recent suicide for my interview. As she portrayed the character of Jessica Savitch the reporter, Savitch the widow was desperately hurting inside. Still processing the events, she poignantly said:

> I'm widowed. His life ended in suicide this past August after a lengthy illness. He had aggravated liver disease brought on by hepatitis that he had had seven years ago, before I knew him. It caused more severe liver dam-

age than anyone realized. The only two parts of my life were my work and my husband. Yes, the other half of my life is gone. I just realized what I said: the other half is not there anymore. There were two parts to my life, and one part . . . one part is not there.

This woman who had so tragically lost her father at an early age had now lost the other love of her life. She described her relationship with Donald as her "very first intimate relationship." Visited with so much despair in her life, Savitch had a profound answer when I asked for her personal definition of happiness:

You see, "happiness" doesn't just come to you. You can't set up a way that it comes to you. The things I thought would make me the happiest didn't, and the other moments did. Other people and fulfillment at work, in concert—these two things make up the formula for happiness. And if you can enjoy them in good health, that's the optimum!

She then spoke about judgment and characterization, echoing a familiar theme in this chapter:

Stars are some of the most unsuccessful people in the world. Never, never, never equate recognizability or earning large sums of money with success. That is not success—although it may be part of it. I see success as internal and external: someone who is able to contribute and to draw some measure of happiness from the contribution.

Savitch found that her professional calling provided a mode for truth and integrity in her personal life:

See, my job is to figure out what is the truth. My whole objective then is to take the message to the people. I have sought to bring this to bear in my personal life too: to be true, to find out what are my truths, to be honest, fair, and compassionate. Most of all, finding out what is truth to yourself is the big thing. I used to think that I would be a good reporter if I just found out what the truth was on a given story, but you first have to understand what basic philosophies you have before you can become a good reporter. You have to understand what you are about in order to see clearly. You have to know yourself and your limitations before you seek to find out truth from other people.

We are all, according to Savitch's profound metaphor, investigators who must know where we stand before we seek the truth from others. She realized that her critical connections and her True Self needed to remain balanced. She was a thoughtful and courageous woman who, through her own determination and discipline, had coped with the tragedies in her life and opened doors for other women. Her wisdom was well beyond her years.

After her death, her contributions were overshadowed by rumors about her personal life, which essentially dissolved her strong reputation. Two weeks after the accident, I met with her assistant in New York City. All traces of her existence seemed eliminated at NBC. The one whose life had been glossed over by the "halo effect" had been harshly judged by the same society that had endowed her with the halo.

Everybody Wants to Be a Star   We began this chapter by talking about mythological figures who did not possess character but were characters. Celebrities are their modern-day equivalents, and we would do well to understand the pitfalls of believing their inaccurate popular images. For some, an illusory fulfillment comes from the quest for one's so-called "fifteen minutes of fame." While potentially exciting and glamorous, such a quest really speaks to the hunger for attention and recognition. And this quest can undermine a search for the True Self.

Even though she enjoyed being a celebrity, Jessica Savitch found the search for popular success unfulfilling. Having pursued it too far, she recognized that she had suffered great personal loss in neglecting her critical connections. In speaking with me about her personal relationships, she emphasized that she needed to establish solid roots in her own personal life.

Savitch's story underscores the potential parody of the term *character*. At the young age of thirty, she had achieved what no other woman had before, but the strength of her own character suffered from the confusion between her genuine character and the characters she played in modern culture, where she was described as the "Golden Girl" (*Newsweek*), the "Marilyn Monroe of TV news," and a "Pop Mythological Woman" (*USA Today*). After her death, the ravenous interest of some dismantled her character and ate away at her worthy legacy. Because she did not identify with her colleagues, many of them even commented that she had been on illicit drugs when she died and that she had severe emotional problems.

I wanted to protect her memory when I saw how others turned on her. The genuine qualities of character—her courage, insight, caring, perseverance, and strength should not have drowned with her. Jessica's extraordinary character in the face of such adversity counts for more than the "character" she was said to have played. At thirty-six her life ended, but her contribution to journalism, to women, and to society will remain.

In the age of information, leaders often shudder at the thought that their private lives and indiscretions could be used against them someday, cloaking their character in scandal. This paranoia depletes many of us, leading many to choose to maintain a low profile than to risk humiliation.

Indeed, we are all human, seeking and needing to grow in character, not wanting to become characters in someone else's drama. The awakening of true coming of age is available to everyone who holds on to the True Self. Let us now look at yet another anchor who has successfully built up his character.

Meeting the Test

If our character is best illustrated by how we respond to crises, Tom Brokaw's character was truly on display during one of our country's most challenging periods—the terrorist attacks of September 11, 2001, and the anthrax attacks that followed. Not only was he thrust into what he called an "out-of-body experience" in having to report on the devastating World Trade Center assault, but he was put into the surreal position of becoming news himself as he became the target of the subsequent anthrax attacks.

We met in November 2001, after the impact of the disaster had somewhat settled, to follow up on some of our earlier conversations. Visibly worn by both the added workload and security procedures, Brokaw put on his familiar stolid face and calmly explained:

> I had no idea that anything like that would happen. But if it had to happen, I'm glad that I was at this stop in my life, in my career (referring to his approaching retirement). I think it requires the kind of professional and personal perspective to get through those long days. The anthrax layer on top of that made it all the more difficult.

Brokaw was the intended recipient of an anthrax letter sent to his office. But it was his assistant Erin who actually opened the letter and was exposed to the deadly virus. Only days before the anthrax incident, Erin had told Brokaw that their office received a lot of "nutty mail" that she never showed to him and that the office was especially vulnerable since September 11. He responded by saying, "Well, we're going to get you out of the mail-opening business." After Erin was exposed, Brokaw said he felt "angry and responsible at a lot of different levels—responsible for her welfare because it was a letter addressed to me."

After the terrorist attacks and the anthrax incident, there was a ton of tension in the news room. Everyone had been pushed beyond their limits, yet according to Brokaw, "everybody performed magnificently." To raise their morale while the staff all took their prescribed dosage of Cipro, Brokaw poured each a shot of Jack Daniels to go along with it. He recalled the scene:

> I went out and bought a bunch of Jack Daniels whiskey and had everybody come in. It was like something out of the old westerns: we just stood

at the bar and had one straight shot of Jack Daniels, trusted each other, toasted them, and went home.

While Brokaw denied being afraid, he nevertheless recognized how disturbing and potentially harmful the letter could have been for him. He had been in many dangerous places before, but he had always managed to make wise decisions. As he said, "It was a random attack. I didn't think it was a part of a sustained effort to knock me off."

Not only did Brokaw raise his troops' morale, but as a voice of the nation, he buoyed millions of Americans with his newscasts. But weeks after September 11, Brokaw found some times too difficult to handle:

> I got unexpectedly emotional in the course of the interview after Erin opened the envelope containing Anthrax. I was just overwhelmed by it. I know that you cannot remove the personal component. I always think that you have to be very careful about how you strike the balance.

Brokaw's poised manner was clearly reflected when controversy arose over television reporters wearing American flag pins in the weeks following the attacks. Although it seemed logical that he would be the first to display the flag—as he had been specifically targeted—his stance was actually detached from the personal attack. In fact, he chose not to wear an American flag pin because he knew that might be interpreted in many ways:

> I think you have to be careful. I know there was a huge emotional wave of patriotism running across the country. I felt it. There was a surge, you know—"By God, you're among us." My job here is to be that place you can turn to before you ask the questions of "military tribunal versus regular trials" or "How involved do we get in Afghanistan?"

Brokaw's sound judgment and honesty led him to feel at ease dealing with this new reality without candy-coating it. Brokaw's goal, even in harried, raucous times, was to get the full story.

Brokaw described his dad as someone from "a pretty rough and tumble background" who had dropped out of school in the third grade.

His mother he described as very bright, "oriented toward books and public affairs." Though her family had lost everything in the Great Depression, they were well educated: her uncles were doctors and lawyers. Tom followed in the intellectual line of his mother, but his father was perhaps an even bigger, awe-inspiring influence on him:

> He was a big presence. He was very strong: red hair, mechanically gifted. He was pretty stern. He really had no parents growing up; he was just kind of thrown into the street. He was tough on us boys at home—but not abusive. He had high expectations. We had a wonderfully mature relationship from an early age.

He characterized his parents as the perfect "yin and yang combination": his mother "bookish, interesting, verbal, placing a premium on what's going on in the world"; his father the "strong, silent type, with a wonderful sense of humor." They both gave Tom confidence and a grasp on the world:

> From books to the world news events, from the workshop to sporting actions, from fishing and hunting to libraries and research. Being good Christians was an underpinning of our lives, but it was not something that took our lives.

Valuing hard work, managing several tasks at once, and striving for excellence were behaviors Brokaw learned early in life and incorporated into his character.

Where did all his poise come from? Like Diane Sawyer, Brokaw was a whiz kid in high school, supported by hard-working parents with whom he had a strong relationship. He admitted to me, though, that when he began college at the University of Iowa, he rode for a while on his reputation of being a "boy wonder." He behaved more like a "jock" (though he did not play college sports) and ended his first couple years "majoring in coeds and beer drinking." Then, at the University of South Dakota, a highly respected professor shocked him into reality. Over dinner one night Brokaw recalls this professor saying, "I've been thinking about what you're going to do with your life, and I believe I have an answer." Brokaw asked his professor what he meant and he replied, "I think you should drop out. You're wasting my time, you're wasting your time, you're wasting your parents' money. Just get out of here for a while, and get it out of your system, whatever it is." This advice floored Brokaw, but also marked a major turning point in his life, permitting him to see himself and his limits.

This wake-up call was soon followed by another, in the form of a devastating letter from his girlfriend, Meredith. She wanted to break up with Brokaw because she found him "so unformed." The simultaneous blows from academic and romantic angles cast Brokaw into a brief period of disillusionment; but he soon returned to college and won back the attention of both his professor and Meredith, the woman he would later marry.

With these as the only set backs he recalls (and temporary setbacks at that), Brokaw calls himself "the world's luckiest guy." While he may have gotten off course in his college days, he could return to the strong roots of his upbringing. He attributes his work ethic to the perseverance of his father. He admitted, "I still measure myself by my parents' values, how they define success, and how they defined the work ethic." In raising his own three daughters, he and his wife model their parenting after their own parents' unconditional love. In all, he knows, "I've had a blessed life."

CHARACTERS, HEROES, AND HEROINES SELF-EXAMINATION

Think about the role models that you looked up to in your childhood. What character qualities attracted you to them?

NAMES	CHARACTER	QUALITIES
1.		
2.		
3.		

NAMES	CHARACTER	QUALITIES
4.		
5.		

Did you find yourself seeking different character models at different points in your life? How so? Which of these character qualities are part of your life?

Do you think that you serve as a model of character qualities for others? If so, which qualities and for whom?

NAMES	CHARACTER	QUALITIES
1.		
2.		
3.		
4.		
5.		

TELEVISION, MOVIES, AND BOOKS: HEROES AND HEROINES

Think back about the heroes and heroines that you had from watching television, going to the movies, and reading.

1. What qualities most appealed to you—and from which individuals?
2. Why do you think you were attracted to those qualities?
3. Did your interest have any effect on you?
4. Which of these experiences had the greatest impact on you personally? Why?

12

⌒∞⌒

BEING FULFILLED

Nothing in excess.
—Ancient Greek maxim,
inscribed in the Temple at Delphi

The Olympic Games are thrilling to watch. This dazzling spectacle assembles athletes from around the world to compete with each other, sometimes establishing new records of strength, speed, and skill. More important, as these athletes test themselves against their own best efforts and those of others, it is all about human potential.

For the ancient Greeks, the Olympics were about more than athletic ability and prowess. Central to the games was the notion of *arete*, the balance of body, mind, and soul. To embody *arete*, an athlete needed not just physical power, but also virtue, valor, nobility, and a drive toward excellence. The games that took place in ancient Greece thus exercised the whole person—just as we have been learning to do in this book. The total balance of *arete* is essentially what we have been talking about all along: our ability to balance our True Self with others and God, keeping body and heart connected with the Spirit.

To illustrate their complete personhood, the athletes in ancient Greece did not wear uniforms or clothing; instead, they competed in the nude, expressing their complete connection to their bodies. This was not about sensuality but was rather about a sense of wholeness and goodness—body, mind, and soul converging in an extraordinary feat. Their nudity also tested their ability to focus on the activity at hand, in which they tapped into the spirit in expression of *arete*. Claiming he had come to the games to honor the athletes who display *arete*, Pindar wrote in 464 B.C.:

> *Truly blessed is he who is surrounded by constant good*
> *repute,*
>   *for the grace who give the bloom of life now favors one,*
>   *then another*
>   *with both the sweet-singing lyre and the variegated notes*
>   *of the flute . . .*
> *Father Zeus, give honor to this hymn for a victor at*
>   *Olympia, and to his now famous arete in boxing.*
> *Grant him grace and reverence among his townsfolk and*
>   *among foreigners.*
> *He travels the straight path which despises hubris,*
>   *and he learned well the righteous precepts of good forefathers.*

But while Pindar and others glorified athletes, some claimed that the idealization of athletics overlooked the excesses of greed, self-glorification, and corruption that some athletes displayed. Athletes' heroization was as much a reality then as it is today.

We see, then, that the Greek athlete is an excellent model for us as we complete our learning about true coming of age. These athletes struggled, as we often do, overemphasizing one aspect of what was meant to be a holistic pursuit; they, too, had to keep the principles behind their feats in view; and they, too, suffered from excess and irrational idealization. Nonetheless, *arete* directed the Olympian athletes in positive ways and toward success in the games, and this principle can do the same for us. In this final chapter, as we embark on our true coming of age, we will see how the idea of *arete* can guide our voyage to fulfillment. In this chapter, we see why we must seek balance through our True Self and our critical connections; we explain how an authentic life integrates our body, mind, and soul; we show how to embark in our gift of life through true coming of age; and we learn how to find fulfillment by fully attuning to our True Self, opening our heart, and embracing our soul.

The Need for Balance

Avoiding extremes and establishing moderation were the basic principles of ancient Greek culture, as reflected in two ancient maxims: *meden agan*, literally translated as "no extremes," and *pan metron ariston*, literally, "measure is always best."

For the Greeks, *amartia*—literally, "missing the mark"—occurs when we do not maintain balance in our life. Aristotle uses the term in defining a tragic character's fatal flaw, though the term is often translated into English today as "sin." In fact, the ancient Greek *amartia*, however, was a violation of personal balance, not of moral law. Only during the Judeo-Christian period of Hellenism, during the first century, did *amartia* become associated with morality. But for the Greeks, whenever a person is pulled into extremes and loses perspective, he or she "misses the mark," drifting from the center of the True Self and submitting to chaos.

Modern research confirms the importance of retaining balance of body, mind, and soul. To a great extent, the renaissance of holistic health and spirituality in recent years is our culture's effort to reclaim this balance. Through mind-body research, scientists have been rediscovering for us the intricate connections of our True Self, heart, and soul, proving that the well-being of the mind is intimately intertwined with that of the body, and vice versa. Though we often forget it, the mind is part of the body: the brain is an organ like every other, dependent on neurotransmitters that communicate between nerves and enable us to act. When we make love, go running, or eat chocolate, the same neurotransmitters sense and register the pleasure of what we feel. Similarly, we find that many conditions (depression, for instance) can be treated successfully with a broad spectrum of interventions—drugs, psychotherapy, spirituality, and alternative therapies ranging from nutrition to biofeedback. Each avenue—body, mind, and soul—provides support for healing. We are undoubtedly healthiest and most complete when we attune to our whole psychosomatic being.

Balance treats stress for what it is—a burden on our bodies. In line with this mind-body research, studies have shown that mental stress depletes our immune reserves, creating both acute and chronic illnesses. Most of us encounter stressors regularly—from positive events, like hosting weddings or parties, to negative ones, like deaths and job loss. The key to dealing with stress is the same as absorbing a blow to the body: to move with the force and thus avoid the loss of balance upon impact. This strategy is also affirmed in Japanese aikido, a holistic tradition that teaches practitioners to move with the ki, or the force: If a force is coming at you, do not fight it head-on and absorb the brunt of it; redirect it, or move with it, elsewhere. In other words, use the intrinsic gifts of the True Self to redirect the force of stressors and maintain your balance.

When we are not alert to the positive and negative energy we encounter, we may find ourselves immobilized, targeted, and disillusioned. As adaptive creatures, we do learn to cope when faced with difficulty; we manage our circumstances, often unconsciously and without reflection. But these automatic survival strategies are not our best option; relied on too often, they too can end up disrupting our balance.

The purpose of this book has been to provide habits of self-management that are better than these autoresponses. When confronted by disillusionment—whether through individual events or their cumulative effect—we begin to ask some of those basic questions we have already raised, ones we may have thought we already answered: Who am I? Is there a God? Why is this happening? To whom can I turn for help?

While we may be able to come up with partial answers to these questions, the deeper problem often remains. Traumatized or disoriented we may have lost our inner compass. Moreover, what we may ultimately lose is contact; we may lose balance in our own self-assessments, our relationships to others, and in our experience of our spirituality.

When the plan we had for life, the one we thought would work, has become confused, we can feel abandoned by everyone—including God. But we can always restore balance and find our answers by reestablishing our True Self and our critical connections.

Balance does not mean that we walk through life as though on a tight rope, struggling to achieve perfection. We have to live fully without an unrealistic sense of control. Each of us is also unique in our coping strategies. Within our unique vessels, we move through the sea toward our goals, prepared to encounter difficulties and absorb them without being consumed by them. We can create *arete*.

In the story that follows, we see how one has pursued his own true coming of age in the spirit of holistic balance and *arete*.

A Grandfather for a Nation

Whenever I have sat down to talk with C. Everett Koop, surgeon general during the Reagan administration, I have always felt like a young boy, listening to the fascinating stories of his grandfather. Koop's tales of his personal experiences are filled with tremendous moral lessons. Beyond his professional accomplishments— innovator in children's surgical practice and namesake of the C. Everett Koop Institute at Dartmouth Medical School—for many years he has been America's "grandfather," exhibiting wisdom, personal convictions, and compassion for humanity's well-being. As a good doctor and a vibrant human being, Koop embraces life's opportunities to learn and grow. He is an example of balance and *arete*, teaching us to live well in all aspects of our life.

When Koop was in medical school, most doctors were uncomfortable with anesthetizing infants and young children; pediatric surgery was relatively unknown in mainstream practice. He thus had few role models. In fact, there were only six pediatric surgeons practicing at that time in the entire country. By the time he was thirty-two, however, he had taken a position as surgeon-in-chief at the Philadelphia Children's Hospital, where he established the country's first neonatal intensive care nursery. Then Koop worked his way up the academic ladder at the University of Pennsylvania School of Medicine, becoming professor of pediatric surgery in 1959. He also went on to found the American Academy of Surgeons and its journal publications. He is widely regarded as a forefather of pediatric surgery.

In the 1960s and 1970s, science and religion were widely viewed as separate paths to healing. But Koop had studied medicine during the 1930s when it was still taught that spirituality had a place in medicine. He had been integrating his faith with his work since his first surgical procedure, amputating a patient's leg when Koop was only nineteen: "I can assure you," he told me, "the procedure was immediately preceded by a short prayer." As a resident, Koop remembered learning from older, wiser clinicians the importance of using a patient's own faith to heal. He explained, "Find those things in each patient's armamentarium which can assist healing and use them. If it is garlic tied to the forehead in a silk stocking for a headache, use it; if it's prayer, use that too." His understanding of faith as a resource for healing is linked to research showing that lifestyle changes can postpone death in 75 percent of ailing patients—while typical rehabilitative procedures, from pills to operations, are only 15 percent effective. Koop elaborated: "I think one of the big problems in medicine is that we don't always give the right medicine to the particular problem." But as a young doctor, while embracing the spiritual and emotional needs of patients, he was still hesitant to bring his own faith fully into the doctor-patient relationship, primarily due to concern for professional boundaries.

In 1968, however, Koop underwent his own personal trauma—and an epiphany. His son David died while rock climbing in New Hampshire. An avid and experienced climber, David was scaling a cliff that suddenly sheared in two, breaking all of his safety ropes in the process.

This horrific event brought Koop to a valley that he had never before seen. Thirty years later, Koop broke into tears when he recalled the event to me, describing his immediate reaction when hearing news of the accident after church:

> I was physically unable to stand; so I leaned into the table and put my arms around my family. I prayed [an] absolutely positive prayer, and I asked to keep my faith in God's will. I think that his death has been the most important experience in my life . . . not only the worst, but the most important.

When Koop first returned to the hospital after David's death, he was not sure he could continue working as a surgeon because he found it difficult to remain professionally detached from the plight of the parents of his young patients. Whenever he approached a dying child or grieving parents, he became overwhelmed by tears himself. Changed by the experience, his empathy led to agony as he faced suffering parents, for in them he now saw his bereaved self. "The loss of a child is unlike any other loss; it upsets both our personal balance and our sense of the natural balance of time."

Koop's words resonate with our theme: he was finding it nearly impossible to redirect the blow of David's death and maintain balance:

> I did; I do. I not only experienced genuine contact with my patients, but genuine contact with God. I had submitted; I trusted. This contact changed me and ever since. It directs me.

Leaning on his religious convictions to move forward after David's death, Koop realized something positive had come out of the traumatic event. His new empathy brought him closer to his patients. He regarded prayer in his hospital ward as a needed outlet for families, a means for enduring a loss. Thus, this mentally tough physician decided to be as authentic and honest as possible about the needs of his patients, their families, and also himself. When a child died in his care, he took it upon himself to deliver the infant's eulogy at the funeral because he felt he shared an important personal connection with the parents and the child.

Now something of a living legend in his field, this devout Christian (employing an unusual fusion of prayer and medicine) would soon meet his second great challenge in life. Nominated by President Reagan in 1981 as surgeon general, Koop was nicknamed "Dr. Kook" by critics who feared his conservative views on abortion. With the political spotlight now on him, the stability and balance he had maintained over his lifetime were upset. His family was "crushed," he said, by the negative opinions surrounding his brutal confirmation process, which lasted eighteen months. "Preeminent in my specialty, I was all of a sudden characterized as an absolute bum," he recalled to me. "There were cartoons showing me as a two-headed monster." He found strength in the letters he received from people around the country telling him they were praying for him during this difficult period: "Their support gave me confidence that the whole world wasn't against me."

Koop prevailed against this onslaught, recognizing that he should restrain his own personal views while he was a government servant. He intended to uphold the rights of individuals according to the law, regardless of his own pro-life opinions.

If abortion was his career's albatross, Koop's work on AIDS was his vindication. AIDS was a new epidemic, and more misconceptions than facts about the disease were in circulation. To quell its spread, Koop researched the virus, contacting analysts, gay activists, and victims. He implemented a national awareness campaign in the nation's schools; using graphic language and stark definition, his campaign promoted sex education as well as abstinence. Some conservatives saw his acknowledgment of sex as a promotion of immorality, but he acted courageously, positively, and decisively, facing the fact that plenty of teenagers do not abstain from sex even after being warned of its potential consequences.

Comparing his work with AIDS to the fight against leprosy, Koop observed, "It's not the same problem, but it is and it isn't." People have known about leprosy for centuries, doctors are still uncertain of how it spreads among some people but not among others. Its variations are also similar to the mutations of the AIDS virus:

We can help in so many ways by example. I would never fear touching a leper. In the same way, I always made a point to touch people with AIDS, so that others would see how you would not contract it.

After working with two different presidential administrations, Koop left Washington in 1985 and returned to the Children's Hospital in Philadelphia. He sees the unification of spirituality and science that is happening today as something that will improve the well-being of patients.

Koop continues to be a spokesman for the balanced integration of mind, body, soul, and spirit. He summarized his approach in a lecture at Johns Hopkins University in 2003: "It makes sense to me to see each of us as a body, soul, and spirit: the body being the material part of us, the soul being the seat of our emotions, the spirit the seat of our religion, or God-consciousness." His simple and moderate message about a balanced, holistic lifestyle, encompassing all aspects of the self, has been cause for his wide appeal and successful impact in and out of public service.

Koop draws on the impact of God in his life and work and derives his personal strength from his True Self. He says that whenever he sits and prays with a family whose child is desperately ill, it is strictly because God has led him to do so. In the face of death, his faith in God gives him a source of peace within and helps him avoid the common questions of Why? and What if? A true vehicle of *arete*, Koop is a doctor of body, mind, and soul and a model for balancing the personal, professional, and spiritual aspects of life.

We see from the lives of Koop and so many others that having virtue is not about following specific rules; it is rather about cultivating character. We find personal excellence by finding truth, both through the True Self and the Spirit. Our virtue will be defined by taking possession of the life we're living today, not focusing on remembering yesterday or preparing for tomorrow. In this way, we are sure to maintain balance in our complicated lives, a balance that one of the world's great spiritual leaders continues to address.

Integrating Faith and
Science, Inner and Outer Life

Draped in the garb of a Buddhist monk, palms pressed together, and bowing before his packed audience at Harvard University's Memorial Church on September 15, 2003, the Dalai Lama, spiritual leader of Tibetan Buddhism, discussed several polarized aspects of modern life: Eastern and Western philosophy, science and religion, and our inner and outer being.

Born in 1935, this defining spiritual leader of modern times and Nobel laureate was enthroned in Lhasa, Tibet, in 1940 at the age of four. He began formal education when he was six years old, culminating in a doctorate in Buddhist philosophy when he was twenty-five.

Immediately addressing education, the Dalai Lama honored his audience "as members of a very august and famous learning center . . . where, in act, all of you have the flame of intelligence—very bright and burning." But he soon asked, "What is the purpose of education?"

> I can answer: The main purpose of education is to bring a happy life or successful life on the individual level, in community and even at a global level. Certainly the purpose of education is not to create trouble on this planet.

Reflecting on the record of modern history, the Dalai Lama observed that although we possess a profoundly sophisticated faculty of intelligence, aligning himself with the definition of true knowledge that we considered among the great religions, "we must combine the mind and the heart: The human intellect is no guarantee to bring happiness . . . the combination of the mind and heart is crucial."

While in Boston, the Dalai Lama participated in convocations with scientists at the Massachusetts Institute of Technology to explore the relationship with faith and science. He affirmed the links for Buddhist monks and science, particularly in the areas of cosmology, neurobiology, physics, and psychology, stating that findings from these areas are very useful details from which Buddhists can learn. Though extolling these benefits, he emphasized that "the most important use for our intelligence is to analyze the inner world." He noted that westerners are overly concerned with material acquisitions and do not emphasize internal life sufficiently:

> I feel that in modern society what is lacking is not being able to pay equal attention to the development of the individual, particularly the basic qualities of good warm-heartedness. We don't pay enough attention to the degree comparable to the attention that we pay towards the brain development through education.

The Dalai Lama inferred the need for both integration and balance of the heart and mind, to develop character in life:

> The practice of love, compassion, kindness, contentment—these things, something very useful, very important for a happy life. If you look at all the various religious traditions they all talk about these things in the same way, all the same message of love, compassion, forgiveness, tolerance, contentment, self-discipline. The philosophies are different and there are many different religious positions. But they all have the very important same message. Therefore, all have the same potential to develop good beliefs. So there is real ground to make harmony.

Reflecting on his own work, he said, "I always try to promote religious harmony." His advice to others: "basically two things—try to increase basic good human qualities and try to be a nice person."

With humor sprinkled throughout his talk, the Dalai Lama opened by saying that if any expected magic from his presentation, they would be disappointed, adding, "If someone really has healing powers, I would like to call them about my knees." In this way the utter seriousness and sobriety of the Dalai Lama's message was brought into the balance he advocated.

Building Your Vessel

The goal of this book has been to help you build a ship for your journey toward true coming of age. Likewise, this book has given you a chart with which to plot the course your ship will sail. These tools of ship and chart are made up of the wisdom we have gathered from the many different stories told here and their influence on our personal paradigm. In this sense, this book has been less like a map or a blueprint and more like a mosaic, a collection of beautiful pieces that you must ultimately arrange for yourself.

As we reach our conclusion, let us contemplate the significance of what we have learned about the adventure of true coming of age:

1. We understand that we possess the True Self and that by using our intrinsic gifts we can strengthen our critical connections.
2. We know that unless we focus on the sea ahead and its possibilities, we will simply choose to stay in our current harbor.
3. We recognize the significance of fully engaging our body, heart, and soul to build a vessel for our journey, allowing their interaction to light our search for purpose.
4. We can then see the various kinds of love and determine whether and how each kind relates to our self, to others, to God, and to our purpose.
5. We understand the importance of knowing our talents and strengths and aligning these with our critical connections.
6. We know how attunement to our physical, emotional, and spiritual dimensions leads us to wholeness and to well-being.
7. We realize that truth consists of our experiences in life, and we see the need to examine whether our beliefs are consistent with that lived truth.
8. We are open to the reality of the Spirit moving in our life and enhancing our understanding of ourselves, giving us perspective on both small things and on the big picture.

9. We see how those who live in truth find fulfillment, and we are able to distinguish a life lived with the marvelous power of the soul from one lived without it.

10. We are determined to fully integrate our lives with our talents, distinguishing achievements and success from meaningful fulfillment.

11. We understand that having integrity and character requires performing actions in accord with our True Self rather than accepting someone else's plan.

12. We know that fulfillment occurs when we draw on our authentic True Self, balanced with our authentic nature—body, heart, and soul.

True coming of age is a gift that we can only give ourselves. It can only be achieved by living through our True Self. As we embark on the journey to understand our True Self, we must be patient and not look for a quick fix to the problems of identity and purpose. Each sea that we travel is different and personal, but if we pursue our quest individually, our authenticity will be unique and lasting. We recognize that we alone determine how we will construct and guide our ship and find fulfillment.

There comes a day when we all must face one of life's many challenges, and we must choose which path to take for our journey. No matter how many people influence us or what cards life deals us, our challenge will not go away unless we deal with it. By resolving these problems, we can undergo the transformational process—True Coming of Age.

Tapping Your True Source of Power

As we make the journey toward true coming of age, and authentically engage our True Self, we increase our connections to others, our opportunities to use our intrinsic gifts, and, quite simply, the choices open to us. Likewise, when we welcome a belief in something greater than ourselves, we are no longer fearful, unable, or unaware. We have the power to change our lives and energetically face our future. We are also called on to share our power with others and not to be isolated. "Our scientific power has outrun our spiritual power. We have guided missiles and misguided men," Martin Luther King, Jr., observed. We must not look only to power outside but must draw out our power from within.

Theologian-sociologist Harvey Cox says, "Not to decide is to decide." Parents often defer to schools to instill values in their children, but public educators find their hands tied by the government in teaching morality. Many people turn to religious institutions for guidance and then do not become members. Our nation, our institutions, and even our individual homes have been ineffective in recognizing and embracing the values so essential for daily life. We have neglected to marshal the spiritual core of our True Self. And yet we wonder why things are awry.

There's a story about a few high school students who were talented underachievers. As part of an educational experiment, this group of students was periodically bused to Princeton for lectures by distinguished physicists, with the hope that these great thinkers would positively influence them. Einstein was among the faculty, as was Robert Oppenheimer, who was instrumental in developing the atomic bomb and later an adamant critic of its use. On one occasion, a young girl in the back of the room raised her hand and wryly asked the panel of great scientists what they thought of ghosts. Two of the physicists quickly and completely dismissed the notion, citing a lack of scientific evidence. Oppenheimer paused after they finished and offered a different response. He said, "That's a fascinating question. I accept the possibility of all things. . . . I believe that it is necessary to find one's own required evidence" before accepting or rejecting the possibility.

Like that girl, we need to ask what may seem to be unexpected questions.

Setting Out on Your Journey

While the Greeks did not know of a connection to the gods, their struggle for understanding meaning was transformed by the considerations of Socrates through Plato, who saw the divine as the path to knowledge that explained ideas about the soul. Our relationship with God centers our authentic life. Access to God as a natural engagement of the True Self moves us ever more deeply to contact.

The mystery of our life is revealed from the connections we make. We must take responsibility for what guides our path: Is it modern society? Early childhood experiences? Relationships? God? Whatever we choose constitutes our important positioning toward our True Self. And so we end this invitation to our journey with a modern Greek vision of life:

ITHAKA

When you start on your journey to Ithaka,
   hope the voyage is a long one,
   full of adventure, full of discovery.

Lestrygonians and Cyclops,
   angry Poseidon—don't be afraid of them:
   you'll never find things like that on your way
   as long as you keep your thoughts raised high,
   as long as a rare excitement,
   stirs your spirit and your body.
Lestrygonians and Cyclops,
   wild Poseidon—you won't encounter them
   unless you bring them along inside your soul,
   unless your soul sets them up in front of you. . . .

Keep Ithaka always in your mind.
Arriving there is what you are destined for.
But do not hurry the journey at all.

Better if it lasts for years,
    so you are old by the time you reach the island,
    wealthy with all you have gained on the way,
    not expecting Ithaka will make you rich.

Ithaka gave you the marvelous journey.
Without her you would have not set out.
She has nothing left to give you now.

And if you find her poor, Ithaka won't have fooled you.
Wise as you have become, so full of experience,
    you will have understood by then what these Ithakas mean.

—C. P. CAVAFY[1]

In the end, we are the inheritors of much wisdom, but we must take possession of our life to be fulfilled. Fulfillment comes through our design. We must pick up our own drafting pencil and draw up our own blueprint.

NOTES

INTRODUCTION

1. The chapters of this book are drawn from clinical examples, longitudinal interviews, and psychohistories by Dr. Chirban over the past twenty years, including Maya Angelou, Desi Arnaz, Jr., Lucille Ball, Billy Bean, Tom Brokaw, Shirley Chisholm, Eileen Collins, Bette Davis, Tom Hanks, Ron Howard, Jeane Kirkpatrick, C. Everett Koop, Jay Leno, Keith Lockhart, Sandra Day O'Connor, Mary Lou Retton, Jessica Savitch, Diane Sawyer, B. F. Skinner, Desmond Tutu, Rosalyn Yalow, and Anastasios Yannoulatos, among others.

2. Please note capitalization in the text refers to terms that relate to God, e.g., "good" is a general judgment as distinct from "Good" originating from God.

CHAPTER 3

1. Winnicott, D. (1965). *The Maturational Process and the Facilitating Environment.* London: Hogarth Press.

2. Thermos, V. (2002). *In Search of the Person: "True" and "False Self" According to Donald Winnicott and St. Gregory Palamas.* Montreal, Quebec: Alexander Press.

CHAPTER 4

1. Offit, A. K. (1983). *The Sexual Self.* New York: Congden and Weed.

2. McDougall, J. (1995). *The Many Faces of Eros: A Psychoanalytic Exploration of Human Sexuality.* New York: W. W. Norton.

CHAPTER 7

1. Easterbrook, Greg. (2002). "The Pew Forum on Religion and Public Life; U.S. Census 2002; The Gallup Organization, Religion in America." *Brookings Review,* January 1, 2002.

2. Skinner, B. F. (1976). *Particulars of My Life*. New York: Knopf.

3. Skinner, B. F. (1983). *A Matter of Consequences*. New York: Knopf.

CHAPTER 8

1. Wilber, Ken. (2000). *Integral Psychology: Consciousness, Spirit, Psychology, Therapy*. Boston: Shambala.

2. Chariton, Igumen of Valamo (Ed.). (1966). Translated by E. Kadloubovsky and E. M. Palmer. *The Art of Prayer: An Orthodox Anthology*. London: Faber and Faber.

3. Koenig, H. G., and H. J. Cohen, (Eds.). (2002). *The Link Between Religion and Health: Psychoneuroimmunology and the Faith Factor*. London: Oxford University Press.

4. Idler, E. L., and S. U. Kasl. (1997). "Religiosity Among Disabled and Nondisabled Persons I: Cross-sectional Patterns in Health Practices, Social Activities, and Well-being." *The Journal of Gerontology* 52B: 300–305.

5. Helm, H. M., J. C. Hays, E. P. Flint, H. G. Koenig, and D. G. Blazer. (2000). "Does Private Religious Activity Prolong Survival? A Six-Year Follow-up Study of 3,851 Older Adults." *The Journal of Gerontology* 55A: M400–M405.

6. Woods, T. E., M. H. Antoni, G. H. Ironson, and D. W. Kling, (1999). "Religiosity Is Associated with Affective and Immune Status in Sympotomatic HIV-infected Gay Men." *Journal of Psychosomatic Research*. 46: 165–176.

7. Byrd, R. C. (1987). "The Therapeutic Effects of Intercessory Prayer in a Coronary Care Unit." *Southern Medical Journal* 81: 826–829.

CHAPTER 9

1. Jung, C. G. (1933). *Modern Man in Search of a Soul*. Translated by W. S. Dell and Carry R. Baynes. New York: Harcourt.

2. Pew Research Center for the People and the Press (2002). "Among Wealthy Nations, U.S. Stands Alone in Its Embrace of Religion," December 19. http://people-press.org/reports/display /php3?ReportID=167.

3. Koslowski, P. (2001). *The Concepts of God, the Origin of the World, and the Image of the Human Person in the World Religions*. Dortdrecht, The Netherlands: Kluwer Academic Publishers.

4. Jayawickrama, N.A. (1990). *The Story of Gotoma Buddhat*. Somerville, MA: Wisdom Publications.

5. Harvey, P. (2000). *An Introduction to Buddhist Ethics*. Cambridge, England: Cambridge University Press.

CHAPTER 12

1. Cavafy, C. P. (1992). *Collected Poems*. Translated by Edmund Keely and Philip Sherrard. Edited by George Savidis. Princeton, NJ: Princeton University Press.

INDIGO SIGNAL HILL
Indigo Store 279
5570 Signal Hill Centre SW
Calgary AB T3H 3P8
(403)246-2221 Fax: (403)242-6815
GST# R897152666

222827 Reg 6 ID 162 2:00 pm 01/06/05

S TRUE COMING OF AG   1 @ 28.95   28.95
S 0071426817
SUBTOTAL   28.95
TAX: GST - 7%   2.03
TOTAL SALES TAX   2.03
TOTAL   30.98
DEBIT CARD PAYMENT   30.98

Exchanges or refunds within 14 days only
with receipt. Items must be in store
bought condition.
Please note we cannot accept a return or
excahnge of magazines or newspapers.